Cybersecurity Fundamentals

T0383730

Cybersecurity Fundamentals
A Real-World Perspective

Dr Kutub Thakur
Dr Al-Sakib Khan Pathan

CRC Press
Taylor & Francis Group
Boca Raton London New York

CRC Press is an imprint of the
Taylor & Francis Group, an **informa** business

First edition published 2020
by CRC Press
6000 Broken Sound Parkway NW, Suite 300, Boca Raton, FL 33487-2742

and by CRC Press
2 Park Square, Milton Park, Abingdon, Oxon, OX14 4RN

© 2020 Taylor & Francis Group, LLC
CRC Press is an imprint of Taylor & Francis Group, LLC

ISBN: 978-0-367-47648-9 (hbk)
ISBN: 978-0-367-47250-4 (pbk)
ISBN: 978-1-003-03562-6 (ebk)

Typeset in Times
by codeMantra

"To my Father and Mother, Billal Thakur and Nurunnahar Parul"

Kutub Thakur

"To my Father, Abdus Salam Khan Pathan, and my Mother, Delowara Khanom"

Al-Sakib Khan Pathan

Contents

Preface

This book describes the detailed concepts of computer networks and cybersecurity. It talks about the types of major computer malware programs and the major cybersecurity attacks that shook the cyber world in recent years. The details of the major attacks and their impacts on the global economy are analyzed. The details of the malware codes that help the hacker initiate hacking attacks on networks are also described in length.

A few chapters are fully dedicated to high-tech cybersecurity programs, devices, and mechanisms that are extensively adopted in modern security systems. The examples of those systems include intrusion detection systems (IDS), intrusion prevention systems (IPS), and security firewalls. The general prevention mechanisms from the cyberattacks are detailed in a couple of dedicated chapters.

Password management with modern technologies that help to create and manage passwords more effectively is described in full detail. This book also covers aspects of wireless networks and their security mechanisms. Details of commonly used wired and Wi-Fi routers are provided with step-by-step procedures to configure and secure them more efficiently.

This book is designed for users to benefit from the following major issues related to the computer and network security:

- Detailed knowledge of computer and networks
- Knowledge of major cybersecurity threats and their impact on the world
- Knowledge of major cyber threats and computer malware programs
- Knowledge of cybersecurity and its importance in the modern world
- Details of major cybersecurity mechanisms
- Cybersecurity aspects of wireless networks and routers
- Step-by-step procedures on how to browse securely on the Internet
- Step-by-step guidelines on how to shop securely on the Internet
- Knowledge of mobile security to secure the mobile devices more effectively
- Details about the types of digital fraud carried out in the cyber environment
- Knowledge of how to make your online presence more secure and reliable
- Details about what to do and what not to do in the web environment to maintain the security of your digital resources
- Details of the major cybersecurity standards that help secure digital activities and resources

We hope that this book will offer great benefits to the students of graduate and under-graduate classes, researchers, and practitioners. This could be a suitable textbook for even non-CS (computer science) students or students who want to learn about basic computer networking, security issues, and cybersecurity issues.

Kutub Thakur, PhD
Professional Security Studies Faculty,
New Jersey City University, NJ 07305-1597, USA
kthakur@njcu.edu

Al-Sakib Khan Pathan, PhD, SMIEEE
Department of Computer Science and Engineering,
Independent University, Dhaka, Bangladesh
spathan@ieee.org

About the Authors

Kutub Thakur is the Director of NJCU Center for Cyber Security, and Assistant Professor and Director of Cybersecurity Program at New Jersey City University. He worked for various private and public entities such as the United Nations, Lehman Brothers, Barclays Capital, ConEdison, City University of New York, and the Metropolitan Transport Authority. He received his PhD in Computer Science with specialization in cybersecurity from Pace University, New York; M.S in Engineering Electrical and Computer Control Systems from the University of Wisconsin; B.S and A.A.S in Computer Systems Technology from the City University of New York. He reviewed for many prestigious journals and published many papers in reputable journals and conferences. His research interests include digital forensics, network security, machine learning, IoT security, privacy, and security and user behavior. He is currently serving/served as the Program Chair for many conferences and workshops. He is also currently supervising/supervised many graduate and doctoral students for their thesis, proposal, and dissertation in the field of cybersecurity.

Al-Sakib Khan Pathan is a Professor of Computer Science and Engineering. Currently, he is with the Independent University, Bangladesh, as an Adjunct Professor. He received his PhD in Computer Engineering in 2009 from Kyung Hee University, South Korea, and BSc degree in Computer Science and Information Technology from Islamic University of Technology (IUT), Bangladesh, in 2003. In his academic career so far, he has worked as a Faculty Member at the CSE Department of Southeast University, Bangladesh, during 2015–2020; Computer Science Department, International Islamic University Malaysia (IIUM), Malaysia, during 2010–2015; at BRACU, Bangladesh, during 2009–2010; and at NSU, Bangladesh, during 2004–2005. He was a Guest Lecturer for the STEP project at the Department of Technical and Vocational Education, Islamic University of Technology, Bangladesh, in 2018. He has also worked as a Researcher at Networking Lab, Kyung Hee University, South

Korea, from September 2005 to August 2009, where he completed his MS leading to PhD. His research interests include wireless sensor networks, network security, cloud computing, and e-services technologies. Currently, he is also working on some multidisciplinary issues. He is a recipient of several awards/best paper awards and has several notable publications in these areas. So far, he has delivered over 20 keynotes and invited speeches at various international conferences and events. He has served as a General Chair, Organizing Committee Member, and Technical Program Committee (TPC) member in numerous top-ranked international conferences/workshops such as INFOCOM, GLOBECOM, ICC, LCN, GreenCom, AINA, WCNC, HPCS, ICA3PP, IWCMC, VTC, HPCC, and SGIoT. He was awarded the IEEE Outstanding Leadership Award for his role in the IEEE GreenCom'13 conference. He is currently serving as the Editor-in-Chief of *International Journal of Computers and Applications*, Taylor & Francis; Associate Technical Editor of *IEEE Communications Magazine*; Editor of *Ad Hoc and Sensor Wireless Networks*, Old City Publishing, *International Journal of Sensor Networks*, Inderscience Publishers, and *Malaysian Journal of Computer Science*; an Associate Editor of *International Journal of Computational Science and Engineering*, Inderscience; Area Editor of *International Journal of Communication Networks and Information Security*; Guest Editor of many special issues of top-ranked journals; and Editor/Author of 21 books. One of his books has been included twice in Intel Corporation's Recommended Reading List for Developers, 2nd half 2013 and 1st half of 2014; three books were included in IEEE Communications Society's (IEEE ComSoc) Best Readings in Communications and Information Systems Security, 2013; two other books were indexed with all the titles (chapters) in Elsevier's acclaimed abstract and citation database, Scopus, in February 2015; and a seventh book is translated to simplified Chinese language from English version. Also, two of his journal papers and one conference paper were included under different categories in IEEE Communications Society's (IEEE ComSoc) Best Readings Topics on Communications and Information Systems Security, 2013. He also serves as a referee of many prestigious journals. He has received awards for his reviewing activities, including one of the most active reviewers of *IAJIT* several times and Elsevier Outstanding Reviewer for *Computer Networks*, *Ad Hoc Networks*, *FGCS*, and *JNCA* in multiple years. He is a Senior Member of the Institute of Electrical and Electronics Engineers (IEEE), USA.

Computers and Networks

1

1.1 INTRODUCTION TO COMPUTERS

Computer is an electronic device that takes the raw data through the input components and processes that into meaningful information and produces that information through the output components of the device for use. A complete unit of modern computer system consists of many components, which can be classified into two major categories – referred to as the software components and the hardware components as shown in Figure 1.1.

The software components consist of the following:

- Firmware
- Operating system or OS software

FIGURE 1.1   Personal computer (PC).

- Device drivers
- Application software

And, the hardware components consist of the following:

- Central processing unit (CPU)
- Data storage
- Input devices
- Output devices (input and output devices are often together called "I/O devices")

Every software and hardware component can consist of many other small hardware and software items, which altogether form a modern computer machine that we use for our day-to-day activities.

1.2 HISTORY OF COMPUTERS

The history of computers dates back to the 19th century when an English mathematician Charles Babbage first designed a computer named as "Analytic Engine". That basic design lays the foundation for the evolution of computers to the modern shape and scale.

The history of computers can be divided into five major eras or generations as described below.

1.2.1 First Generation (1937–1946)

The first-generation computers were based on the vacuum tubes. The first machine was invented by J P Eckert and J W Mauchy between 1943 and 1945. It was a huge machine developed in the state of Pennsylvania in the United States. The name of this machine was Electronic Numerical Integrator and Computer (ENIAC). This machine consisted of over 20 thousand vacuum tubes, 70 thousand resistors, and 10 thousand capacitors. The gigantic machine weighed about 30 tons. When it was first powered up, a big dip in power was observed in many surrounding areas of the state.

1.2.2 Second Generation (1947–1962)

The second-generation computers were based on the transistor technology. The first commercial computer named as Universal Automatic Computer (UNIVAC 1) was based on the transistor technology. It was launched in 1951. IBM launched 650 and 700 series computers in 1953. A large number of computer programming languages emerged in the marketplace. The assembly languages got grounds in this computer era.

1.2.3 Third Generation (1963–1971)

The third-generation computers were based on the integrated circuits or ICs. The advent of silicon material miniaturized the size of the transistors, and ICs were built for the electronic circuitries. The punch cards were replaced by the keyboards and new operating systems emerged, which were able to run more than one application simultaneously. The examples of third-generation computers include IBM 360 & 370 and DPD 11.

1.2.4 Fourth Generation (1971–2010)

The fourth-generation computers became very popular with the masses. These computers were mostly based on the very large-scale integration (VLSI) microprocessors. Many new companies and manufacturers of computers emerged in this tenure. New types of machines were introduced with many different types of operating systems and technologies. Personal computers (PCs), laptops, personal digital assistants (PDAs), and other computer machines were introduced under this generation of computers. Windows, Linux, UNIX, Solaris, and Macintosh operating systems were introduced in this era as well.

1.2.5 Fifth Generation (2010–Present)

The fifth-generation computers are those machines that are substantially powered by the artificial intelligence (AI) and ultra-large-scale integration (ULSI) and robotic processes. Although the use of AI started long before 2010, the higher level of influence started in the present decade. This generation includes the new computers such as IBM Watson, multicore processing machines, distributed processing machines, and the latest AI-enabled mobile devices and tablets.

1.3 COMPONENTS OF MODERN COMPUTER

As a machine, computer has evolved from first-generation computer to the modern day's fifth-generation computer machine by passing through many changes in the software and hardware components. The components explained below form a modern computer device extensively used in our regular life and industries nowadays. A few images of modern computers are shown in Figure 1.2.

1.3.1 Input Devices

The input devices of a computer are those components that are connected to the computer to insert raw data in different formats for processing purpose. A few major input and output devices are shown in Figure 1.3.

The major input devices for our modern computers include the following:

- Keyboard
- Microphone
- Barcode reader
- Camera
- Electronic pen
- Joystick

FIGURE 1.2   Modern computers.

FIGURE 1.3   Computer input/output devices.

- MIDI (Musical Instrument Digital Interface) port
- Pointing devices
- Gamepad
- Touch screen
- Wireless antenna
- USB (Universal Serial Bus) port
- Scanner
- Motion sensor

1.3.2 Output Devices

The output devices of a computer are those components that are connected to the computer for producing meaningful information processed from the raw data inserted through input devices. The major output devices of a modern computer include the following:

- Monitor
- Printer
- Speaker
- Headphone
- Projector
- Plotter
- Computer Output Microfilm (COM)

1.3.3 Central Processing Unit (CPU)

The CPU is the brain of computer that controls the entire functionalities of the machine. It takes the raw data from the input devices, processes the data to generate meaningful information, and sends out the information to output devices or saves it on the data storage. Figure 1.4 shows the CPU unit.

The major components of a CPU include the following:

- Arithmetic logic unit (ALU)
- Random access memory (RAM)
- Read-only memory (ROM)
- Control unit (CU)

FIGURE 1.4   Central processing unit (CPU).

FIGURE 1.5   Data storage devices.

1.3.4 Storage Components

The storage component of a computer is the data storage bank to keep the data saved on the secondary location, where the data can be easily accessed and managed (Figure 1.5).

The storage components include the following:

- Hard disk drive (HDD)
- Flash disk drive (FDD)
- Optical disk drive (ODD)
- Magnetic tapes

1.3.5 Software Components

A computer is the combination of hardware and software components. All hardware components mentioned above are dumb and deaf without the power of software components of a computer. Figure 1.6 shows some of the software running on a computer.

The major software components of a computer include the following:

- OS software
- Component drivers
- Application software
- Utility software
- Firmware

FIGURE 1.6 Computer software.

1.4 FUTURE MACHINES

The pace of advancement in computer science has been much faster than many other technologies. Computer technology not only progressed fast but also impacted heavily on the other technologies and business processes of the world. This fast growth of computer technology made it one of the most unpredictable and volatile technologies of the world. The field of information technology (IT) is the fastest-changing technological sector in the world. See the changing shape of future computers in Figure 1.7.

The future of the computers will be governed by the major prospective technologies as explained in the subsequent subsections:

FIGURE 1.7 Future machines.

FIGURE 1.8   Artificial intelligence concepts.

1.4.1 Artificial Intelligence

AI has been in the field for quite some time, but this technology will impact the computer heavily in the time to come. With the help of augmented reality and virtual reality (AR/VR), voice recognition, text interpretation, image processing, motion detection, and other technologies based on AI technologies, the future of computers looks even smarter and more exciting. The conceptual image of AI is shown in Figure 1.8.

1.4.2 Quantum Computing

The quantum computing idea is not a new one, but its practical existence is still in infancy. There is no high level of quantum information processing, which has yet been completed (at the time of writing this book). Only a few small-scale projects of processing of quantum information in quantum bits (qbits) were successful. When this new field of computing kick starts, the existing binary processing in our modern computers will be heavily impacted with the quantum information processing. The virtual image of quantum computing is shown in Figure 1.9.

1.4.3 Nanotechnology

The size of the hardware, especially in electronics and computer technology, is decreasing exponentially. The size of first data storage based on 18,000 vacuum tubes was about 1,800 ft^2 to keep that tube tank cool. Can you imagine how much data could that huge area store? Yes, that could store up to 18,000 bits of data only.

FIGURE 1.9 Virtual image of quantum computing.

One vacuum tube could store one bit of data for computer processing and storage. The size of the hardware has got reduced to hundreds of thousands of times by this time. Just a small flash of less than a nail size can store billions of bytes of data! The size of the electronic hardware is expected to get reduced even more in the time to come.

The processing of matter to the level of 100th part of a nanometer is referred to as nanotechnology (Figure 1.10). The partnership of nanotechnology and quantum physics will work well in the future, once the technology progresses. The success of quantum and nanotechnology will revolutionize the modern computers to a new level.

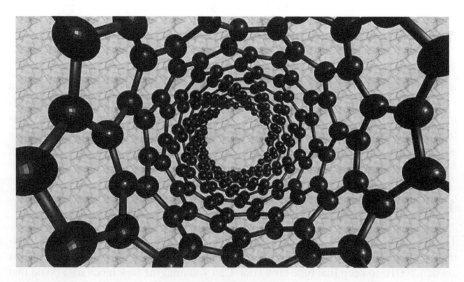

FIGURE 1.10 Conceptual image of nanotechnology.

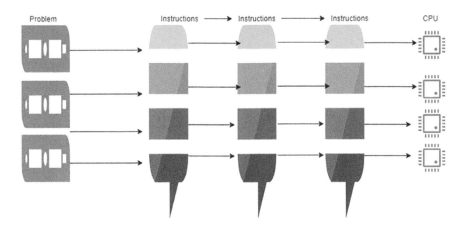

FIGURE 1.11   Schematic diagram of parallel processing.

1.4.4 Parallel Processing

The distribution of computer processing in multiple components comprehensively coordinated with each other has already been extensively used in computer science to increase the processing power of a computer. The virtualization, cloud computing, and distributed processing systems are examples of parallel processing. The implementation of parallel processing at a large scale is going to rock the computer field in the near future. Schematic diagram of parallel processing is shown in Figure 1.11.

1.5 INTRODUCTION TO COMPUTER NETWORKS

Computer network is the combination of two or more computers connected with each other to share their resources, establish communication, and exchange data electronically based on some pre-agreed rules and protocols. The end devices or computers are also known as *hosts*.

A computer network consists of networking devices (e.g., switches, hubs, routers), computer hosts, wired media (copper or fiber cables), wireless media, connectors, and software protocols. Multiple computers are connected with each other through different configurations (physical and logical) known as network topologies. Those computers can be connected through wired or wireless media with the help of media connectors. Figure 1.12 shows the image of a computer network.

This entire hardware configuration is governed by the communication protocols that control the communication rules and patterns in a network. There are many communication topologies, protocols, and network types commonly used in computer networks.

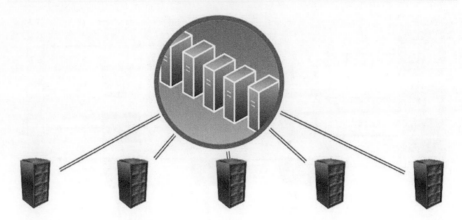

FIGURE 1.12   Computer network.

1.5.1 Network Topologies

Network topology is a type of computer connectivity in which the computers or devices are connected with each other to form a network. These topologies are normally physical references of network connectivity. Figure 1.13 shows the major network topologies used in the modern computer networking.

Major network topologies used in the computer network communication are listed below:

- Star network topology
- Bus network topology

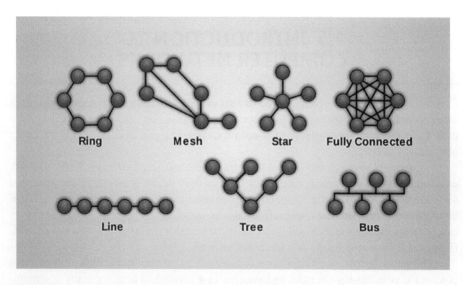

FIGURE 1.13   Network topologies.

- Ring network topology
- Mesh network topology
- Tree topology
- Combination of two or more topologies

1.5.2 Major Network Protocols

The entire communication of computer networks takes place based on the employed network protocols. The digital communication is based on certain rules of interaction (i.e., all requests and responses). The combination of those rules and regulations of the communication between any pair of nodes is known as the network communication protocol. Many network protocols are used for the communication between two nodes. The major principle of communication between two nodes is normally based on client and server as explained below. There are also other principles of communication, such as peer-to-peer communication. Figure 1.14 shows the FTP communications, in which DTP means data transfer process.

A few very important network protocols commonly adopted in the modern network communication are listed below:

- Ethernet for physical and data link OSI (Open Systems Interconnection) layer
- TCP/SPX (Transmission Control Protocol/Sequenced Packet Exchange) at network OSI layer
- IP (Internet Protocol) at transport OSI layer
- HTTP/FTP (Hypertext Transfer Protocol/File Transfer Protocol) upper OSI layers
- DNS (Domain Name System), SMTP (Simple Mail Transfer Protocol) upper OSI layers

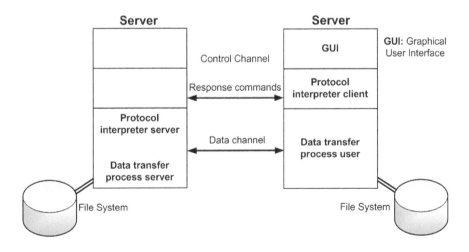

FIGURE 1.14 FTP communications.

1.5.3 Elements of Computer Network

The basic elements of a computer network are hosts, connecting media, and connectors. But the modern communication networks are not that simple. Some of the major elements used to form a modern computer network are as follows:

- Hosts
- Routers
- Switches
- Hubs
- Firewalls
- Servers
- Cables/links
- Protocols
- Connectors

1.5.4 Types of Networks

Broadly speaking, the networks can be classified into three major types irrespective of their connecting media – wireless or wired, which are as follows:

- Local area network (LAN)
- Metropolitan area network (MAN)
- Wide area network (WAN)

These networks are classified in terms of their coverage area. They can be wired, wireless, or even a combination of both.

1.6 THE INTERNET EXPLORED

The Internet is the global network of the networks spread all over the world. This network uses the IP address as the identification address of any node in the Internet. The complete communication stack for the transmission of data across the network is based on the TCP/IP. Internet is a gigantic network that offers multiple types of communication services (conceptual image in Figure 1.15). The major services the Internet offers include the following:

- Voice calls
- Video calls
- Chats
- Fax
- Email

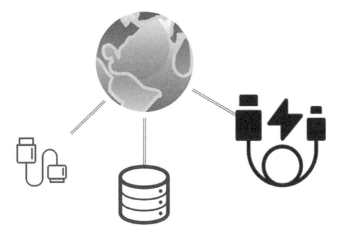

FIGURE 1.15   The Internet explored (conceptual image).

- Social media
- Instant messaging
- Financial services
- Bill payments
- Online shopping
- Video conferring
- TV streaming
- Live movies
- Gaming
- File sharing
- Data transfer
- e-Banking
- Data storage
- e-Marketing
- Remote healthcare
- Remote working
- e-Learning
- Counting

The Internet has revolutionized our day-to-day life. All our business, social, and public activities have changed drastically. Now, we may not even go to the banks frequently but rather, we just contact banks through the Internet. Sending letters to our beloved through post office has almost a very limited scope; rather, we use email, online chat, video call, and other sources of communications to contact with our friends and relatives.

There were more than 4.1 billion Internet users and just a little less than 2 billion websites in the world by the end of 2018. There are more than 2.5 billion Internet-enabled smartphone users in the world today (more or less). The total volume of retail e-commerce sale is expected to cross $4.5 trillion by 2021, and beyond that time, it is expected to increase significantly.

All this happened just because of the power of Internet. The Internet is saving huge costs on communication, data processing, service provisioning, and almost all other fields of our day-to-day life and business activities.

Along with the huge benefits of using Internet, many challenges associated with the use of Internet have also arisen. Among such challenges, the maintenance of security, privacy, and data integrity are the top of all.

1.6.1 History and Evolution of Internet

The history of Internet (Figure 1.16) dates back to 7:28 PM of October 4, 1957, when the first satellite named SPUTNIK was launched by the Soviet Union. It was an era of cold war. The US government was sure to respond. It responded on February 7, 1958, by forming Advanced Research Project Agency, ARPA. Later, it was named as Defense Advanced Research Project Agency, DARPA.

The core objective of this agency was to do research and develop the advanced communication network that will work even in case of damage to certain communication nodes of computers in any kind of war. In 1962, J C R Licklider, who was a scientist in the ARPA project, announced that a network of computers in the United States will continue to operate even in the case of nuclear attack on the United States. This network was later known as ARPA NET.

The packet switching theory was enunciated by Leonard Kleinrock in an MIT (Massachusetts Institute of Technology) publication in 1961, and later, a book was published on the packet switching theory in 1964 by Paul Baran. The packet switching theory laid the foundation stone for the present-day Internet communication. The packet data switching network started working by 1965. In 1969, a revolutionary device was developed named as the interface message processor (IMP). It was the initial version of router, which was able to make data transmission faster and more efficient.

The Stanford University LAN was expanded to connect with the National Science Foundation (NSF) in 1981. Later in 1983, the network was named as NSFNET after the name of National Science Foundation. The TCP was also developed in the same year. In 1985, the restrictions on the NSFNET were reduced by allowing multiple universities of the United States to participate in the research and communication network.

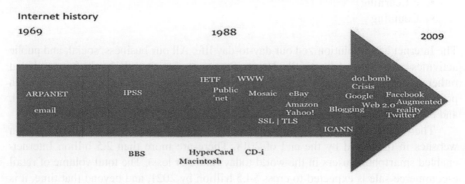

FIGURE 1.16   History of the Internet.

Slowly and gradually, multiple university and other institutes' networks started joining the NSFNET. Subsequently, the NSFNET became the backbone network of this project. In 1989, HTTP was developed by Tim Berners-Lee. The first Internet browser named Mosaic web browser for Internet browsing was developed in 1993.

The policy for the commercial use was also approved in 1993. After the commercial launch in 1993, the NSFNET was discontinued and decommissioned in 1995. In the initial days, the Internet was used only for sharing data and peer-to-peer communication.

Another revolutionary event happened when World Wide Web (WWW) was launched in 1995. This protocol changed the shape and power drastically. Since then, many improvements in the quality of speed, Internet security, and other areas have been noticed till today.

1.7 INTERNET IN TODAY'S WORLD

It was almost impossible 30 years back to think about the scale of impact the Internet would have on our today's lives. Almost each and every activity related to business, social life, personal life, governmental procedures, science and research, education, and even the way we live has been extensively influenced by the impact of Internet. The average Internet penetration of the world was about 55.1% by the middle of 2018. Once the Internet penetration reaches 100% (or, very close), the impact will be enormous on the domains of our modern life (conceptual view, Figure 1.17).

Starting from just a communication tool, Internet evolved into the following services:

- Websites
- Web applications
- Mobile applications
- Cloud computing

FIGURE 1.17   Internet in today's world (conceptual image). (Courtesy ©Shutterstock.com.)

The major sectors that have been revolutionized by the impact of the abovementioned services of the Internet include the following as discussed in the subsequent subsections.

1.7.1 Telecommunication

The traditional communication was restricted to circuit switching-based landlines, telephones, fax, telegraph, and handwritten letters. All those methods were so costly and resource-consuming. But Internet has replaced many of the modern communication technologies by now. The landline phones have been switched to IP-based phones and even video conference calls. The emails have almost replaced the traditional postal services and old faxing methods. Instant messaging, live streaming, chats, recorded messages, and many other things have also been added to the communication sector. The term "tele" basically means "distance", and hence, the term "telecommunication" means "transmission over a distance".

1.7.2 Retail Sales

The traditional sale is being extensively replaced with the online shopping. The "retail sales" has already become a multitrillion economy, and it is growing very fast with the support of various Internet-based platforms. With the advent of mobile e-commerce, the growth is expected to become spectacular in the near future.

1.7.3 Education

The Internet has impacted the education sector heavily. There is huge surge in online learning, remote learning, and e-Learning. Thousands of online courses are available to take remotely from different universities located at any corner of the world. Even the traditional education system in the universities has been heavily influenced by the electronic books, e-libraries, e-classrooms, digital form of multimedia, and other factors.

1.7.4 Business Processes

The business processes are the top beneficiaries of the Internet. Almost every process has been heavily improved by the use of Internet. Digital marketing, e-commerce, m-commerce, customer relationship management (CRM), business process outsourcing (BPO), automated billing/invoicing, enterprise resource planning (ERP), payroll management, remote hiring, enterprise application integration (EAI), business intelligence (BI), and many other new processes have emerged in the business sector. Billions of dollars were saved by using these improved business processes governed by the power of Internet.

Other sectors that benefited a lot from the use of Internet include the following:

- Banking
- Financing
- Insurance
- Healthcare
- R & D (Research and Development)
- Marketing
- Tourism
- Entertainment
- Gaming

1.8 ELEMENTS OF THE INTERNET

The Internet is a gigantic network of thousands of networks connected with each other through backbone connectivity and routers. Let us have a look at the major hardware elements of the modern Internet. Previously, we discussed the core elements of a computer network (in Section 1.5.3), but here, the major elements of the Internet would be mentioned.

1.8.1 Internet Cloud

The Internet cloud (Figure 1.18) is the general name of the entire infrastructure of the Internet. The cloud is an abstract name of Internet, which consists of the small networks like the pieces of clouds making a huge cloud in the sky. The data are uploaded, downloaded, and saved in the cloud while using the Internet services.

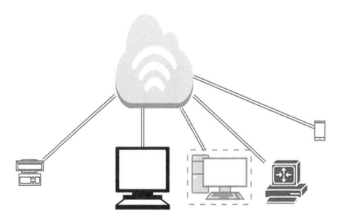

FIGURE 1.18   The Internet cloud.

1.8.2 Edge Router

The edge router is the router which is the first bridge between the Internet cloud and your own network in which your computer is located. The edge router maintains the global record of routes and addresses. This router distributes the packets to the other networks located at different parts of the cloud. Edge router is normally a powerful router to handle a large amount of information about the whole Internet addresses and routes.

1.8.3 Core Router

The core router is a central router within a network and maintains the information of an entire network within the boundaries of a network. Any external packet is handed over to the edge router for distribution in the global cloud. The core router routes and distributes the data packets within the single network or small parts of the corporate network.

Cisco is one of the leading manufacturing companies that produces routers and network elements. It offers numerous types of routers of different capacities. It is also one of the best providers of core routers. A picture of Cisco CRS-X Router Series is shown in Figure 1.19.

1.8.4 Firewalls

Firewalls are the defense wall of the corporate network connected to the Internet. The firewall is normally connected after edge router inside the local network. This device protects the internal devices from the malicious intrusion of unauthorized users.

The latest series of Cisco firewalls include Firepower 9000 series (at the time of writing this book). These firepower firewalls are very powerful and fast, which can handle the traffic throughput up to 225 Gbps. The image of Firepower 9000 series firewall is shown in Figure 1.20.

Normally, firewalls repel the cybercrime attacks if they are properly configured and installed to counter the possible threats. There are basically two major categories of firewalls: hardware firewall and software firewall. A hardware firewall is a physical

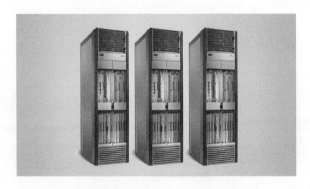

FIGURE 1.19   Cisco CRS-X Router Series.

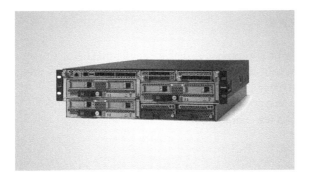

FIGURE 1.20   Firepower 9000 Series Firewall.

device connected with the network, while a software firewall could be installed on each of the computers, phones, or tablets in a network.

1.8.5 Switches

Switches separate the data packets within the corporate network and isolate the small business units within a big corporate network. Switches are also used for the distribution of data packets at the data link layer to the hosts based on the MAC (medium access control) addresses of the hosts.

The latest switches also have capabilities to support three-layer data distribution within multiple subnetworks of a big network. The most powerful layer 3 switches are produced by many companies in the world. Cisco systems, Juniper Corporation, and Teledata are a few to name. Figure 1.21 shows a Cisco Catalyst 9200 Series L2 and L3 Switch.

1.8.6 Hubs

Hubs are packet broadcasting devices within a small local network. The use of hubs has almost vanished nowadays, but still in small networks, hubs are used at a very low scale.

FIGURE 1.21   Cisco Catalyst 9200 Series L2 and L3 Switch.

1.8.7 Servers

The servers are the heavy computers that are configured to cater to the requests received from the hosts within the network or from the external networks (Internet cloud). There are many types of servers commonly used in the Internet. An image of a Dell EMC PowerEdge Server Series is shown in Figure 1.22.

The names of a few main servers are listed below:

- DNS server
- Voice server
- Media server
- Web server
- FTP server
- HTTP server
- File server
- Proxy server
- Application server
- IRC (Internet Relay Chat) server
- Chat server
- Mail server
- Database server
- Game server

1.8.8 Connectivity

All devices are connected to the network through different media, topologies, and strategies. A host is normally connected to the local switch/router through network cable or wirelessly. The routers are normally connected to the edge routers through Gigabit Ethernet copper or fiber cables. The connection between edge router and the backbone depends on the volume of bandwidth. Normally, the connection between edge routers to the backbone is done through either fiber or satellite links. The backbone of

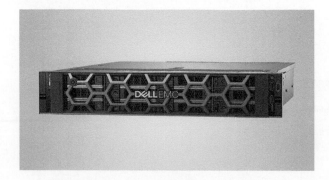

FIGURE 1.22   Dell EMC PowerEdge Server Series.

FIGURE 1.23   Connectivity – different types of cable connectors.

the Internet is normally either undersea fiber cables or satellite links across the major regions of the world. Different types of connectors are shown in Figure 1.23.

1.8.9 Hosts

Hosts are the end terminals that use the Internet services. Hosts can be computers, mobile devices, tablets, watches, printers, fax, and any other such devices. The hosts normally access the Internet services through host or client applications like web browser and other custom applications for the specific services.

The client software tools are installed on the host to access the server through server–client communication. The other formats of communication are also used on the computer networks such as peer-to-peer communication.

1.9 INTERNET SOFTWARE INFRASTRUCTURE & PROTOCOLS

Every hardware component of the Internet uses unique software to perform the desired tasks associated with that particular device. A router has its own OS that performs the functions of routing, route calculation, filters, and other activities. Similarly, the switches have their own system software to perform their respective duties.

Every server has its own software application that runs on it to cater to the requests coming from different clients either inside the network or outside the network. Different servers have different operating systems and their respective application software that runs on the OS of the servers. A conceptual view of Internet software infrastructure and protocols is shown in Figure 1.24.

Let us have a look at the major software infrastructures and protocols used in the Internet in length.

FIGURE 1.24   Internet software infrastructure and protocols.

1.9.1 IP Address

Internet protocol uses the IP address for routing. It is a logical address consisting of 32 bits of binary digits – zeros and ones. For the writing simplicity, IP address is written in the dotted notations like 11110000.11110000.11110000.11110000. This is a unique address for every node in the Internet. Every port connected to the Internet has a unique IP address. This dotted notation is converted to dotted decimal notation like 123.123.123.123.

There are two versions of IP address known as IPv4 and IPv6. The IPv4 version (Figure 1.25) is extensively used in the Internet. To extend the number of IP addresses for future growth, IPv6 version is introduced.

IPv4 address is categorized into different classes. The total number of IPs in IP version 4 would be 4,294,967,296 (2^{32}). Table 1.1 shows the IP classes, IP address ranges, and total number of hosts allowed in every class of IP addresses (all for IPv4).

The IPv6 offers much more than IPv4. The total number of IPv6 would be (2^{128}). That number will be equal to 340,282,366,920,938,463,463,374,607,431,768,211,456!

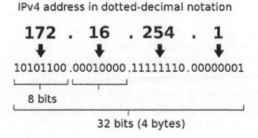

FIGURE 1.25   IP address – IPv4.

TABLE 1.1   IPv4 Address Classes

IP CLASS	IP ADDRESS RANGE	TOTAL NUMBERS
Class A	1.0.0.1 to 126.255.255.254	16 million hosts on 127 networks each
Class B	128.1.0.1 to 191.255.255.254	65,000 hosts on 16,000 networks each
Class C	192.0.1.1 to 223.255.254.254	254 hosts on 2 million networks each
Class D	224.0.0.0 to 239.255.255.255	Reserved for multicasting
Class E	240.0.0.0 to 254.255.255.254	Reserved for R & D and future use

TABLE 1.2   IPv4 Address Registry Names and Covered Regions

REGISTRY NAME	COVERED REGION
APNIC (Asia-Pacific Network Information Center)	Asia-Pacific region
AFRINIC (Africa National Information Center)	Africa region
ARIN (American Registry for Internet Numbers)	North America and few Caribbean countries
LACNIC (Latin American and Caribbean National Information Center)	Latin American countries and a few Caribbean countries
RIPE NCC (Reseaux IP European Network Coordination Center)	Europe, Central Asia, and the Middle East countries

Internationally, the IP address is managed and governed by the International Assigned Number Authority, IANA. There are sub-registries or authorities for the regional IP distribution. Those regional registries are listed in Table 1.2.

1.9.2 DNS Server

DNS is a type of server that deals with the conversion of domain into IP address. It is also known as domain name resolution server. Why is DNS used in the Internet? The reason behind using DNS is very simple. The names of the websites on the Internet are identified by the domain names like: http://www.abcd.com, but the transmission of data to communicate with the website server is done through IP address. Then, how is it possible for the routers to understand the domain name? It is the responsibility of DNS server (Figure 1.26). The IP address is sent to designated DNS server that returns the IP address of the domain. The routing of the data packets is then done through IP addresses.

It is very difficult for a person/user to remember a large number of IP addresses to access the desired websites. A user visits hundreds of websites on a daily and weekly basis; hence, it is very difficult for a user to remember IP addresses of all those websites.

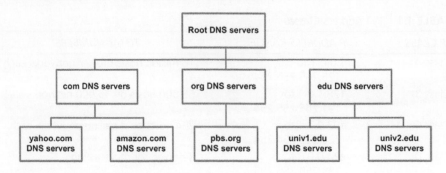

FIGURE 1.26   DNS server hierarchy. Various levels: LDNS (local DNS), ADNS (authoritative DNS), and gTLD (generic top-level domain).

The domain names are comparatively easy to remember. So, people type the domain name (technically known as URL – Uniform Resource Locator) in the web browser.

The DNS server comes into play to convert the domain name into the IP address associated with that particular domain name. Thus, the routing at the backend is done through IP addresses, which normally go unnoticed in the eyes of the Internet user. All these activities take place at the background between host, router, and DNS server.

There are many hundreds of DNS servers located in many countries of the world. All those DNS servers are linked with the major 13 servers named as DNS root name servers. All these 13 servers are located in the United States (10), Stockholm (1), Tokyo (1), and Amsterdam (1). The names of those root name servers are "A" through "M".

You can also use many other public DNS servers such as Google DNS, OpenNIC, Cloudflare, and Verizon, which can be used as both primary and secondary DNS servers. You can use the DNS services of these servers without any fee or charges.

1.9.3 TCP/IP Protocol

TCP/IP is a protocol suite used by the Internet for routing the data packets across the network of the networks. The TCP/IP suite works on the network, transport, and session layers of the seven-layer OSI model. Any network that wants to connect with the Internet should use TCP/IP for the abovementioned three layers. The flow of working requests and responses is explained in Figure 1.27 (figure taken from YouTube).

Another protocol used in parallel with the TCP is User Datagram Protocol (UDP). UDP is used instead of TCP in certain applications to improve performance rather than error correction. TCP is a connection-oriented protocol that checks the errors and has a flow control to provide accuracy. In real-time applications, UDP is preferred to improve the speed and performance of the data transmission.

The data packet received from the data link layer is wrapped with the headers containing IP address and related overloads and is handed over to the TCP or UDP to add its header for further transmission through different upper-layer protocols. The same process repeats in the reverse order to retrieve the data for the network destination.

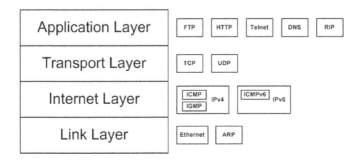

FIGURE 1.27   TCP/IP suite layers.

1.9.4 HTTP

HTTP (Figure 1.28) is server–client data communication protocol. It is an application-level protocol that communicates with the server through user agents such as web browsers, mobile apps, voice browser, web crawlers, and other similar kinds of client software agents.

The communication is based on request/response. Client sends request to the server through a port number (normally 80) of network layer to seek some information. At network layer, HTTP can communicate with both the TCP and UDP in the Internet stack through any designated port. The server responds with the response message that contains the requested message. The hypertext resources involved in this communication protocol include the URLs, HTML files, and other content.

HTTP was first introduced in 1990 by Tim Berners-Lee. This is the part of the TCP/IP suite used in the Internet communication. The latest version of this protocol is HTTP 2.0 released in 2015. The first version of this protocol was named as HTTP 0.9.

1.9.5 World Wide Web (WWW)

World Wide Web or precisely "WWW" (Figure 1.29) is the name of the combination of both web users and the resources that use the HTTP for communication. Many people confuse the terms: WWW and the Internet. In fact, they are different things.

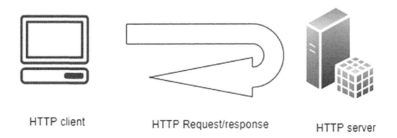

HTTP client   HTTP Request/response   HTTP server

FIGURE 1.28   Hypertext Transfer Protocol.

FIGURE 1.29   World Wide Web (WWW) – conceptual image.

The Internet is a gigantic network of networks, which may use different protocols for their communication at local network level, while WWW is the combination of all information including all web resources and users that use the HTTP.

WWW was introduced by Tim Berners-Lee first in 1989 by creating WWW server at CERN in the UK. It was publically available for use from 1991 when the public-level Internet was started. The WWW network-based information is governed and regulated by World Wide Web Consortium precisely referred to as W3C.

SAMPLE QUESTIONS AND ANSWERS FOR WHAT WE HAVE LEARNED IN CHAPTER 1

Q1. What is an output device of a computer?

A1: An output device of a computer is a component that is connected to the computer for producing meaningful information processed from the raw data inserted through input devices.

Examples: monitor, speaker.

Q2. What are storage components? Name some of them.

A2: The storage component of a computer is the data storage bank to keep the data saved on the secondary location, where the data can be easily accessed and managed.

The storage components include the following:

- Hard disk drive (HDD)
- Flash disk drive (FDD)
- Optical disk drive (ODD)
- Magnetic tapes

Q3. What are the major prospective technologies that could govern the future computers?

A3: AI, quantum computing, nanotechnology, and parallel processing.

Q4. What are the basic elements of a computer network?

A4: The basic elements of a computer network are hosts, connecting media, and connectors. But the modern communication networks are not that simple. Some of the major elements used to form a modern computer network are as follows:

- Hosts
- Routers
- Switches
- Hubs
- Firewalls
- Servers
- Cables/links
- Protocols
- Connectors

Q5. What is Internet? Name some of the major hardware elements of the modern Internet.

A5: The Internet is a gigantic network of thousands of networks connected with each other through backbone connectivity and routers. Some of the major hardware elements of modern Internet are as follows:

- Internet cloud (general name of the entire infrastructure of the Internet)
- Edge router
- Core router
- Firewalls (hardware version)
- Switches
- Hubs
- Servers

Q6. What is the basic difference between WWW and the Internet?

A6: Many people confuse the terms: WWW (World Wide Web) and the Internet. In fact, they are different things.

The Internet is a gigantic network of networks, which may use different protocols for their communication at local network level, while WWW is the combination of all information including all web resources and users that use the HTTP.

SOURCES

http://www.just.edu.jo/~mqais/CIS99/PDF/Ch.01_Introduction_%20to_computers.pdf.
https://en.wikiversity.org/wiki/What_is_a_computer%3F.

https://all-free-download.com/free-vector/download/computer-accessories-03-vector_155669.html.

http://people.bu.edu/baws/brief%20computer%20history.html.

https://www.webopedia.com/DidYouKnow/Hardware_Software/FiveGenerations.asp#fifth-generation.

https://www.geeksforgeeks.org/generations-of-computer/.

https://fcit.usf.edu/network/.

http://www.internetlivestats.com.

https://www.internetsociety.org/internet/history-internet/brief-history-internet/.

https://www.internetworldstats.com/stats.htm.

https://www.iana.org/numbers.

https://www.cse.wustl.edu/~jain/tutorials/ftp/t_2tcp.pdf.

https://www.w3.org/Protocols/rfc2616/rfc2616-sec1.html.

https://web.stanford.edu/class/cs344g/www-1992.pdf.

https://homepage.cs.uri.edu/faculty/wolfe/book/Readings/Reading03.htm.

Baran, P. *On Distributed Communications*, RAND Corporation, 1964 (last accessed 7 March 2020) https://www.rand.org/content/dam/rand/pubs/research_memoranda/2006/RM3420.pdf.

Cybersecurity Basics

2

2.1 INTRODUCTION

The short definition of cybersecurity is, "The protection of software, hardware, and data resources connected and stored on the Internet is known as the cybersecurity". From an individual to a large corporation, everybody is concerned about the security of their online data, software, and information.

The protection of the personal, financial data, commercial data, business-critical information, operational continuity, data integrity, and availability of online software services fall in the cybersecurity domain. Regulating the physical access and controlling the malicious intrusion, allowing the authorized access, encrypting the valuable information, and safeguarding the privacy are the components of cybersecurity.

Cybersecurity is one of the most important domains in the field of information technology. There are two spellings for it, "Cybersecurity" and "Cyber Security". In this book, we preferred using the former spelling. Cybersecurity is basically the name of standard practices that involve the people, technology, and processes in an organization, in a team, or even in a stand-alone environment in which the computers with the valuable data are connected to the Internet or the Intranet. Cybersecurity deals with the different procedures that create an environment of full security.

Cybersecurity widely relates to the technological processes and procedures to keep the valuable data and software resources safe and secure from the external threats emerging through the Internet, but the physical security is also a big component that affects the cybersecurity both directly and indirectly.

In our modern technological environments, software resources are the core components for almost all businesses, public life activities, governmental organizations, defense systems, and many other fields. The availability, integrity, and confidentiality of those software resources make your life run smoothly. The failure of any of the above three major components – integrity, availability, and confidentiality, will bring our entire life to a halt.

Nowadays, physical security is also becoming a part of cybersecurity issue. With the advent of Internet of Things (IoT) technology, the automation of home, factories, commercial areas, buildings, places, and many other installations is becoming a very commonplace practice. Thus, the entire physical security of any installation will also be influenced by the cybersecurity threats through the Internet. Meanwhile, the impact of physical security on the cybersecurity is already huge. Any small breach in the physical security can definitely pose a great threat to the cybersecurity as well.

Cybersecurity can be classified into multiple elements as mentioned below:

- Network security (NS)
- Information security (IS)
- Application security (AS)
- Business continuity planning (BCP)/disaster recovery
- Leadership commitment
- Operational security (OPSEC)
- End-user education

It is very important to note that cybersecurity is not just a one-time measure. It is a continuous process of security awareness, strategic planning, implementation, monitoring, and evaluation.

So, cybersecurity is a vast field in the information technology environment, which covers from human behaviors to the technological procedures that impact directly or indirectly the security of valuable resources stored and connected to the network.

2.2 IMPORTANCE OF CYBERSECURITY

According to the latest predictions from the Gartner research organization, the total global spending in the field of cybersecurity is expected to cross the US$124 billion mark in 2019 with a huge growth of over 8.7%.

The growth rate of security spending in 2018 as compared to that of 2017 was estimated at about 12.4%. The total spending in 2018 is estimated at about US$114 billion. The total global spending related to cybersecurity is expected to cross the US$1 trillion mark by 2022. Thus, this huge cybersecurity spending will make it one of the biggest spending domains in the information technology field.

The history of cybersecurity is very old, which dates back to 1903 when an insulting message coded in the Morse code was sent out to the John A Fleming by Nevil Maskelyne. This message marks as the first cyberattack in the form of malicious communication through distance communication between two connected devices. Cyber hacking has evolved over the past 115 years and has become very sophisticated, advanced, and high tech so that you cannot catch easily.

Many kinds of software and hardware tools are being extensively used in the modern hacker attacks on the networks, computers, storage devices, servers, applications, and vulnerable codes. The security of network has got much sophisticated in the present days due to the strong security features and capabilities of powerful firewalls. Still, the applications and software programs are the most vulnerable areas for the hackers to attack on.

According to the *Cybersecurity Ventures* latest predictions, the cost of global damages incurred due to the cybercrimes will cross the US$6 trillion mark from the total damages of US$3 trillion in 2015. If you look at these statistics, you will come to know the gravity of the cybersecurity threats (conceptual picture is shown in Figure 2.1).

The average cost of one single cybersecurity breach in 2018 is estimated to be about US$3.86 million, which is about 6.4% higher of the same in the previous year. The cybersecurity cost is continuously rising not only in terms of total loss of the organization but also in terms of the number of cybersecurity attacks. The new forms and features of cyber threats are emerging in the marketplace. The hackers have become so advanced that they create new and out-of-the-box ideas to attack the systems, networks, services, and data to steal the valuable IT resources.

The average cost of deploying the automated security system is very high. The average cost of automated security system implementation is about US$2.88 million. This huge amount is definitely out of the affordability of many small and medium-sized companies all over the world. To cope up with those increasing security threats, it is very crucial for the small and medium-sized companies to strictly follow the standard practices devised by the regulatory authorities and industry standard organizations.

If a proper compliance of the guidelines issued by the cybersecurity standard organizations is done, a substantial success in averting any big cybersecurity breach can be achieved easily.

FIGURE 2.1 Cybersecurity is important! (conceptual picture of a warning sign).

2.3 INTRODUCTION TO CYBERATTACKS

What is cyberattack? Getting access to the legitimate systems – servers, computers, network, or software programs – illegally and establishing control over the legitimate systems for carrying out malicious activities such as information stealth, data damage, system damage, and interruption in smooth operations of the legitimate networks and systems (Figure 2.2).

A cyberattack is a deliberate and malicious electronic attempt by one party, which may be either an organization or an individual to breach into the cyber environment of the other party – an individual or an organization – to steal, delete, or damage the valuable information.

The main objective of the attacker is to get benefits from that malicious act. Many organizations from the enemy countries try to destroy the important information to inflict losses to the enemy countries and their institutes. In short, the core purpose of cyberattack is always to inflict losses to the targeted entity.

The main areas of attacks include the following:

- Data servers
- Application servers
- Storage servers
- Financial information

FIGURE 2.2 Various types of cyberattacks.

- Operational systems
- Computer networks

There are numerous types and methods used for attacking the cyber environments of the other people. A few very important ones include the following:

- Malware attacks
- Phishing attacks
- Structured Language Query, SQL Injection
- Denial-of-service (DoS) attacks
- Man-in-the-middle (MITM) attacks

The successful number of cyberattacks per company has increased by 27.4% in 2017 as compared to 2016. The total number of successful cybersecurity attacks in 2017 was recorded as 130 attacks per company, as compared to 102 cyberattacks in 2016. The average annualized cost pertaining to cybersecurity is about US$11.7 million per company. That is unimaginably huge!

2.4 OBJECTIVES OF CYBERATTACKS

The objectives of cyberattacks (Figure 2.3 – concept) may vary from person to person and from organization to organization. For instance, many individual hackers attack the computers of other organizations or individuals to get financial benefits. An organization may steal the information from its competitor to achieve competitive edge.

FIGURE 2.3 Objectives of cyberattacks (conceptual picture).

Some enemy government-sponsored organizations may steal information from the other country to damage its capabilities or steal the information for countermeasure preparations. Some of the main objectives of a hacker for conducting cyberattacks are listed below:

- Achieving monetary gains
- Damaging the brand value of the other party
- Inflicting damages through cyberterrorism
- Obtaining government and business secrets
- Warfare cyberattacks
- Growth hacking email campaign

All of the abovementioned objectives can be achieved when any one or all of the following systems and data breaches are achieved by a hacker. Breaching "CIA" triad – confidentiality, integrity, and availability – makes a successful cyberattack. Let us now have a look at the major technical breaches of a successful cyberattack.

2.4.1 Confidentiality Breach

The breach of confidentiality occurs when the personal information or data provided by a client of an organization under certain data confidentiality agreements is either intentionally or unintentionally disclosed to the third party without getting consent from the client.

A hacker attacks the customer data stored on a server of an organization. Often it is done through multiple ways to get access to the information, which is provided to the organization in confidence. The confidentiality breach can inflict financial losses to the client. Even the sense of insecurity is often unbearable for the user. The personal data is compromised and misused for further hacking of data and other information associated with the confidential data.

There are many rules and regulations in place in many countries of the globe to sue the company that discloses the confidential information to the third party without any consent from the concerned client. Normally, the confidentiality breach occurs unintentionally through cyber hacking. The main sources of confidentiality breach include the following:

- Theft of employee laptops
- Leaving computers with confidential information unattended
- Providing unauthorized access to the unconcerned person
- Unauthorized access by hacker through malware
- Consulting company employees violating confidentiality agreements
- Unlawful use of information for personal or business gains

The examples of confidential data include the following:

- Intellectual property
- Personal identity information

- Credit card information
- Bank account information
- Personal health information
- Business or trade secrets

The examples of big confidential data breaches in recent years include the Marriot data breach (500 million) in 2018, Equifax data breach (143 million) in 2017, and Adult Friend Finder data breach (412 million) in 2016.

All those breaches affected hundreds of millions of accounts of personal information. The human error and internal employees are the major sources of confidentiality breaches. The external hacker is also a big threat, but much lesser than the former ones if the proper cybersecurity measures are taken for the confidential data security.

2.4.2 Availability Breach

The availability breach occurs when the authorized user is unable to access online services or personal information that he/she is authorized for. The denial or unavailability of the authorized digital resources is known as the availability breach.

The main malicious activities used for disrupting the availability of the services or information are done through DoS attacks or network intrusion. Once the hacker gets success in intruding into the network, he/she establishes the control over the servers illegally and denies the authorized access of the legitimate users to the resources or services.

The main sources of breach of availability may include the following:

- Failure of hardware
- Malfunction of software
- Choking of data bandwidth
- Redundant arrangement failures
- DoS attacks

It should be clarified here that DoS is basically a situation or a condition, which can also occur due to unintentional causes like software bug, hardware failure, environmental conditions, and other external issues; however, when an active attacker intentionally causes a DoS situation, it is called DoS attack (i.e., deliberate attempt to attack the availability of data or services).

The examples of breach of availability of services and data include failure of Google Cloud in February 2018 and failure of Equinix in March 2018.

2.4.3 Integrity Breach

Any data stored on the service provider's server should remain accurate, consistent, and valid for the entire period of data stay on the server. Normally, data is stored and transported in the encrypted forms for maintaining the confidentiality of the data. The data changes its formats, but at the end of the day, the data should be valid and meaningful.

Any activity that damages the data consistency, validity, and accuracy is known as the data integrity breach activity. The integrity breach may corrupt the data, and then, it may not be useful anymore.

The hackers achieve the data integrity breach through multiple ways as mentioned below:

- Introduction of malware on the server
- Undoable malicious encryption of data
- Manipulation of original data
- Introduction of viruses
- Malicious insiders

The examples of data integrity attacks include the introduction of Stuxnet worm to manipulate the Iranian Nuclear Program Data in 2010 and World Anti-Doping Agency data manipulation in 2016.

SAMPLE QUESTIONS AND ANSWERS FOR WHAT WE HAVE LEARNED IN CHAPTER 2

Q1. Define cybersecurity.

A1: The short definition of cybersecurity is, "The protection of software, hardware, and data resources connected and stored on the Internet is known as the cybersecurity". From an individual to a large corporation, everybody is concerned about the security of their online data, software, and information.

The protection of the personal, financial data, commercial data, business-critical information, operational continuity, data integrity, and availability of online software services fall in the cybersecurity domain. Regulating the physical access and controlling the malicious intrusion, allowing the authorized access, encrypting the valuable information, and safeguarding the privacy are the components of cybersecurity.

Q2. What is a cyberattack?

A2: A cyberattack is a deliberate and malicious electronic attempt by one party, which may be either an organization or an individual to breach into the cyber environment of the other party – an individual or an organization – to steal, delete, or damage the valuable information.

Q3. What are confidential data? Name some examples.

A3: Confidential data are sensitive data that should not be known by someone or some party who is not authorized to read or see that. Often, these are about personal data or data that may have significant implications when exposed to the public arena. Some examples of confidential data include the following:

- Intellectual property
- Personal identity information
- Credit card information
- Bank account information
- Personal health information
- Business or trade secrets

Q4. What are the major sources of breach of availability?

A4: The main sources of breach of availability may include the following:

- Failure of hardware
- Malfunction of software
- Choking of data bandwidth
- Redundant arrangement failures
- Denial-of-service (DoS) attacks

Q5. How could the hackers breach integrity of data?

A5: The hackers achieve the data integrity breach through multiple ways as mentioned below:

- Introduction of malware on the server
- Undoable malicious encryption of data
- Manipulation of original data
- Introduction of viruses
- Malicious insiders

SOURCES

https://www.freepik.com/
https://www.cisco.com/c/en/us/products/security/what-is-cybersecurity.html.
https://www.itgovernance.co.uk/what-is-cybersecurity.
https://www.gartner.com/en/newsroom/press-releases/2018-08-15-gartner-forecasts-worldwide-information-security-spending-to-exceed-124-billion-in-2019.
https://cybersecurityventures.com/hackerpocalypse-cybercrime-report-2016/.
https://www.ibm.com/security/data-breach.
https://www.accenture.com/t20170926T072837Z__w__/us-en/_acnmedia/PDF-61/Accenture-2017-CostCyberCrimeStudy.pdf.
https://www.markeluk.com/articles/what-is-a-breach-of-confidentiality.
https://www.unco.edu/hipaa/breach-confidentiality/.

https://www.csoonline.com/article/2130877/data-breach/the-biggest-data-breaches-of-the-21st-century.html.

https://whatis.techtarget.com/definition/Confidentiality-integrity-and-availability-CIA.

https://guardtime.com/blog/target-a-confidentiality-or-integrity-breach.

https://digitalguardian.com/blog/what-data-integrity-data-protection-101.

https://www.itsecurityguru.org/2016/11/29/2017-year-data-integrity-breach/.

Types of Cyberattacks

3

3.1 INTRODUCTION

According to the information of University of Maryland research report, there is a hacker attack after every 39 seconds (on an average) on a computer connected with the Internet. That means any computer connected to the Internet sustains 2,244 malicious attacks every day!

All those attacks on the computers are carried out through different formats and modules of cyberattacks. There are many established formats of cyberattacks, which are very well known in the market, but the hackers always try out new and sophisticated ways to exploit the vulnerabilities in the computers and networks to strike. Newer formats and ways of cyberattacks (conceptual image in Figure 3.1) are being developed in the market to bypass the recognized security measures.

Let us have a look at the most common types of techniques adopted in day-to-day cyberattacks on networks and computers to either steal valuable data or disrupt the continuity of online services on the Internet.

FIGURE 3.1   Cyberattack concept.

3.2 DENIAL OF SERVICE (DoS)

Denial of Service or DoS is an Internet security-related event in which the hackers attack a particular server running some Internet services to prevent it from working normal or to stop the services. In this case, the servers are overwhelmed with the flooding of superfluous messages (Figure 3.2).

The hacker actively exploits the server vulnerability and sends the bombardment of automated requests and messages to that particular server to respond. The server gets overwhelmed and choked and stops working normal. In certain cases, the service stops working due to overloaded server. These kinds of malicious attacks prevent the

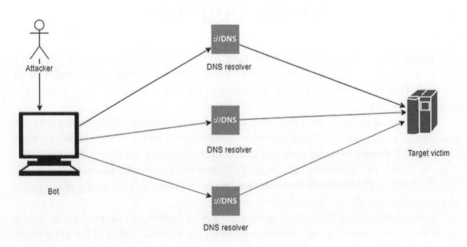

FIGURE 3.2   DoS attack.

legitimate users from accessing the online services (hence, the services are disrupted or stopped for the legitimate clients/users).

The major symptoms of being the victim of DoS attacks (for a legitimate user) include the following:

- Inability in accessing a website
- Delay in accessing online service
- Huge delays in file opening on the websites
- Increased volume of spam emails
- Degradation of performance of services

The impact of the DoS attack can be mitigated by taking the following steps:

- Routing the malicious traffic
- Using load balancers to avoid heavy malicious traffic to strive the server
- Using intrusion detection systems
- Using intrusion prevention systems
- Using security firewalls

Main types of DoS attacks include the following:

- DNS (Domain Name System) server attack
- HTTP (Hypertext Transfer Protocol) server attack
- ICMP (Internet Control Message Protocol) flooding
- Network attack or buffer overflow attack
- Large name files attack on the network or server
- Ping of death attack
- SYN flood attack on TCP (Transmission Control Protocol) handshake protocol
- Shrew attack

3.3 DISTRIBUTED DENIAL OF SERVICE (DDoS)

Distributed denial of service or precisely DDoS is a type of DoS attack. Like the DoS attack, in this type of cyberattack, the servers are jammed or overwhelmed with the malicious traffic to prevent the legitimate users from accessing their accounts or legitimate online services. However, the main difference between DoS and DDoS attacks is that the DoS attack is targeted from a specific origination of traffic to attack the victim server, while in the DDoS attack case, multiple sources of traffic are used to attack the victim server (at the same time). DDoS attack is more lethal than the DoS attack. The prevention of DDoS attacks is very difficult as compared to the normal DoS attacks (Figure 3.3).

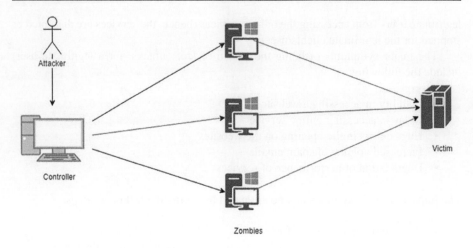

FIGURE 3.3   Distributed denial of service (DDoS).

In the DDoS attack, the hacker uses controller machine to hack multiple vulnerable machines around the globe. Then, all those infected machines will be controlled by the software program running on the attacker's server. That controller sends instructions to the infected machine on which the hacker has already established the control to send automated requests (traffic) to the targeted victim machine. Then, all those "zombies" start attacking the target from multiple Internet Protocol (IP) sources to bring the server to almost a *halt*.

It is more difficult to prevent DDoS attack than the usual DoS attack. In this attack, many computers from different parts become the part of this deadly attack without any approval and knowledge of the owner of the computer.

DDoS attacks are carried out in different ways; the main types of DDoS attacks are listed below:

- Connection-based application-layer attacks, i.e., HTTP, DNS, web servers, and others
- Connectionless volumetric attacks from multiple botnets
- State table exhaustion attacks
- And all other techniques used in the DoS attacks

3.4 MAN-IN-THE-MIDDLE (MITM) ATTACKS

In the "Man-in-the-Middle" or MITM cyberattack, the hacker intercepts the normal connection between the user and the web server without any knowledge of both user and server. The legitimate communication link between the two entities is exploited, intercepted, and decrypted to steal the personal information for malicious use (Figure 3.4).

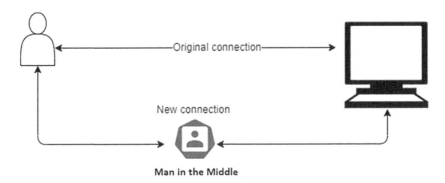

FIGURE 3.4   MITM attacks.

MITM attack consists of three major steps. In the first step, the hacker scans the vulnerabilities of the system and network. Once the vulnerabilities are known, the phishing emails are sent to users; those emails contain the wrong addresses of your services or bank accounts. In the third step, they decrypt your information for stealing purpose.

Let us take an example to better understand the issue of MITM attack. Sometimes, you get an email that looks like it was sent from your bank or your other financial institute. That is a *phishing* email, which asks you to click certain link for the verification of your account, phone number, or any other information. Once you click that link, the link takes you to the web server, which looks like your bank website but in reality, that is not your bank website. You insert your credentials to login. Thus, you provide your bank information to the hacker.

Finally, the hacker obtains your password and uses that password to take some information or valuable item from your account. This entire process is known as the MITM cyberattack. The major types of MITM attacks include the following.

- DNS spoofing
- HTTP spoofing
- IP spoofing
- Email hijacking
- SSL (Secure Sockets Layer) hijacking
- Wi-Fi network eavesdropping
- Stealing the cookies set on the browsers

3.5 CRYPTOJACKING

Cryptojacking is a relatively new form of cyberattack to be used for stealing the "cryptocurrency". This attack mines processor's power through malicious software on the cryptocurrency miner machines of the legitimate users. In this form of cyberattack, the processing power of the legitimate cryptocurrency machines is hijacked and used for cryptocurrency mining to earn rewards.

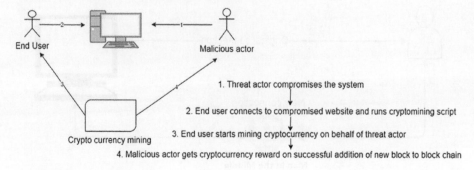

FIGURE 3.5   Cryptojacking.

The cryptocurrency, especially the Bitcoin, has become so costly during the past 1 year. Hence, the attraction and benefits of the cryptocurrency soared so high in the past couple of years. The hackers were also enticed with this lucrative business. They started capturing the cryptocurrency rewards by using computer processing power of other people.

Normally, cryptocurrency is used to verify the cryptocurrency transactions, and in return, the servers that verify the hashed transactions of cryptocurrency are rewarded with a fraction of Bitcoin. This is known as *mining*. The cryptocurrency mining requires huge processing power to verify the complex hashed codes. So, hackers started using the computing power of the legitimate users in their names.

In this method of hacking, a malware is installed on the servers of the cryptocurrency miners. That software uses the power of the machines in the name of the malicious users. Thus, the reward earned through legitimate verification of transactions goes to the account of the hacker.

The step-by-step procedure of cryptojacking is shown in Figure 3.5.

Cryptojacking is done through the injection of CoinHive software into different websites, browsers, and operating systems. This software is maliciously installed on other's resources to run crypto-mining software to earn the rewards. It has been noted that thousands of computers were used for this purpose by just a single hacker to earn substantial amount of money in the form of Bitcoin.

3.6 SQL INJECTION

Structured Query Language (SQL) injection (Figure 3.6) is a type of malicious practice to steal the valuable data from the database server. This method exploits the vulnerabilities in the traditional Active Server Page (ASP) websites, PHP applications, and SQL server forms. The traditional ASP and hypertext preprocessor (PHP)-powered websites generate the dynamic SQL within the front end of the application. The malicious user appends an SQL command in the back end of the SQL form field. The objective of that command is to break the original SQL script and run the malicious script attached with the SQL form.

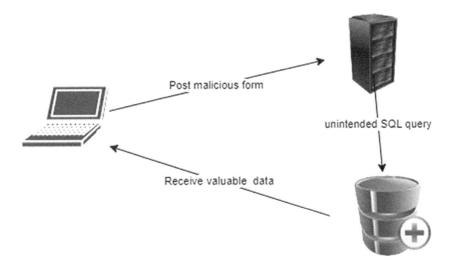

Post malicious form

unintended SQL query

Receive valuable data

FIGURE 3.6 SQL injection.

The malicious code gets data from the SQL database server and sends to the computer of the hacker. Thus, the valuable information is compromised through SQL injections. However, the release of latest ASP.NET and standard practices for creating software code have somewhat reduced SQL injection attacks in the recent years.

According to the web application attack statistics 2017, SQL injection is the second largest source of web application malicious attacks with 21.6% of the total web application attacks preceded by the cross-site scripting (XSS) with 31.6% and followed by path traverse with 11.4%.

IT, banks and e-transaction website, and government websites were the top three fields badly affected by the web application attacks that were predominated by the XSS and SQL injection attacks.

3.7 SPAMMING

Spamming in the IT field is the name of sending junk mails and messages to the users in bulk without getting consent from the users (conceptual image, Figure 3.7). It is a form of bombardment of products for marketing purposes. The hackers also use spamming for spreading malware, viruses, phishing, Trojans, worms, and spyware. A large source of security threats is extensively used in numerous types of cyberattacks.

Spamming is a widespread form of malicious attacks used to send the unsolicited messages through different modes of messaging such as instant messages, emails, social network messages, ads, mobile phone messages, and social groups. All these activities are directed to get marketing gains by attacking the users incessantly through unsolicited messages.

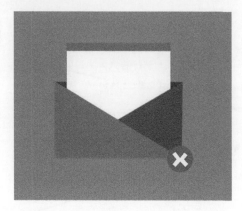

FIGURE 3.7   Spamming (unwanted emails – conceptual image).

The word "spam" comes from the luncheon meat introduced around in the middle of the 20th century. That spam contained repeated layers of meat. So, the repeated layers of messages are collectively known as the spamming in the modern field of technology.

Till the middle of 2018, the spam emails accounted for over 45% of all emails shared on the Internet, according to the Propeller research conducted in the first quarter of 2018. In this spamming traffic, advertising, adult-related materials, and finance-related matters are the top three domains in the spamming email messages.

According to the research, more than 14.5 billion emails were sent out on the Internet on a daily basis in the starting months of the 2018. The senders of the spam emails all around the world collectively earn about US$7,000 per day. Thus, it is still an attractive business for many individuals and businesses.

3.8 CYBERTERRORISM

The term "cyberterrorism" (conceptual image in Figure 3.8) was coined many years back in 1980 by Barry Colin. The term got more attention in beginning of the 21st century. Many new methods and modules have emerged on the cyberspace arena.

Cyberterrorism is a type of cybercrime to attack or threat to attack the computer systems, mission-critical data, or computer networks either to damage the cyber resources or to steal the critical information that can pose a great threat to the security of public lives, government systems, or even the defense systems of a country. The objectives of cyberterrorism include the sabotage of political and social fabric through coercion or intimidation tactics.

The main examples of cyberterrorism include the disruption of public utilities such as water supplies, electricity, healthcare, and other such systems. The coercive activities include the honey trap and other blackmailing tactics that can lead to the compromise on the governmental or security system information. All these activities can lead to economic system instability, explosion, plane crash, and other actions that cause serious

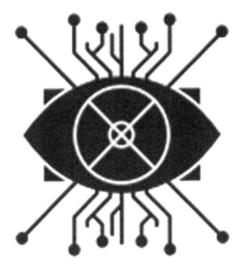

FIGURE 3.8   Cyberterrorism (conceptual image).

injuries or death to a person or a group of people in a country. The terrorist attacks are normally destructive in nature to inflict huge losses to the planned targets rather than getting some money or economic benefits.

The core objective behind cyberterrorism is either to inflict direct physical, monetary, political, and social damages on the targeted entity or to prepare for the lethal attacks in the future on the premeditated targets. Cyberterrorism is becoming a huge menace for the entire civilized world horn locked in the conflict of civilizations and different ideologies. New forms and formats of cyberterrorism are surfacing to inflict serious damages to the legitimate systems, governments, and societies.

Intimidation and coercive activities to destabilize the societies, governments, and other institutions to gain the religious, social, ideological, and political gains fall under the broader category of cyberterrorism. These activities are carried out to gain control and power through illegal way.

All traditional hacking tools such as phishing, worms, malwares, Trojan horses, and viruses can be used to pave the way for a large-scale and massive cyberattack that can result in severe loss and damage to the public lives, societies, government system, and other critical infrastructures.

3.9 DIGITAL PROPERTY MISAPPROPRIATION

The digital property misappropriation (Figure 3.9) is the illegal or fraudulent use of the digital resources like software and digital content, including e-books, audios, videos, images, writings, paintings, and the likes without the permission of the owner of that digital property.

FIGURE 3.9   Digital property misappropriation (concept).

According to the latest research conducted by the Transparency Market Research Inc., in 2017, the total global market value of digital property misappropriation is expected to reach the US$6.76 billion mark by 2025 with over 14.3% CAGR (compound annual growth rate) between 2017 and 2025. This huge amount of money is used illegally by different rogue companies, people, and countries to use the digital property without paying any royalty to the owner of that particular digital asset. In other words, over US$6 billion are misappropriated in the global economy!

There are many local and international rules that govern the prevention of the misappropriation of the legitimate digital assets, but the implementation of those laws in full force is still far away from the realization. Among such laws, patents, copyrights, trademarks, and other such rules are already in force to safeguard the rights of the owners of the digital property in the global market.

The major steps powered by the modern technology to safeguard the digital properties include data encryption, digital access control, user controls, and others. Once the data has been transferred into the hands of malicious users, they can misappropriate that digital asset in different ways. So, the effectiveness of the technological-based measures is still not sufficient to fully safeguard the misuse of the digital assets of legitimate owners of the property.

3.10 ZERO-DAY EXPLOITATION

Zero-day exploitation (Figure 3.10) commonly known as Zero-Day or 0-Day is a vulnerability in the computer software system that is known exactly on the same day when the malicious attacks exploit that vulnerability. In this attack, there is almost no time to patch up the vulnerability of the software because it was known at the same time when the attack occurred and no time was available for the software engineers to tackle this issue.

According to the WatchGuard Threat Lab research report 2018, there is as much as 33% rise in the zero-day attacks by the middle of 2018. In the third quarter 2018 report, it was found that 28.9% of the total malware attacks accounted for the zero-day exploitation.

FIGURE 3.10   Zero-day exploitation (unknown issue – conceptual image).

The total number of zero-day attacks has increased in 2017 as compared to the previous years. The total number of verified zero-day attacks in 2017 was recorded as 1,522 as compared to 1,262 in 2016. The reason behind this increased number of zero-day attack is the increased sophistication of malicious users and hackers. In zero-day vulnerabilities, the malwares are installed silently on the computers without any notable movement or change, but it explodes immediately as it is detected by the computer security personnel. In certain cases, the malware automatically encrypts the data before sending to its command control center established by the hackers. Due to the high sophistication of the malware program, it goes unnoticed for a longer period to exploit the known fault of the system.

Either to avert or to reduce the impact of the zero-day vulnerabilities, many companies run incentivized programs for the hackers to find out the zero-day vulnerability against the pre-announced bounty commonly referred to as bug bounty rewards. Google has paid over US$3 million in the name of bug bounty rewards in 2017.

3.11 PHISHING

Phishing (Figure 3.11) is a type of cyberattack in which the targeted person is bombarded with the emails that look very similar to the emails coming from their banks, insurance companies, and other service providers. The hacker targets the people through emails to get their sensitive and personal information related to their financial and other account information disguising as the genuine and trustworthy individuals.

The main target of the phishing attack is to get the information about the credit card number, ATM pin codes, passwords, user name, and the related information. Once the information has been collected, the hackers use that information to steal the money or other valuable digital assets. This attack is normally used for the financial theft from the bank accounts. The marketing strategies and campaigns also use similar kinds of tactics to increase the sales of the products.

FIGURE 3.11   Phishing (conceptual image).

There are three major modes of phishing used in the modern phishing activities as listed below:

- Telephone calls commonly referred to as voice phishing, or vishing
- Emails referred to as general phishing
- Small text messages (SMS) referred to as smishing

The core objective in all three modes of phishing is to steal the identity of the legitimate user by alluring via different modes of communications.

3.12 DIGITAL VANDALISM

The digital or cyber vandalism is a very destructive form of cybersecurity threat, which is increasing very fast nowadays. In digital vandalism, the data, computer, or networks are either damaged or manipulated so that the genuine objectives of the IT system are changed badly. When cyberspace is used for digital vandalism, that is cyber vandalism. Hence, these are basically the same in context (Figure 3.12).

In a digital vandalism attack, the malware either removes the useful data from the websites or manipulates the information in such a way that the meaning of the information is reversed. Thus, a bad impact on the reputation of the source is created.

The increasing competition in the field of global businesses has changed the way people deal with the competitors to obtain the competitive edge. Many black-hat marketing tactics are also used to malign the reputation of the competitor services or products. This campaign of cyber vandalism is also used in many political, social, and personal defamation cases. It is comparatively difficult to catch and sue the culprits due to the sophisticated attacks by the hackers from unknown locations.

For instance, in 2016 US elections, the wiki page of Donald Trump was removed and then recreated with many changes and creating mocking slogans on the web page.

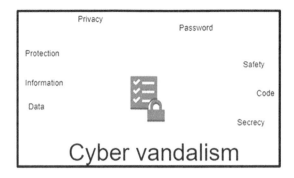

FIGURE 3.12   Cyber/digital vandalism (conceptual image).

The main reason behind this act was to malign the image of Donald Trump and his campaign in the elections.

Digital vandalism directly affects the reputation and brand name of the company, person, or an institute. It has become very critical today because of fierce competition in the marketplace. Many hackers damage the brands of a particular company or entity and indirectly provide the benefit to its competitor in the market.

3.13 CYBERSTALKING

Cyberstalking (concept shown in Figure 3.13) is one of the most serious problems in the domain of cyberspace. Women are the most affected population of cyberstalking. Cyberstalking is a form of harassing and threatening. It is also known as cyberbullying

FIGURE 3.13   Cyberstalking.

in other terms. In this form of cyberattack, the organizations, groups, or individuals are harassed to agree upon some undesirable conditions in relationship or business.

Cyberstalking is a systematic approach of harassing done through email, phones, SMS, chats, and other forms of communication. The main components used in the communication to threaten the targeted entity include defaming, false allegations, slandering, and other forms of blackmailing.

Digital cyberstalking is similar to the offline or physical stalking done in the streets, at home, or at shopping centers through different traditional modes of communication. The impact of the cyberstalking on the teenage group is much pervasive and widespread. They happen to be so sensitive and less mature to handle the pressure of blackmailing targeted on them. In certain conditions, people succumb to the pressure and commit some serious life-threatening acts such as suicide and other such things.

The impact of cyberstalking in Asian countries is very high due to the traditional social structures and many taboos spread in the society. So, the cyberstalking should be discouraged very aggressively at the root levels.

The other common names of cyberstalking are Internet stalking, online stalking, and e-stalking. In many countries, cyberstalking is a punishable crime.

3.14 CYBER FRAUDS AND FORGERY

Cyber frauds and forgery is also a new form of cyberattack in the modern digital world. In this form of crime, the digitally stored documents are forged to form the counterfeit documents. This crime is increased during the recent years due to the availability of high-tech devices like computer software, printers, scanners, cameras, and other tools (Figure 3.14).

FIGURE 3.14 Cyber frauds and forgery (concept).

In cyber frauds, the fake and counterfeit currency is also a big component. Traditionally, it was very difficult to create fake currency because it required a high level of technology, machinery, and tools. But now it is much easier with the help of ink jet printers and modern software tools.

Many documents used for the immigration, education, jobs, and security clearance were found fabricated with the help of modern cyber tools. Although all these crimes are punishable under the laws, catching such frauds without any particular tools and training is almost impossible. Many counterfeit checks, coupons, stationery, bills, and other documents are becoming more prone to forgery and fraud in the market.

SAMPLE QUESTIONS AND ANSWERS FOR WHAT WE HAVE LEARNED IN CHAPTER 3

Q1. What is DoS Attack? What are the general symptoms?

A1: Denial of service or DoS is an Internet security-related event in which the hackers attack a particular server running some Internet services to prevent it from working normal or to stop the services. In this case, the servers are overwhelmed with the flooding of superfluous messages.

The major symptoms of being the victim of DoS attacks (for a legitimate user) include the following:

- Inability in accessing a website
- Delay in accessing online service
- Huge delays in file opening on the websites
- Increased volume of spam emails
- Degradation of performance of services

Q2. What is the difference between DoS and DoS attack?

A2: Whenever legitimate service is denied for a user for some invalid cause, DoS situation may occur which means the service is not given. This can happen due to software bug, hardware failure, environmental conditions, and other external issues; however, when an active attacker intentionally causes a DoS situation, it is called DoS attack. That means, to be considered as an attack, there must be an active attacker behind that to make data and services unavailable to the user who needs it via legal means.

Q3. What is MITM?

A3: In the "Man-in-the-Middle" or MITM cyberattack, the hacker intercepts the normal connection between the user and the web server without any knowledge of both user and server. The legitimate communication link between the two entities is exploited, intercepted, and decrypted to steal the personal information for malicious use.

Q4. What is Cryptojacking?

A4: Cryptojacking is a relatively new form of cyberattack to be used for stealing the "cryptocurrency". This attack mines processor's power through malicious software on the cryptocurrency miner machines of the legitimate users. In this form of cyberattack, the processing power of the legitimate cryptocurrency machines is hijacked and used for cryptocurrency mining to earn rewards.

Q5. Why could cyberstalking be dangerous? Explain.

A5: Cyberstalking is a systematic approach of harassing done through email, phones, SMS (short message service), chats, and other forms of communication. The main components used in the communication to threaten the targeted entity include defaming, false allegations, slandering, and other forms of blackmailing.

Digital cyberstalking is similar to the offline or physical stalking done in the streets, at home, or at shopping centers through different traditional modes of communication. The impact of the cyberstalking on the teenage group is much pervasive and widespread. They happen to be so sensitive and less mature to handle the pressure of blackmailing targeted on them. In certain conditions, people succumb to the pressure and commit some serious life-threatening acts such as suicide and other such things. Hence, it could really affect the mental health of the youth within some period of time.

SOURCES

https://www.securitymagazine.com/articles/87787-hackers-attack-every-39-seconds.
https://www.ptsecurity.com/upload/corporate/ww-en/analytics/Web-application-attacks-2018-eng.pdf.
https://issuu.com/larapace/docs/computer_related_forgery_and_fraud.
https://www.researchgate.net/publication/251329429_Forgery_and_Computer_Fraud.
https://www.computerhope.com/jargon/c/computer-fraud.htm.
https://social.technet.microsoft.com/Forums/exchange/en-US/2086dd81-cc0d-424a-8123-f4d5578ba74e/what-is-spam-how-they-attack?forum=exchangesvrsecuremessaginglegacy.
https://en.wikipedia.org/wiki/Denial-of-service_attack.
https://www.britannica.com/topic/cybercrime/Counterfeiting-and-forgery.
https://www.cloudflare.com/learning/ddos/what-is-a-ddos-attack/.
https://searchsecurity.techtarget.com/definition/denial-of-service.
https://securebox.comodo.com/ssl-sniffing/ddos-attacks/.
https://us.norton.com/internetsecurity-wifi-what-is-a-man-in-the-middle-attack.html.
https://www.enisa.europa.eu/publications/info-notes/cryptojacking-cryptomining-in-the-browser.
https://crypto.stanford.edu/cs142/lectures/16-sql-inj.pdf.
https://cdn.ttgtmedia.com/rms/pdf/Cherry_Securing_SQL_Chap6.pdf.
https://www.propellercrm.com/blog/email-spam-statistics.
https://www.symantec.com/avcenter/reference/cyberterrorism.pdf.
https://en.wikipedia.org/wiki/Cyberterrorism.
https://www.transparencymarketresearch.com/intellectual-property-software-market.html.

https://www.nap.edu/read/9601/chapter/7#163.

https://www.watchguard.com/wgrd-resource-center/infographic/ internet-security-insights-q3-2018.

https://www.trendmicro.com/content/dam/trendmicro/global/en/business/products/network/ integrated-atp/vulnerability-tracker-feb-2018.pdf.

https://www.itproportal.com/2016/07/18/digital-vandalism-the-latest-security-threat/.

https://usa.kaspersky.com/resource-center/threats/computer-vandalism.

https://study.com/academy/lesson/vandalism-in-digital-crime-types-evidence.html.

Mohammed, M. and Pathan, A-S.K., *Automatic Defense against Zero-day Polymorphic Worms in Communication Networks*. ISBN 9781466557277, CRC Press, Taylor & Francis Group, Boca Raton, FL, 2013.

Pathan, A.-S.K. and Kindy, D.A., "Lethality of SQL injection against current and future internet-technologies," *International Journal of Computational Science and Engineering*, Vol. 9, No. 4, 2014, Inderscience Publishers, pp. 386–394.

Sharma, G. and Sheetal, K., "Advanced multi-factor user authentication scheme for E-governance applications in smart cities," *International Journal of Computers and Applications*, Taylor & Francis, Vol. 41, No. 4, 2019, pp. 312–327.

Thakur, K., Shan, J., and Pathan, A.-S.K., "Innovations of Phishing Defense: The mechanism, measurement and defense strategies," *International Journal of Communication Networks and Information Security*, Vol. 10, No. 1, April 2018, pp. 19–27.

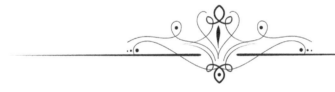

Recent Cyberattacks and Their Impact

4

4.1 INTRODUCTION

Cyberattack comes down heavily on the companies, businesses, governments, and other organizations. It costs billions of dollars to the affected entities across the globe. According to the UK Center for Strategic and International Studies, the estimated global losses due to the cyberattacks were about US$400 billion per annum in 2017.

Higher volumes of losses incurred due to the cyberattacks have increased the cyber insurance business exponentially. According to the Allianz Insurance Corporation, the cyber insurance premiums are expected to cross the US$20 billion mark by 2025 from the present volume of just under US$4 billion. With the elevated wrath of cyberattacks, the insurance business is expected to grow at over 40% CAGR (compound annual growth rate) in the next 5–7 years.

The recent cyberattack on the Equifax consumer credit rating agency devastated the reputation and business of the company with an estimated loss of over

US$150 million or so. Thus, the cyberattacks are posing huge threats to businesses in the times to come. Let us have a look at a few top cyberattacks that took place in the recent years.

4.2 EQUIFAX DATA THEFT

Equifax (Figure 4.1) is a consumer credit rating agency based in Atlanta, USA. The company handles over 820 million consumers and over 91 million companies round the world. The company has also a very huge database of employees working with more than 7,100 employees. The company has many details of the consumers such as salaries, personal information, credit card numbers, driving license numbers, medical records, and many other such critical information.

Between the mid of May 2017 and the end of July 2017, hackers got access to the Equifax database by exploiting the vulnerabilities present in the official website of the company, and started stealing the consumer information continuously for over 2 months without being noticed or caught. The company security team detected the malicious activity on July 29, 2017. But by that time, it was too late for the security team to contain the wide-scale damage wreaked on the company.

More than 143 million consumers' data were stolen. That information included consumer names, birth certificates, physical addresses, credit card information, driving license, medical information, and much more. The total number of stolen credit card numbers was about 209,000. More than 182,000 important documents of the people were stolen.

This huge data breach cost the company over US$4 billion according to a report published in the *Time* magazine. It is very important to note that data theft losses cannot be calculated accurately, and the liquidated damages of the company are very large.

FIGURE 4.1 Equifax.

Such a company suffers in multiple ways for many months and years to come. The reputation of the company goes down, and the over market performance and business processes are struck badly. In fact, in this case, the company sustained a huge blow when its shares dipped by over 20% in less than a week's period. The litigation and the regulations substantially increased on the company. A huge disruption in the business processes and services leads to the mayhem situation in the company and in the consumer base of the company.

Reuters news agency with reference to different analysts and experts termed it the biggest cyberattack in the history of digital crimes in terms of the total loss of revenue for a single company. It was also estimated that the average cost of a single cyberattack in 2017 has increased tremendously to more than US$11 million as compared to the average cost of a single attack in 2016.

The losses to Equifax Company will continue incurring for many months and even years. Having noticed this huge loss inflicted upon Equifax, companies across the world are extremely caught in dilemma. All companies across the world are facing a bigger challenge to maintain their business processes secure and smooth.

There is catch-22 situation in between the cost of the cyberattack and maintenance of high level of cybersecurity in the online environment. Many enterprises choose not to adopt the security policy, which in certain case can cause them serious damages in their businesses. This trend of ignoring the implementation of security policy on the basis of high cost is pervasive in small businesses.

4.3 VPNFILTER CYBERATTACK

VPNFilter (Figure 4.2) was a malware that originated from Russia. Initially, Ukraine was the main target of this malware, but later, it affected over 500,000 routers worldwide. This malware was based on the man-in-the-middle (MITM) cyberattack. This attack badly affected numerous routers of Ukraine.

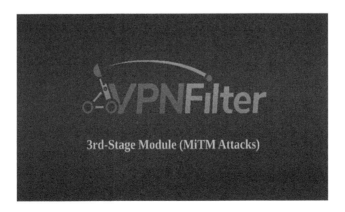

FIGURE 4.2   VPNFilter cyberattack.

This malware maintains its presence on the routers even the router is rebooted; therefore, the router becomes a big nuisance for the cybersecurity people for many days and months. This malware was developed with multiple stages and based on modular principle. This attack is also known as the Internet of Things (IoT) attack. According to the FBI reports, VPNFilter malware was spread by a Russian group named Fancy Bear.

This malware affects the IoT routers and network-attached storage (NAS) via multistage infections. It has infected more than 500 thousand routers in more than 54 countries worldwide. Especially, the impact of these attacks on Ukraine has been extremely high. The first Ukraine blackout in 2015 also used the first-stage malware of this new format of cyberattack.

The most vulnerable routers for this malware include D-Link, Linksys, MikroTik, Asus, TP-Link, Netgear, and many others. All these routers are used in the Internet access for the physical automation and IoT systems in homes, industries, and commercial areas.

This malware has three fundamental stages to attack a networking device:

Stage one: A worm is installed on router that maintains its presence even after rebooting of the device.

Stage two: The body of the malware contains the code to effectively respond to the third-stage instructions.

Stage three: This stage contains multiple modules to run on the router devices. These modules are the instructions to the second-stage body of the code to change the routes, spy the routing information, stop the industrial automation, and many other functions. The modules of this stage are continuously increasing. In this stage, some communication plugins start communicating over the Tor server (Tor is basically free and open-source software to enable anonymous communication) for spying and sniffing the data packets.

This malware has incurred huge losses to many industries, households, private places, commercial entities, and many others. This malware is evolving into new modules. It is using different command and control servers for attacking different parts and countries of the world. The attackers also change settings as per the need of the cyberattack to make it more lethal.

The modification in the VPNFilter attacks cannot be ruled out in near future. More sophisticated and more dangerous third-stage plugins can surface anytime and anywhere in the world.

4.4 WANNACRY RANSOM ATTACK

If you have already seen the above screen on your computer, you were the victim of WannaCry ransomware attack. This attack was unleashed to the world in May 2017, when many of the computers from more than 150 countries were affected by this cyberattack (Figure 4.3).

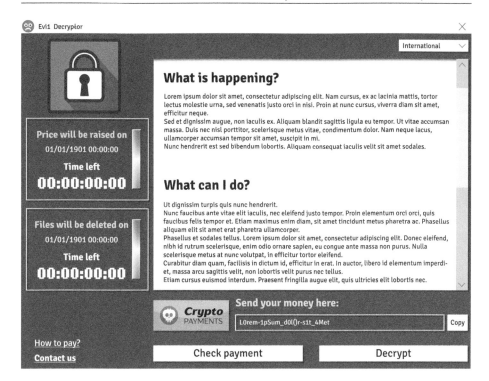

FIGURE 4.3   WannaCry ransomware attack.

This cyberattack is a type of ransomware attack that was initiated to extort money in the form of Bitcoin (a form of digital currency). Many countries and investigating agencies believe that the WannaCry attack was started by the North Korean authorities or the agencies working for North Korean government.

WannaCry is also known very well with the following names:

- WannaCryptor
- WannaCrypt0r
- WannaCrypt0r 2.0
- Wanna Decryptor
- Wanna Decryptor 2.0

This ransomware attack affected between 200 and 300 thousand computers across the world. The hackers would encrypt the data files on the computers and would decrypt them for a ransom or extortion money ranging from US$300 to US$600. Hackers wanted that money through Bitcoin cryptocurrency to be transferred to their Bitcoin digital wallets.

According to different news reports, the total impact of the WannaCry ransomware attack was equal to about US$4 billion. This huge loss was incurred due to the lost productivity, extortion, and other related matters.

The main target of this attack was the computers with Windows operating systems. WannaCry used the EternalBlue exploit, which was developed by some national security agencies, as per reports, to propagate the code to other computers. WannaCry would use the EternalBlue exploit present in the implementation of server message block (SMB) protocol on Microsoft Windows operating system. The malicious code (a form of crypto worm) would encrypt the important data files on the computer and would ask for the extortion money to decrypt the files.

Once the demanded amount of ransom in the form of bitcoin was paid, the hacker would offer you the decryption key to decrypt the files. The attack was stopped within a few days due to fast release of patch and the discovery of a kill switch, which would stop the malicious code to further propagate. Thus, the over effect was limited to a few billion dollars; otherwise, the damage could have been much worse than the present evaluation.

The newer version of this ransomware also surfaced in the month of August 2018 in Taiwan. This new variant of WannaCry ransomware badly affected the operations of the company for a certain time. The name of that chip manufacturing company in Taiwan was Taiwan Semiconductor Manufacturing Company (TSMC). The production of the company was shut temporarily, when more than one thousand computers of the company were affected with WannaCry ransomware attack. The automation processes of the company were badly affected.

4.5 PETA CYBERATTACK

Irrespective of its history, Petya cyberattack (Figure 4.4) was unleashed in the computer world on May 27, 2017, to target the main businesses such as power grids, gas stations, energy production companies, banks, airports, bus stations, and other communication-based systems. The main target of this ransomware was Ukraine because

FIGURE 4.4 Petya cyberattack.

more than 80% of its impact was noted in the Ukraine after one day of attack. Russia and Germany were other major countries where the impact of the Petya attacks was noticed extensively.

The first version of the Petya ransomware was noticed in March 2016. This first version would propagate with the infected email attachments. This version was not able to make a big impact on the global IT market. Another variant of the first version of Petya was caught in May 2016 with a secondary payload, but this version was also unsuccessful in inflicting huge damage to the information world.

The second version of the Petya was more dangerous, fast, and powerful to break into the legitimate systems and encrypt the files permanently. The second version that created havoc in the IT world surfaced on May 27, 2017. This new variant of the Petya would propagate through the EternalBlue exploit that would compromise the security of Microsoft Windows SMB.

It is important to note that the WannaCry ransomware attack also used the EternalBlue vulnerability in the Windows-based computers to establish full access to the computers. There was a substantial difference between the first version of Petya discovered in 2016 and the second version of the same discovered in May 2017; therefore, many people call the second version of ransomware as NotPetya too.

Petya was named after the name of a Russian satellite shown in the James Bond's film Golden Eye. That satellite was shown to have been carrying the atomic bomb named as Golden Eye in the film to create electromagnetic pulse when detonated.

The Petya malware would use a payload, which would infect the master boot record (MBR) of a computer. Then, it would modify the Windows Boot Loader by overwriting it. And at the third step, the malicious code would force the system to restart. When the system restarts, the data files are encrypted and damaged while restarting the system.

The estimated damages done by the Petya ransomware were about US$10 billion. The main reason of this huge cost was the attack on energy companies and power grids. The services of those companies directly impact the services and performance of the other businesses. Thus, the impact swelled exponentially. The cost of Petya was much higher than that of WannaCry ransomware attack.

The speed and power of the attack was very high. The ransomware started from Ukraine on the 27th day of May 2017 and infected thousands of machines in hundreds of companies in the country. The impact of the same malware was also noticed in the other countries of Europe such as Germany, Hungry, France, Italy, UK, and the United States on the same day. Germany was the second most affected country from the impact of Petya malware attack after Ukraine.

The attack unleashed its bad impact on many industries and companies in the United States across all states of the country. Many major companies felt the jolt of this nasty attack. The impact of this ransomware also traveled back to Russia and other European and Asian countries too. The main cause for spreading of this ransomware so fast was that the code was propagating with the software updates of ME Docs, which were already exploited by the Petya crypto worm.

Summary of the main points of Petya ransomware attack:

• First detected in March 2016
• Second time detected in May 2016

- Major attack surfaced on May 27, 2017
- Total damage was about US$10 billion (estimated)
- Big damage to a company – Maersk SeaLand Inc.
- Maersk's revenue loss was about US$300 million.
- Major companies affected by Petya include Cadbury, Australia; JNPT Container, India; Mondelez International, USA; DHL Logistics, Germany; and many others.

4.6 US ELECTION MANIPULATION

The heat of sharp discussions regarding the US elections 2016 is being still felt in different segments of the US society. There were many heated arguments during and past election. The arguments started from the streets to courts of law. Indeed, there are so many arguments and counterarguments about the involvement of Russian hackers in the manipulation of the US elections in 2016 (Figure 4.5 shows the main candidates in that election).

Many media channels reported that the Russian hackers manipulated the elections in more than 39 states before the voting started. The Russian hackers exploited the faults and vulnerabilities of the US election system to alter the voter data and influence the voters about whom to vote. It was also noticed that a few hackers tried to delete the voter data from the US system so that a particular party may be put in the advantageous position.

The American election system has many online vote register websites, software companies, and online sharing of important voting information for gathering the party support. All these systems were tried to be exploited and used in their favor.

FIGURE 4.5   US election manipulation (main candidates in 2016).

Both the Office of the Director of National Security and the Department of Homeland Security jointly confirmed that there were substantial clues that the Russian hackers with the instructions of the Russian government systematically hacked the emails and other sources of information including online services to damage the credibility of the US elections. The main target of the Russian hackers and authorities was to meddle into the election systems and influence the voters so that the position of the Hillary Clinton is damaged and political instability is created.

Russian hackers hacked the Democratic National Committee (DNC) servers and the personal Gmail account of John Podesta who was the election campaign head of Hillary Clinton. The emails from his personal email accounts were leaked to the WikiLeaks; thus, the issue created a huge controversy in the country over the meddling of Russian hackers and authorities in the US elections. The hacking of the DNC server was done by the Russian military intelligence service (GRU).

Meanwhile, a series of fake news were also spread on the social media from the IDs operating from different parts of the world as well as from Russia. There are many deniers of any involvement of the Russian hackers in this entire process, but there are many recorded incidents and deliberate attempts to manipulate the election or the voters' minds or records and so on. The main points of this entire hacking event are given below:

- The buzz of Russian meddling in elections 2016 started in the middle of the 2016 or even before.
- On October 7, 2016, both the Department of Homeland Security and the Office of the Director of National Intelligence publically expressed confidence of the involvement of Russian hackers to meddle the elections.
- Obama administration warned Putin administration to stop interference in the elections through red tape phone.
- In December 2016, President Obama ordered investigation of Russian involvement and interference in elections from 2008 onward.
- Bipartisan investigation was called upon by the democrat senators in December 2016.
- President-elect rejected the demand in December 2016.
- Thirty-five Russian diplomats were expelled from the country on December 29, 2016.
- First round of sanctions imposed on Russia in March 2017.
- In June 2018, new sanctions were imposed by the US Department of Treasury on the account of Russian meddling in the elections.
- Director James Comey of FBI was dismissed by Trump administration in May 2017.

The hacking of elections was already tested by the Russian hackers in the Ukraine elections in 2014. A powerful distributed denial-of-service (DDoS) attack was launched to disrupt the Ukrainian elections at that time.

The same types of allegations also surfaced in the provincial elections of Gujarat state in India. A UK-based company was alleged for meddling in the Gujarat elections in the favor of Congress party to defeat the incumbent party.

4.7 POWER GRID HACKING

The US power grid hacking attack (Figure 4.6) surfaced in March 2018. In fact, there were attempts to strike down the power systems of the country back in early 2016. According to the Department of Homeland Security and other investigating agencies, those attacks were carried out in the wake of the "Cyber Actor" program initiated by the Russian government back in 2016.

Earlier than this attempt, Russians succeeded in disrupting the power grid in Ukraine in 2015. In that attack, more than 200 thousand people were deprived from the power supply for a long period. The main target of the hackers in power grid attacks is to target the power generation. Once the hackers get access to the power generation systems, they try to stop the generation units so that the power is fully disrupted in the targeted area.

In the US grid cyberattack, the hackers used the traditional techniques to get important information about the user accounts and credentials. For that purpose, the hackers used the emails, diverted websites, and similar kinds of phishing techniques to collect the critical information about the power accounts.

According to the investigation report, the hackers used "spearphishing" technique to get information about the users. They send emails to the users in the power companies from the accounts that the user has already interacted with. Once the user opens the email and clicks on the attachment, the malicious code starts running on the machine to collect confidential/personal information.

Similarly, another technique known as "waterholing" was also used for getting the critical information. The websites that the users in the energy sector visit were altered

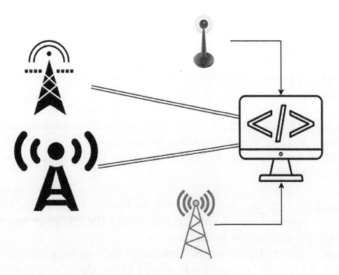

FIGURE 4.6   Power grid hacking (conceptual image).

in the way that they looked similar to the genuine websites. Thus, the confidential information was collected.

The Department of Homeland Security revealed that the majority of the critical information was collected from within the organizations that work directly with the power grids and other infrastructures. They used the phishing methods in most of the cases to collect the information. The hackers were not able to succeed the way they wanted to damage the power systems of the country, but they made the US government realize that these kinds of hacker attacks can have serious impacts on the country:

- Hackers can target infrastructure such as power grid, power generation, water supply, and aviation.
- The hacking impact on sewerage can flood the US cities with the sewer water.
- Utilities such as water, electricity, gas, and transportation can be stopped.

The major points of the US grid cyberattack are summarized below:

- First cyberattack on the USA grid, water, aviation and other critical infrastructures surfaced in March 2016.
- First attack was conducted by the "Cyber Actors", which is a Russian secret cyber team to attack the critical installation and infrastructures of the adversaries.
- FBI and Department of Homeland Security confirmed the involvement of Russian cyber actors.
- In the first attempt, some of the critical manufacturing and commercial installations were also attempted to hack.
- On March 15, 2018, the US government announced that the major power grid and other infrastructures were attacked by the Russian hackers.
- Spearphishing and waterholing techniques were used for getting the critical information for intrusion into the networks.
- Symantec report published in October 2017 citing the government report said there was a Russian code found in the malware used for infrastructure attacks.
- Symantec reported that Dragon Fly hacking campaign is on from 2014 to disrupt the energy and power services.
- Dragon Fly 2.0 started from the end of 2015.
- Dragon Fly 2.0 campaign is in the base of power grid attacks in the Europe and the United States, according to the Symantec report.

The details of the impact of the grid attack were not disclosed. The report just pointed out that the main purpose of this attack was not to sabotage the power system; it was just meant for the scouting purpose. But the gravity of this scouting is huge. Pentagon and associated agencies are preparing for higher level of security and emergency plans for power grid repairing in the possible shortest time.

4.8 SHADOW NETWORK ATTACK

The Shadow Network attack (Figure 4.7) is highly sophisticated and powerful espionage attack originated from the People's Republic of China (PRC). It was a huge and comprehensive attack to spy on the Indian government's secret information and Dalai Lama's activities. The attack was so highly coordinated and sophisticated that it was very difficult to break initially.

The Shadow Network cyberattack was unleashed in 2010. The main target of this espionage attack was to get access to the classified information, emails, and documents related to the office of Dalai Lama, Indian government, government's computer networks, and security-related organizations. This attack was first detected by the researchers working at the Information Warfare Monitor. This is the second largest cyber-based espionage attack originated from the PRC.

The first espionage attack originated from China is named as the GhostNet, which was discovered by the same organization that discovered the second espionage attack, "The Shadow Network". The first attack was discovered in March 2009. That attack was simultaneously spying on more than 103 countries and hundreds of organizations, offices, foreign embassies, and many other installations.

The Shadow Network attack exploited the Internet and social media services extensively to spy on the different organizations and office locations simultaneously. The major cloud-based and social services that were exploited included Yahoo Mail, Twitter, Blogspot, Baidu, Google Groups, and others. These websites were used to host malicious code (malware). When these websites were used, the malware infected the computers and started spying on the communication and data on the computers and local networks.

The main points and impact of the Shadow Network cyberattack are summarized below:

- Shadow Network was an espionage cyberattack with the focus on targeting Indian government and Tibetan exile leader Dalai Lama.
- Originated from PRC.
- Chengdu was the city of origination in the province of Sichuan.

FIGURE 4.7   Shadow Network attack.

- Surfaced through Information Warfare Monitor report named as "Shadows in the Cloud: Investigating Cyber Espionage 2.0".
- The investigating report was released on April 6, 2010.
- Prior to this, GhostNet investigation report was released in 2009.
- Cloud services and social media were exploited for malware spreading.
- The investigation was done with the collaboration of researchers working at Shadowserver Foundation (USA) and Info Warfare Monitor (Canada).
- Shadow Network was also detected to a very low level during the investigation of GhostNet, but after the release of the GhostNet report, many Shadow Network servers went offline.
- Still the espionage of Indian authorities and Dalai Lama was continuing.
- The researchers found that many computers at the Office of His Holiness the Dalai Lama (OHHDL) were compromised with the Shadow Network malware.
- More than 1,500 emails were copied from Dalai Lama office.
- A large number of Indian government's sensitive documents were stolen.
- Indian missile system, Indian state security plans, and many other such documents were stolen from the computers.
- The documents related to the Indian policy and relationship with the African countries, Middle Eastern countries, and Russia were also stolen.

The gravity of this theft is very high in terms of the strained relationships between India and China. Both countries were at the verge of war in 2017 due to the Doklam standoff. Both countries are emerging powers of the region with many differences in terms of the international boundary demarcation and other issues.

4.9 GITHUB DDoS ATTACK 2018

The distributed denial of service or DDoS is a very common technique to overwhelm any online or cloud-based service with the huge influx of the traffic from multiple locations directed to the targeted sever. Hundreds of thousands of DDoS cyberattacks have already taken place in the world till now. We talked about this kind of attack before. However, the GitHub DDoS attack that brought the entire service of the GitHub to standstill was the most powerful and lethal DDoS cyberattack in the history of the cybercrimes (at the time of writing this book). This attack is suspected to have originated from the PRC. The attack was carried out on the GitHub services on February 28, 2018. During the attack, the server services were unavailable for about 5 minutes (Figure 4.8).

The major points and the subsequent impact on the global market are summarized in the following important points:

- The largest DDoS attack in the history
- Service outage occurred between 17:21 and 17:26 UTC on February 28, 2018.

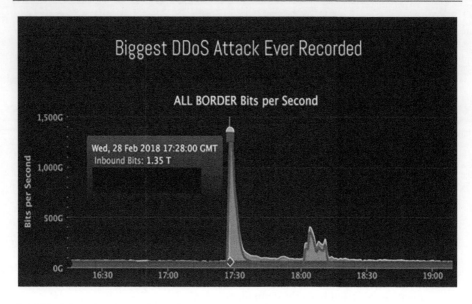

FIGURE 4.8 GitHub DDoS attack 2018.

- Intermittent service availability between 17:26 and 17:30 on the same date.
- Conducted through the amplification vector that used the memcached over the UDP (User Datagram Protocol). Memcached is a general-purpose distributed memory-caching system.
- Memcached instances were badly abused to conduct this attack.
- IP spoofing was used to direct the memcached response to the targeted server.
- Amplification factor of memcached is 51 thousand times, so each byte of sender data was amplified to 51 bytes and sent to the target.
- At the peak time of the attack, the total data rate sent to the target was about 1.35 Tbps.
- 126.9 packets were sent per second to the target.
- Akamai Prolexic helped GitHub to route traffic through its scrubbing centers to block the malicious traffic.
- The attack lasted for about 8 minutes after the traffic was diverted through scrubbing center of Akamai Prolexic.
- The impact of this attack on the software development community was huge because millions of software users use the GitHub services.

The DDoS attacks are normally carried out to disrupt the services. Commonly, there is no threat to the data stored on the target servers. Hence, the disruption of the online services is restored to the normal operation once the attack is stopped. But the service disruption for even a short duration of big service can cost millions of dollars to the company as well as to the users. Apart from the financial loss, there could be loss of confidence or reliability of the offered services.

4.10 UNDER ARMOR ACCOUNT HACKING

Under Armour is a US-based manufacturer of popular brands of sports equipment, footwear, and casual apparels for leisure and sporting events. The company is headquartered in Baltimore, Maryland. The company has many commercial apps and brands that contribute extensively to the company's business. Among such applications, MyFitnessPal is one of the most popular mobile applications in the United States (Figure 4.9).

MyFitnessPal has millions of users who use this application for maintaining their fitness. This application helps the users about their intake calories, workouts, sports, and other health-related issues. The application also hosts over 2 million different types of healthy foods with their complete details and nutrition values.

MyFitnessPal was created in 2005 by two brothers, but later, it was acquired by the Under Armour Corporation. The acquisition of the app cost the Under Armour US$475 million in 2015. The application was hacked and data of more than 150 million users were stolen in a cyberattack on the application database in February 2018. This was one of the largest data breaches in the history of cyber hacking.

The main points of this cyberattack on the MyFitnessPal application database are summarized below:

- The attack took place in the last days of February 2018.
- The company was able to know only in the last days of March 2018.
- Under Armour announced publicly on March 30, 2018, that the data of MyFitnessPal app has been compromised.
- More than 150 million accounts were compromised.
- The shares of Under Armour fell by over 4.6% in the trading.
- The data stolen in the cyberattack included usernames, passwords, and email addresses.
- The stolen data did not comprise driving license, credit card, or social security numbers.
- It is one of the top five big data breaches till today.

According to the Under Armour information, all users were notified immediately through a procedure to change their passwords. The remaining useful data would be the email addresses, which can be used by the spammers for marketing and other cyber tactics. By large, both the company and the users have not sustained future potential threats due to this data breach.

Under Armour

Data breach

FIGURE 4.9   Under Armor account hacking.

SAMPLE QUESTIONS AND ANSWERS FOR WHAT WE HAVE LEARNED IN CHAPTER 4

Q1. What is a malware?

A1: A malware is basically an unwanted software or programming code that runs on a computer and may cause harm or jeopardize the normal functions of a computer.

Q2. What is WannaCry ransomware?

A2: WannaCry is a ransomware crypto worm, which targeted computers (when it first appeared) running the Microsoft Windows operating system by encrypting data and demanding ransom payments in the Bitcoin cryptocurrency. In plain words, this is a kind of malware which attacks a computer and locks it demanding some ransom or payment to get it unlocked.

Q3. What kinds of impact power grid hacking can do?

A3: Power grid hacking is potentially very dangerous. These kinds of hacker attacks can have serious impacts on the country:

- Hackers can target infrastructure such as power grid, power generation, water supply, and aviation.
- The hacking impact on sewerage can flood the US cities with the sewer water.
- Utilities such as water, electricity, gas, and transportation can be stopped.

Q4. Name at least five well-known attacks which could have significant impact on the systems.

A4:

- VPNFilter cyberattack
- WannaCry ransomware attack
- Petya cyberattack
- Power grid hacking
- Shadow Network attack

Q5. Name some variants or other names of the WannaCry ransomware.

A5: WannaCry is also known very well with the following names:

- WannaCryptor
- WannaCrypt0r
- WannaCrypt0r 2.0
- Wanna Decryptor
- Wanna Decryptor 2.0

SOURCES

https://www.nytimes.com/2017/09/07/business/equifax-cyberattack.html

https://www.bbc.com/news/business-42687937

http://time.com/money/4936732/equifaxs-massive-data-breach-has-cost-the-company-4-billion-so-far/

https://en.wikipedia.org/wiki/VPNFilter

https://www.wespeakiot.com/vpn-filter-malware-attacks-router-and-nas-systems/

https://en.wikipedia.org/wiki/Petya_(malware)

https://cloudblogs.microsoft.com/microsoftsecure/2018/02/05/overview-of-petya-a-rapid-cyberattack/

https://en.wikipedia.org/wiki/WannaCry_ransomware_attack

https://www.zdnet.com/article/wannacry-ransomware-crisis-one-year-on-are-we-ready-for-the-next-global-cyber-attack/

https://www.wired.com/story/notpetya-cyberattack-ukraine-russia-code-crashed-the-world/

https://www.vox.com/world/2017/6/13/15791744/russia-election-39-states-hack-putin-trump-sessions

https://www.cfr.org/backgrounder/russia-trump-and-2016-us-election

https://en.wikipedia.org/wiki/Russian_interference_in_the_2016_United_States_elections

https://www.csoonline.com/article/3177209/security/why-the-ukraine-power-grid-attacks-should-raise-alarm.html

https://www.symantec.com/blogs/threat-intelligence/dragonfly-energy-sector-cyber-attacks

https://www.independent.co.uk/life-style/gadgets-and-tech/news/russian-hacking-attacks-us-power-grid-sewage-explosions-a8462691.html

https://www.bloomberg.com/news/articles/2018-03-15/russian-hackers-attacking-u-s-power-grid-aviation-fbi-warns

https://www.nytimes.com/2018/07/27/us/politics/russian-hackers-electric-grid-elections-.html

https://www.npr.org/2018/03/23/596044821/russia-hacked-u-s-power-grid-so-what-will-the-trump-administration-do-about-it

https://resources.infosecinstitute.com/shadow-network-part/#gref

https://en.wikipedia.org/wiki/Shadow_Network

https://www.nbcnews.com/tech/security/under-armour-says-data-hacked-150m-myfitnesspal-app-accounts-n861406

https://www.bloomberg.com/news/articles/2018-03-29/under-armour-says-150-million-myfitnesspal-accounts-were-hacked

https://www.forbes.com/sites/paullamkin/2018/03/30/under-armour-admits-huge-myfitness-pal-data-hack/#ef63930cc54f

Types of Computer Malware

5.1 INTRODUCTION

The malware is a computer software program maliciously developed to install on the computers without any consent of the users. The main objective of such ill-conceived programs is to either establish the access to the targeted computers without any permission of the user or to install the program to create annoyance for the users.

The annoyance can include pranks, data theft, data damage, computer malfunction, service blockage, and spying on the users. In most of the cases, the malware programs are installed on the targeted computers to achieve different types of goals, which may include getting financial favor, knowing the business strategies, compromising the defense, sabotaging the governmental system, and many others.

All those malicious objectives are achieved by introducing different kinds of malicious programs, which are classified into different categories in the field of information technology. The main types of malware software programs are explained in the subsequent sections in this chapter.

5.2 VIRUSES

A computer virus is a malicious computer program, which is designed to alter the computer functions, slow down the computer performance, and damage the valuable files on the computer drive. The virus programs are executable files when run on any machine by mistake, or through any trick or click, it will get activated and will start altering the computer configurations and the process, which are used for smooth operation of the computer (Figure 5.1).

The virus programs have the capability to copy into multiple files and, thus, overwhelm the computer processes and data storage. As mentioned earlier, the virus programs are designed to propagate to other machines when some data is transferred from an infected computer to the other one. The main sources of virus propagation include the following:

- Copying on hard drive
- Data copying through flash
- Email attachments
- Short text messages
- Scam websites
- Scam social media links
- Infected file downloading from Internet
- Visiting infected websites

The viruses are just programs in the form of executable files. They do not get activate without running those executable files on your computers. If you got a virus program

FIGURE 5.1   Viruses.

on your computer, but it has not been executed on your computer, your computer is not infected as yet. As soon as you execute that file by either clicking or running some legitimate programs on which the virus files are attached, the virus becomes active and starts doing its designed job.

The objectives of spreading a virus may include the following:

- Amusement, fun, and prank
- Altering computer functioning
- Corrupting data files on computer
- Stealing credentials
- Sending spamming emails from your computer
- Erasing valuable data
- Damaging hard drives
- And others.

In the modern world, the creation of computer virus is motivated by gaining some financial benefits on the Internet. That may include stealing data and selling it to the third party, or even using that data for malicious financial transactions.

The main symptoms of a virus-infected computer may include the following:

- Frequent appearance of pop-ups and other annoyance
- Changes in the home screen and other settings
- Redirecting your online surfing to certain websites
- Large-scale incoming and outgoing emails
- Slowing down of the performance of your computer
- Running of unknown programs on your computer
- Changes in your passwords, especially the admin passwords
- System starts crashing frequently
- Restarting of your computer unexpectedly
- Any other unexpected error or behavior of the computer or the computing machine.

The solution to the menace of computer virus is to use updated antivirus software from well-known antivirus software companies. It is very important to note that antivirus programs should be regularly updated to cope with the increasing threat of computer viruses.

It is very important to note that some of the stubborn viruses are very difficult to remove permanently from your computers because they intrude into the system through legitimate programs; hence, it becomes almost impossible for the standard antivirus software to delete completely from the computer. In such conditions, when the viruses penetrate into the system through legitimate program installation, the antivirus just quarantines the viruses into the vaults.

Another important thing about the modern virus is that the number of virus attacks in the cyber world is reducing continuously. At the present time, the average ratio of viruses is less than 10% of all malware spread through the Internet or other sources.

If you take care while using any external data storage, email attachment, websites, or any file downloads, you can save your computer from virus infections easily. Always follow the security guidelines while browsing the Internet and also take precautionary measures while downloading, accessing, or copying any data on your computer. Always scan the external data sources with the updated antivirus to make sure there is no malicious program attached to the data you are trying to copy on your computer.

We can save our computers from the attack of nasty viruses by taking the following measures:

- Avoid using insecure websites.
- Do not open fake websites that allure you for some free incentives.
- Always keep your antivirus software updated.
- Always keep operating system (OS) of your computer updated.
- Turn on the security firewall settings.
- Always configure your browser for high level of security.
- Free and insecure plugins should not be installed on your browsers.
- Do not use your credit cards on the websites that do not comply with the Payment Card Industry Data Security Standard (PCI DSS) guidelines for secure transactions.
- Never insert flash cards (i.e., pen drive) or other storage devices into your computer without scanning and knowing about the type of data.
- Never open emails and their attachments from unknown people and email address.

5.3 TROJAN HORSE

Trojan horse (Figure 5.2) in this field is also a malicious computer program that may look very meek and harmless, but it can pave the way for a bigger attack on your computer and valuable data. It collects the information about the user behavior, credentials, and other activities on the computer silently and sends those to its command and control center from where the other malicious attacks can originate.

Hackers use Trojan to open the backdoor on your computer to access your computer and establish control on your machine.

The concept of the Trojan horse in the modern computer terminology resembles 100% with the story of Trojan horse in the Greek mythology. According to the old mythology, the Greek developed a wooden Trojan horse, which would house many soldiers inside the wooden compartment of the Trojan horse. The people of the Troy city would pull the Trojan to the city and the soldiers hidden inside the Trojan horse would come out in the night and open the gates of the cities. They would call their fellow soldiers to come in and overrun the city to conquer.

The concept of Trojan horse in computer security is also same. A Trojan horse comes in through some social engineering tactics such as emails, disguised links, and

FIGURE 5.2   Trojan horse.

other sources. They would sit on the computers and start spying, making changes in credentials and doing other such malicious activities.

The main objectives of Trojan horse are to spy on the user activities and send back to its master control. Based on the information, backdoor access on the computer is created to get control over the computer for malicious activities.

The Trojan horses cannot replicate as the virus or computer worms can do. They are like spies working silently on your computers to accomplish their malicious acts for which the Trojan horses are designed and propagated.

Generally recognized activities of a Trojan horse on an infected computer include the following:

- Collecting data and sending to command and control center
- Copying the files and credential information
- Blocking of the data
- Altering the useful data
- Reducing the performance of computer
- Deleting some useful data files

There are numerous types of Trojan horses used in the modern cybercriminal activities. A few very important ones are mentioned below:

- Trojan Spy
- Trojan Mail Finder
- Trojan Proxy
- Trojan Clicker
- Trojan Ransom
- Trojan SMS
- Trojan Dropper

- Trojan Fake AV
- Trojan Game Theft
- Trojan Backdoor
- Trojan DDoS

Trojan horses are used for the secretive attacks on the computers to open backdoors on the computers so that more lethal cyberattacks can be unleashed on the targeted computers. How can we recognize that the computer has been infected by the Trojan horse attack? One can diagnose by the symptoms of Trojan horse attack, which are listed below:

- Performance degrades significantly.
- Internet speed slows down.
- Problem in Internet browsing occurs.
- Many Internet browser pop-ups may appear.
- Your computer security application can warn you through security pop-ups.
- Computer starts working itself without your instructions.
- Some crucial applications will stop working and unwanted applications will load without any control on them.
- A large number of spam emails appear in your inbox.
- Your contacts may receive emails that you did not send to them.
- Loading of computer takes much longer.
- Your data files are deleted or modified.

The working principles of all these types of Trojan horses are same, but the designated objectives and goals are different.

According to the statistics, in the year 2016, Trojan horse-based cyber infections accounted for about 74.99%. This huge ratio of Trojan malware indicates that how useful the Trojans are for the hackers. Trojan dropper is the second biggest threat in 2018, according to the Kaspersky Lab research.

Trojan horses may apparently look less dangerous, but in fact, they are very dangerous in an online business environment. Trojan horses pave the ways for many serious cybercrimes for the hackers, and those cybercrimes may include financial gains, data theft, spamming, and many others.

5.4 ROOTKIT

Rootkit is a type of malware that gets the administrator-level privileges on the OS of the computer without showing its presence on the computer. The main feature of rootkit is that it hides from being detected easily, but maintains the control over the OS to perform its designated tasks on the system. The normal behavior of the OS is subverted by the rootkit malware on the system (Figure 5.3).

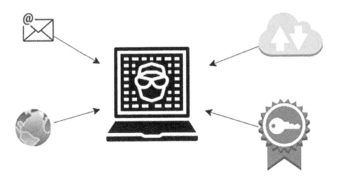

FIGURE 5.3   Rootkit.

The subversion of the operating process is to control the system. As we know, all applications on the computer, including the antivirus, anti-malware, and other security-related applications, use the application programming interfaces or APIs provided by the OS. A powerful rootkit gets control on those APIs and establishes the full control on the system. For instance, windows browser program sends a request to the OS API to find a certain file on the computer. The OS responds to the browser through API about that file.

The rootkit malware subverts the request sent to the OS from reaching to the desired API and responds with fake responses. Moreover, you request the OS to start the antivirus or anti-malware application to scan your computer; the request is interrupted from reaching to the OS. The rootkit interrupts the request and sends you a fake response that the program you requested for is not working at this time.

Rootkit is considered as one of the nastiest forms of malware programs that is not easily detected and removed from your computer once it has established the privileges to access and control the OS through available vulnerabilities in the OS and other applications.

There are three main goals of a rootkit on a computer as mentioned below:

- Running freely without any restrictions of having been caught and deleted
- Hiding from the system applications and the user of the computer
- Stealing personal information, passwords, and installing other malicious programs on the computer so that the compromised computer can be used for attacking the other computers on the network

The major ways in which the rootkits subvert the OS of the computer include the following:

- By changing the API addresses of the legitimate applications' APIs with the address of code of the rootkit. This procedure of subverting the OS functioning is known as the API hooking.
- By hiding the code in the unused area of the hard disk where the APIs of OS do not see it. Then, the *ATAPI.sys* driver is changed in such way that when it loads, it will direct that space to find the rootkit code on the hard drive.

- Getting access to the master boot record or MBR. In certain cases, the rootkit gets access to the MBR. In that case, the rootkit code is able to subvert OS at its will because it gets the control over the loading of the applications in the memory. So, it can easily restrict certain applications to load in the memory.

There are numerous types of rootkits based on the objective and point of attack on the systems. A few very well-known and important rootkits are listed below:

- Memory rootkits
- Kernel rootkits
- Bootkit rootkits
- Firmware rootkits
- Library rootkits
- Application rootkits

For a normal user of the computer, it may be very difficult to recognize that the computer has been infected by the rootkits. If the computer shows the following symptoms, then you should suspect that the computer has been infected by the rootkit attack.

- Modifications in the dates and time of computer
- Slowing down of the computer
- Unexpected system error messages
- Many programs, especially computer security-related programs, fail to start
- Substantial redirects on browsers
- Appearance of blue screen of death

Rootkits travel through the standard ways of the propagation of viruses, worms, and other malware programs. Those include the following:

- Infected downloads
- Peer-to-peer file sharing
- Unknown emails
- Short text messages (SMS)

It is very difficult to detect and remove the rootkit from your computer once it has established the control over the OS APIs. Normally, the rootkit remains unnoticed on the machine and keeps doing its job. For remaining many days on the computer, the system becomes a rogue machine and many malicious programs start running on the machine. Those programs will be used for different malicious activities.

You will find the behavior of OS very irritating with the passage of time. One day you may see a cryptic blue screen of death and your computer will never load again normal. Now, you will have to reinstall and configure your computer from the scratch.

But you can still take the following steps to avert from getting rootkits control of your computer.

- Always visit the legitimate and secure websites.
- Do not download free and compromised products.
- Open emails and their attachments from known people only.
- Never open attachments in SMS and other messages.
- Activate firewall on your system.
- Activate intrusion prevention system (IPS).
- Activate access control lists (ACLs) on the system and network.
- Scan and clean flash or other data traveling devices before opening the files.
- Use the latest anti-rootkit tools with Security Technology and Response (STAR).
- Keep your anti-malware up to date.
- Keep OS up to date.

Many new software tools have also been created by the major computer security software providers such as Norton, Avast, Panda, and Kaspersky. All those tools are able to detect the rootkits if present on your computer. They are also able to remove the nastiest forms of the rootkits on your computer easily.

5.5 SPYWARE

Spyware is a software code or program, which is installed on the computers without letting the user know about it. The main objective of this program is to monitor online activities, computer using habits, and personal interests (Figure 5.4).

A spyware snoops the way user uses the Internet. In most cases, the spyware programs are used to learn the habits of the computer users so that proper and focused digital marketing campaign through emails and other online sources can be implemented.

Today, the importance of privacy has become very critical. By the introduction of General Data Protection Regulation (GDPR) law in the European Union (EU) countries, the importance of the privacy has been made the integral part of any online service.

A few years back, the NSA (National Security Agency) data snooping jolted the entire world. In that security surveillance, the privacy of the online people all over the

FIGURE 5.4 Spyware (conceptual image).

world was compromised. The tougher laws and regulations were brought into force all over the world to maintain the security and privacy of the online users.

Thus, privacy has become a matter of great importance for the individuals as well as for all businesses and enterprises all over the globe. At the initial stages, the attack of spyware is not even noticed, but slowly and gradually, the impact of the spyware unleashes on your system as well as personally on you. The symptoms of a spyware attack on your computer may include the following:

- System performance slows down
- Any program stops working properly
- Many changes in browser tools bar and plugins appear
- Advertisements appear on your screen incessantly
- Internet bandwidth chokes
- Search engine and other preferences change

But in harsher attacks of spyware, the usernames and passwords of different services can also be captured and sent back to the command and control center for more lethal cyberattacks on your personal accounts and data. The total spending on the digital marketing in the United States only is expected to cross US$120 billion by 2021.

So, to make most of this huge spending in the marketing, the businesses use multiple ways to gather the information about the interest and habits of the users.

Owing to the expanding volume of online advertisement, digital marketing, and electronic commerce, the number of spyware is also increasing in the marketplace. Newer types of spyware are being launched to spy on the behavior of the online users. The main categories of the spyware are listed below:

- Modem hijacker spyware
- Browser hijacker spyware
- Keyboard logger spyware
- Commercial spyware
- Majority of adware programs broadly fall under spyware category

The artificial intelligence, spyware, and other similar types of sources are the major tools for the modern businesses to implement their digital marketing campaigns towards the right direction. The information about the user behavior is used to focus the digital marketing more accurately to the targeted audiences.

A few years back, Panda Lab conducted a large-scale scanning of the computer in 2008. The study found that more than 10 million computers were affected with some kinds of spywares out of the 67 million computers scanned in the research.

Technically, the spyware once installed on the computer gets into computer registries and, thus, makes them bulkier. So, the performance of the computer also degrades with the passage of time. Meanwhile, a spyware can also pave the way for the other malware programs, which can lead to the failure of the computer.

The longer the spyware dwell on your computer, the nastier they would get. Your computer becomes so vulnerable and many other hackers would attack on the vulnerabilities of your computer, and malicious codes would start downloading on your system. Thus, the machine becomes a hub of malicious activities for the hackers to exploit.

In today's Internet, where our behavior is tracked through multiple legitimate ways powered by artificial intelligence, it is very difficult to save ourselves from the impact of the spywares. But some precautions can be taken to reduce the impact of spyware on our computer. A few important measures to reduce the impact of spyware are listed below:

- Always close the advertisement pop-up windows by clicking on "X" red button or ALT+F4 shortcut key.
- Do not click the OK, NO, YES, or any other link on the pop-up window.
- Be very careful while visiting new websites or redirected websites.
- Do not download free software tools unless you are sure or confident about the source.
- Do not be lured by the tempting offers.
- Do not open emails and their attachments form unknown senders.
- Do not rely on free help for removing anti-spyware links; they are normally spyware themselves in many cases.
- Keep your OS up to date.
- Install a genuine spyware software from renowned companies.
- Keep your anti-spyware up to date.
- Activate firewall settings.
- Increase the security level of your browser to high.

A normal computer can also be turned into a zombie machine with severe assault of spyware to launch cyberattacks such as spamming and other activities from that computer. This case may be much serious in terms of the security of your computer and data files located on your computer.

5.6 WORMS

The main feature of a computer worms and viruses is that they replicate themselves in order to spread to other computers on the network or through other data transmission media.

Computer worms (Figure 5.5) are the types of malware software programs that replicate on the computers to consume the major portions of the computer resources such as bandwidth, hard disk, and memory.

The basic objective of a worm is to spread over the computers in a network by exploiting the vulnerabilities in the computer OS and other vulnerabilities in the computer networks. They are considered to be harmless without payloads. The worms without any payloads or payload-free worms just consume the resource of the computer

FIGURE 5.5   Worms (conceptual image).

and do no other harms. But when additional payloads are added to the worms, they can become dangerous in installing other malicious programs hidden in the payloads.

Those payloads may install backdoors and other spying codes on the computer to compromise your security and data by sending them to the command and control center located elsewhere. But the role of worm in that entire process is just to transport payloads and install on the networks. But worm itself is again a free replicating and a free wanderer program without posing any serious danger to the data or system.

The history of creating computer worms is very interesting. The first worm code named as "tapeworm" to replicate on 100 different nodes for a communication was created at Xerox Palo Alto Research Center by John Shoch.

The purpose of that code was to analyze traffic patterns of a communication network based on Ethernet. This worm was created to save the time of code creation on every single machine individually. So, that worm code replicated on all machines on the network. It was not a maliciously intended code.

The first maliciously intended worm code surfaced in 1988 when Morris worm shocked the entire world of Internet. Morris worm was created by Robert Morris Jr. He was a student at Cornell University at that time, but he released the worm from MIT. That landed him in a legal pursuit and subsequently US$10,050 fine and 3 years of suspended imprisonment. That worm brought more than 6,000 servers down at that time. The total estimated number of servers on the Internet was about 60,000 at that time.

Hence, the ratio of the servers that went down due to Morris worm was about 10% of the entire Internet. The estimated cost of that worm attack was between US$0.1 million and US$10 million. After that worm attack, many other worms were released on the Internet through different sources. A few very important worms are listed below:

- Blaster worm
- MyDoom worm
- Code Red worm
- ILOVEYOU worm
- CIH worm

The extreme impact of the computer worms without any dangerous payloads can cause slowing down of the computer, choking of the bandwidth, and reducing the size of hard disk. The other part of the worm in terms of the hazards it can cause is the *payload*, which can be any other code to install backdoor or compromise any vulnerability to establish communication with the command and control server (as we mentioned earlier). Those payloads can also damage the valuable data files, steal username and passwords, and spy on the daily activities of the users.

The main points of a worm can be summarized as follows:

- It replicates and spreads.
- It exploits communication protocol vulnerabilities on networks.
- It exploits OSs on the computers.
- They are harmless in nature without any payloads.
- Payloads on the worms can be harmful like virus or other malicious attacks.
- They infect the computers without any interaction from the user.
- Bandwidth, storage space, and memory can be consumed with uncontrolled replication.
- Worms with payloads can wreak havoc on your computer security.
- They pave the way for other lethal cyberattacks such as spamming zombie, distributed denial of service (DDoS), and data theft.

As mentioned earlier, the worms are usually harmless to the computer and valuable data in normal conditions. But it can be dangerous in certain conditions when the worms are used for paving the way for other lethal cybercrimes. Once we know this, the question that arises is, "*How can we recognize that computer is infected by some worms?*" Indeed, a worm-infected computer can be recognized by certain symptoms. Those symptoms are listed below:

- Some errors related to the OS and system files appear.
- The modified files disappear or do not open.
- Firewall warnings may pop-up in certain cases.
- Strange icons or files appear on the desktop.
- Computer generates unknown errors in sounds, messages, or even in images.
- The performance of computer slows down.
- Sometimes computer may hang or freeze.
- In extreme conditions, system may crash frequently.
- In extreme cases, you will find emails sent to your contacts without your knowledge.

The worms can be prevented by taking the following measures and guidelines:

- Always keep OS updated with software patches.
- Always take care in opening emails and its attachments from unknown source.
- Activate the security firewall.
- Use anti-spyware and antivirus software from reliable companies or parties.

- Always keep antivirus software updated.
- Use packet filters on the network.
- Implement ACL and null route configuration on switches and routers.

Some of the dangerous worms that left huge impact on the Internet include SQL Slammer, which infected more than 90% of the hosts on the Internet. The other notorious worms include Code Red, Blaster, and others.

5.7 ADWARE

According to the Statista (company), the total spending on digital advertisement in 2018 was more than US$266 billion, which will increase to over US$517 by 2023 (estimated figure). Different tactics are used by the marketers to make their digital marketing campaigns effective. One of those tactics is the use of adware (Figure 5.6) to make their marketing or advertisement strategies more focused and effective.

As the name "Adware" implies, it is a computer program that forces the Internet users to visit a particular web page, pop-up window, or an on-page advertisement to watch.

Adware has become a very popular tool for digital marketing teams to draw attention of the users to a particular product or service. The adware code uses different ways to propagate and find the suitable targets so that the focused audience is figured out for a particular product.

You might have come across some annoying links and pages while browsing the Internet. When you click on those pages or links, you are redirected to another page that promotes a particular product or service. In some cases, pop-up windows appear with promotional content for a particular product. This is all done with the help of adware programs.

ADWARE

FIGURE 5.6 Adware.

A few very important symptoms of your computer to have been affected by the adware include the following:

- Frequent redirects
- Huge number of spam emails
- Frequent pop-up windows of offers
- Bombardment of product ads in browser
- Heavy outgoing and incoming traffic
- Slowing down of Internet connection

So, an adware is a software code that is used to force the users to see a particular advertisement or promotional content on any website, pop-up window, or a commercial advertisement. The adware software programs are created by the hired programmers for a particular company, which pays the programmers for such codes.

You can avoid adware or reduce them by taking the following measures:

- Activate pop-up blocker on your browser.
- Use your common sense what to click and what not.
- Activate the firewall.
- Install an anti-adware software.
- Update the anti-adware software regularly.
- Try to avoid free downloads, which may contain adware codes.
- Ask a question to those who know to learn about anything you are not sure about.

This is very important to note that adware is normally not so dangerous to damage your computer or valuable data; so there is no need to panic at all. These malware programs only focus on your behavior to study and send you the targeted advertisements that you may be interested in.

As mentioned earlier, adware is powered by a gigantic industry that uses different ways to advertise their products and services. Many rogue companies and marketers use the adware as their tools to earn from their marketing campaigns; so, they launch new types of adware on the Internet to get benefit from them. Till today, hundreds of adware programs have been detected on the Internet, and a few very important among those adware codes are listed below:

- DeskAd adware
- SpyTrooper adware
- WebCake adware
- WebSparkle adware
- 1ClickDownloader adware
- Aartemis search adware
- AnyWhereMe toolbar adware
- AllSearchApp adware
- GetSavin adware
- Hotspot Shield adware

This is very critical to note that some advertisements may be genuine and some may be fake and harmful for your system. Those advertisements carry other forms of malicious code, which may lead to some kind of dangerous impact on your computer and valuable data. So, you should always remain very careful while clicking on those advertisement pages and pop-up messages that allure you to click.

Many marketing companies launch advertisement campaigns to earn substantial amount of money. When you click any advertisement, the marketing company gets paid for every visit that the Internet users pay to the website or every click that the Internet users apply on the advertisement.

5.8 SCAREWARE

Scareware is a type of malware, which pops up in window with a serious warning about any virus threat on your computer. But in reality, there is no threat or virus on your computer except that hoax, which appeared on your screen! (Figure 5.7).

The alert looks very genuine from certain reputable websites, but they are not genuine websites, i.e., they just look like genuine. This message normally prompts the users to download or call some numbers to get help. The main objective behind the *Scareware* is to sell fake and bogus products. In certain cases, the hackers trick the

FIGURE 5.7 Scareware.

users to input the credit card, personal, and bank information on their website. Once you provide that information, your data has been compromised for malicious financial transactions and uses.

The use of scareware has been also found in the entertainment pranks. But the ratio of the pranks is low as compared to the malicious use for launching some kinds of cybercrimes on the targeted people who suffer the impact.

Another use of the scareware trick is to force the user to download some free anti-virus software to clean your computer from those viruses that the website has detected. In reality, that free antivirus is itself a dangerous software program, which can control your computer and start damaging your system or stealing your data. So, the scareware can be the foundation of many dangerous cyberattacks.

The main objectives of spreading scare may include the following:

- Selling fake products
- Stealing personal and bank information
- Installing viruses and other malicious codes for cybercrimes
- Blackmailing for some ransom
- Prank for fun

You can avoid the impact of scareware by taking the following steps:

- Do not panic at all.
- Check if your antivirus is working well.
- Run a virus scan via your own antivirus.
- Check if your antivirus is up to date.
- Search about the legitimacy of that website, which alerts you of virus on your computer.
- Search for the legitimacy of the message you see on your computer; sometimes simple Internet search reveals the reality.
- Never rely on free software in such conditions.
- Purchase a genuine antivirus and install if you have none installed on your computer.
- Keep the antivirus up to date.

The hackers use the social engineering tactics to force you to follow the instructions they give you. So, always use your common sense and remain calm and cool to deal with the situation.

The scareware programs can be spread through the following mentioned tricks:

- Social engineering
- Short text message (SMS)
- Emails and email attachments
- Through adware
- Through faulty websites

If you fall prey to those hackers, you may lose control of your computer and data. The hackers may then force you to pay ransom before you can get the access to your computer and valuable data on your computer.

5.9 BROWSER HIJACKER

You might have been in the situation when the default settings of your browser were changed. For example, your default search engine was changed to a new one without getting permission from you. When you observe this situation, be sure that your computer's browser has been hijacked by the malicious program, which is altering the settings of your browser and creating a way for the malicious programs to intrude in (Figure 5.8).

In some cases, you might have seen that some unknown plugins have been installed and activated on your browser. Although you have not downloaded or installed on your browser, still they are there and active. This is another strong symptom of your browser to have been compromised through the browser hijacking software.

The main reason behind these kinds of activities is a certain malicious code known as browser hijacker malware. This code is used to pave the way for different kinds of cyberattacks on your computer or to the other computers on your network.

Browser hijacker is also a malicious computer code that is normally downloaded on your computer via some free software applications. The malware changes the browser settings on your computer when you install that free software on your computer. The main objective of browser hijacker software is to force the users to visit certain websites for improving the volume of traffic on that particular website. When the traffic of a website is improved, the website gets higher revenue of online advertisement.

FIGURE 5.8   Browser hijacker.

The browser hijacker malware can also be used for stealing personal information, user accounts, and other information for financial benefits. The symptoms and impact of browser hijacker malware may include the following:

- Slow browsing speed
- Multiple tool bars on the browser
- Redirecting your search queries to websites that you have not set as default
- A large number of pop-up windows and ads appear on your browser

You can save your browser from being hijacked by the browser hijacker malware by taking the following measures:

- Avoid free downloads as much as possible.
- Disable unwanted tool bars.
- Remove or disable unwanted plugins.
- Set your default search engine.
- Install anti-malware erasers; however, be careful whether that is authentic.
- Use common sense while downloading and Internet browsing.
- Avoid browsing random websites that contain contents that may not be ethically correct.

SAMPLE QUESTIONS AND ANSWERS FOR WHAT WE HAVE LEARNED IN CHAPTER 5

Q1. What is a computer virus?

A1: A computer virus is a malicious computer program, which is designed to alter the computer functions, slow down the computer performance, and damage the valuable files on the computer drive. The virus programs are executable files when run on any machine by mistake, or through any trick or click, it will get activated and will start altering the computer configurations and the process, which are used for smooth operation of the computer.

Q2. State the main sources of virus propagation.

A2: The main sources of virus propagation include the following:

- Copying on hard drive
- Data copying through flash
- Email attachments
- Short text messages
- Scam websites
- Scam social media links
- Infected file downloading from Internet
- Visiting infected websites

Q3. How is the name Trojan horse given?

A3: The concept of the Trojan horse in the modern computer terminology resembles 100% with the story of Trojan horse in the Greek mythology. According to the old mythology, the Greek developed a wooden Trojan horse, which would house many soldiers inside the wooden compartment of the Trojan horse. The people of the Troy city would pull the Trojan to the city and the soldiers hidden inside the Trojan horse would come out in the night and open the gates of the cities. They would call their fellow soldiers to come in and overrun the city to conquer. This is the same concept behind Trojan horse attack.

Q4. Why is rootkit malware considered one of the nastiest?

A4: The rootkit malware subverts the request sent to the operating system from reaching to the desired API (application programming interface) and responds with fake responses. Moreover, when someone requests the operating system to start the antivirus or anti-malware application to scan the computer, the request is interrupted from reaching to the operating system. The rootkit interrupts the request and sends the user a fake response that the requested program is not working at that time.

Rootkit is considered as one of the nastiest forms of malware programs that is not easily detected and removed from a computer once it has established the privileges to access and control the OS through available vulnerabilities in the OS and other applications.

- VPNFilter cyberattack
- WannaCry ransomware attack
- Petya cyberattack
- Power grid hacking
- Shadow Network attack

Q5. What is the main purpose of a spyware?

A5: A spyware snoops the way user uses the Internet. In most cases, the spyware programs are used to learn the habits of the computer users so that proper and focused digital marketing campaign through emails and other online sources can be implemented.

SOURCES

https://pdfs.semanticscholar.org/165a/99278492f06ba54853a35215f76c7627f5da.pdf
https://cdn.ttgtmedia.com/searchSecurity/downloads/Szor_Ch9.pdf
https://us.norton.com/internetsecurity-malware-what-is-a-computer-virus.html
https://en.wikipedia.org/wiki/Computer_virus
https://searchsecurity.techtarget.com/definition/Trojan-horse
https://enterprise.comodo.com/what-is-trojan-horse-virus.php

https://www.kaspersky.com/resource-center/threats/trojans
https://enterprise.comodo.com/trojan-horse-malware-effects.php
https://securelist.com/it-threat-evolution-q2-2018-statistics/87170/
https://www.computerhope.com/jargon/s/spyware.htm
https://www.forbes.com/sites/forrester/2017/01/26/us-digital-marketing-spend-will-near-
    120-billion-by-2021/#5c0dfb89278b
https://us.norton.com/internetsecurity-malware-what-is-a-computer-worm.html
https://searchsecurity.techtarget.com/definition/worm
https://en.wikipedia.org/wiki/Computer_worm
http://www.ciscopress.com/articles/article.asp?p=662902&seqNum=2
https://us.norton.com/internetsecurity-malware-what-are-browser-hijackers.html
https://www.sans.org/reading-room/whitepapers/incident/scareware-traversing-world-
    web-app-exploit-33333
https://www.symantec.com/content/dam/symantec/docs/security-center/white-papers/rootkits-
    12-en.pdf
https://www.statista.com/outlook/216/100/digital-advertising/worldwide
https://www.veracode.com/security/computer-worm
https://ehs.siu.edu/_common/documents/IT%20newsletter/vol-1-no21.pdf
http://www.computergeeksonline.net/blog/5-tell-tale-signs-of-rootkit-virus-infection/
https://antivirus.comodo.com/blog/computer-safety/what-is-rootkit/
https://www.quikteks.com/malware/adware/
https://itstillworks.com/different-types-spyware-6457947.html
https://usa.kaspersky.com/resource-center/threats/adware-pornware-riskware
https://www.lifewire.com/spyware-prevention-tips-153401
https://www.us-cert.gov/ncas/tips/ST04-016
https://www.researchgate.net/publication/299580232_Computer_Worm_Classification
https://infosecwriters.com/text_resources/pdf/Computer_Worms_Past_Present_and_Future.pdf

Securing Your Computers

6

6.1 INTRODUCTION

Computers have become an integral part of our daily life. We use computers so extensively that our personal and public matters and activities are fully under the influence of computers. We communicate through computers, we buy through computers, we sell through computers, we travel with the help of computer-based systems, we work through computers, we are paid through computers, and even we order our foods through computers.

The computers have drastically changed the way we lived our lives a few decades back. In the 1970s, when the first microprocessor was developed, nobody thought of that chip to influence the way it has done in today's modern life. After the development of Internet and World Wide Web, the influence of computers has become eminent on all fields and activities of life.

As the dependency of the people on computers increased, the issues with security of the computer expanded exponentially. No one was aware of the dark side of the impact of computer till the first malicious program hit the Internet resulting in huge losses to the public lives and businesses. The demand for the security of computers started to increase exponentially in the modern field of information technology.

There are many kinds of threats to the computers, communication networks, and all physical infrastructures that use the power of computer for their operations. The threats to the computers can be divided into two major parts:

• Traditional physical security threats
• Cybersecurity threats

The physical threat can be further classified into the following:

• Overt physical threats
• Covert physical threat

Similarly, the cybersecurity threat can be classified into the following:

• Computer security
• Network security
• Data security

In this chapter, we are going to talk about how to secure your computer from the cyber threats.

From the beginning of cybersecurity threats, the number of hackers is increasing very fast. Hundreds of thousands of hacker attacks take place annually on the Internet in this era. The list of FBI's most wanted cybercriminals is increasing continuously. The total number of cybercriminals included in the most wanted list of FBI expanded to 63 in the first month of 2019. Majority of those cybercriminals belong to the countries that are hostile to the US policies.

Starting from just a few thousand dollar loss, the cost of cyberattacks has soared to millions of dollars and, in certain cases, even billions of dollars. The gravity of the cyberattacks can be imagined by the latest statistics released by MacAfee Inc. According to the MacAfee research, the total loss due to cybercrimes worldwide was estimated at about US$600 billion in 2017.

The intensity of cybercrime is not going to decrease in near future. With the advancements of the technology, the hackers are also becoming very sophisticated and advanced in attacking the computers. Newer ideas, tools, techniques are being applied by the hackers to damage the cyber environment. Some rogue countries and regimes also encourage the cybercrimes on their adversaries.

Terrorism (of any form) is another important driver that encourages the sophistication and advancement in the cyberattacks to inflict huge damages and losses to the humanity and peaceful world. The main crimes that are used to attack the computers include data theft, identity theft, blackmailing, ransom collecting, utility service interruption, government disruption, and many other activities that leave serious effects on the public life of a country or a society.

The cyberterrorism extensively and sophisticatedly uses the latest information technology to design and implement the lethal attacks against the communication networks, utility controlling computer systems, governmental networks, defense systems, and many other important IT-related infrastructures that can leave widespread impact on the life of common people, governments, and societies.

The new aspect of the cyberterrorism has also surfaced in the recent years that the "terrorists" or "terrorist organizations" who are driven by any kind of ideology to inflict harm on normal human life or properties, use the information technology and cybercrimes as the tools for fund raising because the traditional ways of fund raising have been severely blocked across the world through stringent financial regulations.

How to stop all those cybercrime-related activities in the modern fully connected systems worldwide? The simple answer is to secure your cyber infrastructure both physically and electronically. Let us have a look at the major components used for securing our computers.

6.2 FIREWALL SETTINGS

Firewall is the first line of defense for a computer, when it is connected through the Internet or other networks. A firewall is a type of security software that is able to check and monitor traffic coming from certain sources and leaving for a certain port or destination (Figure 6.1).

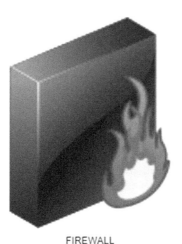

FIREWALL

FIGURE 6.1 Firewall (conceptual image).

Firewall software is used as the first line of defense for any kind of security threat originating from the external sources in a connected environment. It is also the last security checkpost for any traffic originating from your computer.

Many firewalls monitor both incoming and outgoing traffics, but some firewalls only focus on the incoming traffic because the main threat normally originates from the external sources sitting on the other side of the firewall.

It is imperative to note that the software applications that we use on our computers use the communication port numbers at transport layer of the Open Systems Interconnection (OSI) model. The firewall checks the port numbers of the traffic to make sure that the traffic is originated from the authorized sources and is terminating at the genuine port.

If there is any kind of irregularity in the traffic, the firewall is able to detect the suspicious activities and to generate an alert for the same. It is also able to close the port for incoming traffic if it is configured for the auto-blocking malicious activities.

In most of the cyberattacks, the hackers use the untrusted connections to access the vulnerable applications on the computer to launch some malicious software code to install on your computers using those unauthorized connections. Firewall is able to detect any untrusted connection and stop it from intruding into the security measures of the system. Thus, the hacker is caught at the first defense line of the computer before performing any malicious activity on the computers.

There are numerous firewall security software available in the market. You can get so many firewalls for free too, but it is always not recommended to get the free security software for your computer with critical information. Always purchase the firewall security software by paying their price. The paid software are more robust and highly featured to capture numerous kinds of threats originating from the malicious users.

A few very important firewall software that are known for having many great features and capabilities are mentioned below:

- ZoneAlarm Pro Firewall
- Comodo Firewall
- Norton Security Standard Firewall
- Kaspersky Internet Security with Firewall
- Bitdefender Security Firewall
- TinyWall Firewall Software

It is always a great idea to activate the high-level security settings on firewall, but it may irritate you with many warnings and alerts. So, always try to configure firewall settings to allow all programs and their connections to monitor.

If you have many applications that you do not use, you should remove those applications from your computer to make your computer less prone to the external threats. Windows operating system (OS) comes with integrated firewall software. It is activated by default, and you need to configure your security firewall for stronger security settings.

The Windows-based firewall does not monitor the outgoing traffic from your computer, but it focuses mainly on the incoming traffic to monitor any kinds of threats originating from the adversary sources.

6.3 ANTIVIRUS SOFTWARE

Antivirus is one of the fundamental security tools that are recommended for every computer whether it is connected to the external world through Internet or even it operates in a stand-alone position or in the silos (Figure 6.2).

Antivirus software is a security software utility that is able to detect different types of viruses and malware programs on computers. It is also able to remove, delete, and quarantine a virus that has already affected the computer.

There are many types of viruses that commonly spread on the Internet at a very high rate; among such viruses are Trojan horses, worms, viruses, rootkits, and other rogue programs. These viruses are very dangerous for damaging your valuable data on your computer. They use different types of application and system vulnerabilities to get them installed on the computer. Slowly and gradually, they start damaging, coping, or deleting your valuable data. At some point, your will lose your data completely without any remedy to the data recovery.

Hackers and malicious attackers use different types of viruses for different purposes to launch some of the lethal cyberattacks on the networks and computers on the Internet. So, you should always be very well aware of the damage those viruses can inflict on your computers.

The viruses also start duplicating on the computer and, thus, reduce the performance of your computer by filling up the free space on your disk, using the excessive memory, and choking data bandwidth and other resources of the computer and networks. Many viruses create backdoors on the computers and start sending your valuable information and control to the handlers of the viruses (through backdoor).

Once the control of your computer is transferred to the hackers, your computer starts acting as a source of cybercrime by attacking the other computers on the network. Your computer becomes a "Zombie" for hacker attacks. In certain cases, your

FIGURE 6.2   Antivirus software.

computer may crash completely without leaving any possibility of data and system recovery.

There are some good antivirus software programs, which are available in **FREE** as well as paid versions. You can choose any of those versions from the reputed antivirus software providers. For computers with critical information and personal data, it is **NOT** recommended to use free antivirus software because those software programs offer limited capabilities and features. And, those limited capabilities are not sufficient for stopping certain viruses that are more powerful and more dangerous to your computers.

Almost all available antivirus software programs have multiple features such as virus cleaner, spyware cleaner, Trojan horse detection, performance improvements, and other standard features required for keeping your computer clean. But the paid versions of those antivirus software are more robust and have additional deeper features to cope with many dangers of the cybercrimes.

So, it is always recommended to get a paid version of the top-notch antivirus software programs on the computers with critical information and personal data. A few names of the top-notch antivirus software programs are mentioned below:

- Panda Premium Antivirus
- AVG Internet Security
- Microsoft Security Essentials
- McAfee Total Protection
- Comodo Antivirus Software
- Avira Antivirus Pro
- Avast Security Ultimate
- Norton Security

Free versions of these would have limited functionalities and features. Hence, they may not be able to protect the computer in the best possible way. If your computer contains sensitive information, you will need your free version to be converted or upgraded to the paid premium version (by paying the fee online).

Most of the antivirus are set to update their versions automatically by default, but in some cases, if the antivirus software update is not turned on, activate it. You should also take of the following important points for keeping your computer free from viruses.

- Make sure your antivirus software automatically starts with the starting of your computer.
- Antivirus is always "on" while the computer is on.
- Always download and install the latest updates from the vendors to update the virus definition database.
- Regularly run quick scans on your computer.
- Run full scans occasionally after a few weeks.
- Always scan the data transfer media before copying any data.
- Take notice of all warnings and alerts generated by the antivirus software.

If you take care of the abovementioned points, you will be able to keep your computer free from viruses attacking on your computer system and valuable data.

6.4 ANTI-SPYWARE SOFTWARE

Spyware (Figure 6.3) is one of the most critical tools for launching cyberattacks on the targeted networks, services, or the computer servers. Spywares are the malicious code design to spy on the activities of the user for getting information about the behavior of the user or to steal crucial information from the computers and online user accounts.

The spyware codes are also extensively launched by the black-hat marketers to track the Internet user's behavior so that the advertisement campaigns can be started with proper focus on the targeted market segments suitable for their online marketing campaigns.

One form of the dangerous spyware code is known as the keylogger, which is used to track and record the keys pressed. This software code could become very dangerous because it records all keystrokes and sends to the command and control center run by the attacker. By this kind of malicious program, the hackers steal the information such as usernames, passwords, and other codes or pin numbers used for your financial activities and other valuable transactions through the Internet.

Good anti-spyware software can easily detect these nasty codes that reside on your computer, check for your behavior, and steal your bank and other critical information. If you have already installed a full version of any antivirus software on your computer, you might have purchased the anti-spyware already. Many modern antivirus packages are also included with the spyware tools. If there is no such security software on your computer, you may download one from the reputed companies to secure your computer from malicious spying on your computer.

Spyware codes normally spread through free downloads, free websites, and other such free sources available on the Internet. So, it is highly recommended to use the paid version of the software from the trusted security companies.

FIGURE 6.3   Anti-spyware software (conceptual image).

A few very well-trusted anti-spyware software companies are listed below; you can choose any one of them to download the anti-spyware security software.

- SuperAntiSpyware software
- Spybot – Search and Destroy
- Adaware software
- SpywareBlaster
- AVAST Antivirus (embedded)
- AVG Antivirus (embedded)
- MalwareBytes Spyware
- Emsisoft Emergency Kit

You can download and use any of the abovementioned anti-spyware software tools to keep your computer safe from spyware programs. These programs make your information as well as your system exposed to the hackers. Take the following measures to make your spyware protection more robust and effective:

- Use reliable and dedicated antispyware software.
- Many anti-spyware software embedded with the antivirus ignore minor spyware programs.
- Always keep your anti-spyware software up to date.
- Scan your computer regularly for any kind of spyware on your computer.
- Always be vigilant while visiting the unknown websites.
- Major source of spyware spreading is infected websites.
- Deal strictly with the pop-ups and alluring offers by clicking "x" on it.
- Set your browser settings to block pop-up ads.
- Do not open emails from the unknown senders.

By taking all of the above measures carefully, you can save your computer from big spyware attacks to prevent your data from damages.

6.5 ANTI-SPAM SOFTWARE

Spamming is one of the major sources of spreading malware programs on the Internet. Many spammers send malicious code, such as spyware, malware, and viruses, through different kinds of unsolicited emails from different sources. The first spam email is considered to have been delivered through digital communication system about 40 years ago, in 1978 or so (Figure 6.4).

But the email spamming remedies date back to the middle of the 1990s when it became nastier for the companies and email users to sort out the good and bad emails. A huge time was consumed on reading those unsolicited emails, which caused a huge loss to the company productivity.

FIGURE 6.4   Anti-spam software.

At that time, two IT engineers started working on this problem by sorting out the Internet Protocol (IP) addresses, servers, locations, company names, and other information from where the spamming emails were originating. That list was later used on the routers to filter the spamming emails through the Border Gateway Protocol (BGP) on the Internet.

They named it as the Mail Abuse Prevention System (MAPS). The name was a bit difficult, so they reversed the order of the words to make it SPAM. This list was later converted as real-time blackhole list precisely referred to as RBL.

A large majority of the public email servers such as Google, Yahoo, and Hotmail have successfully tracked and identified more than 99% of the spam emails and send them directly to their spam or junk folders. Thus, a huge time and energy of the email user is saved. But this problem is still a matter of concern for many small and big organizations across the world.

According to the latest research (at the time when this was being written) released by digital trends website (https://www.digitaltrends.com), the strike rate of spam emails has increased from 13.4% in 2017 to 14.2% in 2018. If this trend persists for a few years, the nuisance of spamming emails will soar again. The spammers are becoming more sophisticated and sending personalized emails and using other phishing techniques to make the spamming more dangerous in the years to come.

A large ratio of over 31% of the spam emails contain malicious links. If the strike rate of clicking continues to increase, the threat of cyberattacks will also increase substantially. The increase in the cyberattacks will inflict damages to the global economy exponentially.

The major anti-spamming software and services include the following:

- Hornetsecurity spam filter service
- SpamTitan anti-spam software
- MailCleaner anti-spam software
- SpamPhobia anti-spam
- Spambrella anti-spam service provider
- FireTrust MailWasher Service

You can also use customized services and software tools for safeguarding your company employees from the nuisance of spam emails.

As mentioned earlier, the success rate of the anti-spam software tools or anti-spam email cleaning services is about 99% or so. Still, there is a chance of the spam emails to pass through to the inbox of the users. Therefore, you need to take care of your emails too.

Other than using the anti-spamming email solutions, you should also take care of the following points while using emails.

- Never open emails from unknown users.
- Never click on the links or attachments of spam emails.
- Always keep the volume of spam emails in mind; if there is any spike in the emails, consult with your cybersecurity person or service provider.

It is highly recommended that all users should report about any spam email that has passed through the company filter to the administrator of the services. This will improve the efficiency of the spam blocking services.

6.6 SECURITY UPDATES

Computers perform different types of functions and activities based on the software code that runs not only the hardware of the computer, but also the software utilities that we use. No software code is 100% perfect. There may be some flaws, bugs, and other vulnerabilities in all types of software programs.

These bugs or vulnerabilities in the software programs may be present in the OS, drivers, application software, utility software, and network software. The vulnerabilities in the websites and web-based applications can also be a major issue that can pose security threat.

Hackers and cybercriminals use those vulnerabilities, flaws, bugs, and obsolete features to attack the computers and the networks. The security professionals always keep a close eye on the code, features of the code, bugs, possible vulnerabilities, and other security-related aspects to make improvements in the system and application software.

The modification and improvement in the software tools with new software patches or new version releases are known as the updates. The updates are very critical not only for the security of your computer, data, and network, but also for the other people connected with you and your computer network.

If you do not update (Figure 6.5) your software regularly, you would definitely remain at the risk, but your computer once infected, will also pose the threats for the other users on the Internet because your computer may turn into a zombie and spread security threats to other computers of the people known to you and the people connected on your network.

For keeping your computer updated with the security patches, you should need to install patches and install newer versions of the following applications:

- Use the latest version of the OS of your choice.
- Always install OS software updates regularly without any delay.
- Always use genuine security software programs.
- Avoid using free programs, which may bring some malware accompanied with them.
- Always put your security applications on auto-updating option.
- Update every software application that you use on your computer.
- Remove all applications that you do not use.
- Always use the latest versions of the software utilities and applications on your computer.
- Do not use the cracked version of software applications, it may be very dangerous for your data and computer security.
- Never delay in installing downloaded updates.

By taking all of the abovementioned measures carefully, you can save your data, computer, and applications from big dangers. Meanwhile, you also help in making the Internet more secure for the people you know and the other people connected on your network.

FIGURE 6.5   Security updates (concept).

6.7 SECURE BROWSING SETTINGS

The vulnerabilities in the browsers are extensively exploited by the hackers and malicious attackers to intrude into the computer systems for carrying out cybercrime activities such as data theft, identity theft, data corruption, ransom attacks, spamming, and other activities.

Many browsers are used by the Internet users; among such commonly used browsers, Google Chrome (Figure 6.6), Windows Explorer, Mozilla Firefox, and Netscape are a few very important ones to name.

Every browser has its own capabilities and security features. Windows explorer has been among the oldest browsers used by many windows users worldwide. Presently, Mozilla Firefox is one of the most popular browsers used for Internet surfing and accessing the other online web services. The other one competing with it is Google Chrome. Google Chrome and Mozilla Firefox are releasing their security patches and software features more frequently as compared to the other browsers. That is the reason that many people prefer using these two very important browsers for majority of the OSs including Linux, Windows, Mac, and others.

Every browser has numerous settings that relate performance, security, privacy, and other plugins and functions. While using the browsers, you should take special care of all those features and capabilities, especially the security settings. You should configure your browsers with high level of security and privacy settings to make sure that hackers would not be able to exploit the possible vulnerabilities in low security settings of a browser.

You should set the browser to safe browsing mode. Meanwhile, the settings should also not allow the tracking of the traffic request and turn on the SSL (Secure Sockets Layer) and HTTPS (Hypertext Transfer Protocol Secure) certificate settings. All these

FIGURE 6.6   Secure your browser.

security-related settings would help you stay away from the malicious attacks of the hackers. Your browser should be configured for automatic installation of plugins. You should install plugins only when you are 100% sure about that plugin and you trust that vendor.

The privacy settings of the browser should also be restricted to high level of privacy. Your location, personal information, login and passwords, and other information should also be not configured to show or save for every user on the computer. You should also set separate user group for accessing the computer resources. It is always recommended not to use the administrator account for normal activities such as emailing, Internet surfing, normal home or office work, or other such routine activities.

If you are not logged in as administrator, then any malicious attempt to install some code on your computer would be difficult for the hackers. The malicious program will be prompted with logging in as administrator to install any new program.

Thus, your computer will remain safe from hidden attempts to install some malicious programs on your computer, and you will also be alerted for any attempt to alter the settings of your computer or any attempt to install some malicious programs on your computer.

Let us summarize the main settings of your browser to keep your computer safe from any malicious attempt to alter your computer resources and settings.

- Set privacy settings to high level.
- Use separate strong password-based user groups.
- Do not save passwords on browsers.
- Do not login as an administrator unless you really need it.
- Activate the safe browsing settings on the browser.
- Your browsing traffic should be attached with "Do Not Track" request.
- Activate SSL and HTTPS settings.
- All pop-ups, plugins, and other activities should be denied or asked to get permission from the computer admin
- Computer resources and content access settings should be very strong.
- Always check for harmful software installed on your browser or computer.

6.8 SCAN DEVICES BEFORE DATA TRANSFER

Data traveling and other devices to run or transfer data from one point to another one have been the major transporters of viruses, worms, Trojans, and other malicious codes. Among such devices are flash drives, CDs, DVDs, floppies, external hard drive, and any other data transferring devices (Figure 6.7).

All those devices should be properly scanned with the updated antivirus and anti-malware software to detect and kill any malicious programs attached to the data. After scanning the devices fully, you can copy or transfer data between the devices; this will reduce the threat of viruses to infect your computer.

FIGURE 6.7   Scan device before data transfer.

6.9 SOCIAL ENGINEERING ATTACK PRECAUTIONS

Social engineering is very important source for unleashing a cybercrime on your data, personal information, and bank account information. In this form of cyberattack, different media such as text messages, chatting, group discussion, telephone call, and emails are used to communicate with you to exploit your innocence or ignorance. This is also a part of cyber frauds (Figure 6.8).

You might have noticed that you get an email from a legitimate-looking source that you got a prize through a lucky draw or you got a big job opportunity in a big organization. That email looks like it has been sent from a legitimate company and you will be lured by the presentation of the content.

The hacker on the other end of the communication tries to use the social behavior to influence your thoughts and asks you to provide your personal information including the bank account and other information.

When they receive this information, they request you for some processing fee and may ask for credit card information. If you provide this information, they would use it maliciously to damage you to steal money from your banks or from your credit card. If you send the money they ask for, they will go away and will not appear again.

The main objective of such social engineering attacks is to achieve the financial benefits from the unsuspecting people. They also use the text messages, phone calls, and other mediums for the same purpose. In those cases, the in-person communication

FIGURE 6.8   Social engineering attack (concept).

is used so efficiently that you will not doubt on their sincerity at any point of time. They use very professional manners to talk with you so politely and effectively that you start believing in their conversation and provide the information they like to get from you.

Hackers use the social engineering tactics to spread malware in your mobile and computer device through emails, attached documents, and messages. Once you click the emails and its attachments, the viruses embedded in those emails download and get installed on your computer or mobile device. Thus, those viruses start carrying out the activities that they are designed for by the hackers sitting at the remote site.

So, never open emails, text messages, or other messages from unknown people. If you see any kind of such alluring message from the unknown, just delete it without any second thoughts!

As it could be noticed, the protection mechanisms of many of the issues are very much similar, and hence, knowing the common security measures is imperative in today's world whenever one uses Internet and its services.

6.10 MISCELLANEOUS TIPS

All of the abovementioned issues are the major components of keeping your computer free from the viruses and other cyberattacks. There are many other factors that are also very important for keeping your computer free from viruses. These miscellaneous tips could play very crucial role in your personal behavior towards the computer security (Figure 6.9).

As we know, the security is a continuous process, and it is not possible to achieve it by acting on it once. You will have to adopt different recommendations and industry

FIGURE 6.9   Miscellaneous tips.

guidelines in your behavior so that you can make your habit 100% in compliance with the computer security standards and procedures.

The main tips for keeping your computer free from viruses are listed below:

- Never use the cracked software.
- Never use free software.
- Never save your passwords on your computer or browsers.
- Do not provide critical information on telephone, email, or SMS.
- Do not open files sent by unknown people.
- Do not visit faulty websites.
- Set your browser settings at high security and privacy.
- Always create separate users for a computer.
- Create a guest account with minimum privileges, if required.
- Uninstall all apps that are not in use.
- Do not install unknown applications.
- Always install the plugins that you deem necessary for your use.
- Avoid to use free applications.
- Always update your applications.
- Use latest versions of an OS.
- Use latest versions of applications.
- Never miss a security patch or update at all.
- Daily check for the security updates.
- Turn off your computer if you are not using it.
- Turn off the Internet router, if not used for a certain period of time.
- Take security as a serious matter in your life.
- Regularly check for the security guidelines.

- Always make a copy of your valuable data.
- Create checkpoints on your computer.
- Run scheduled virus scans regularly.
- Always download something from the reliable websites.
- Never try to use the public data sharing websites for exchanging data.
- Use highly secure and reliable data sharing and collaboration platforms for data transfers.
- Use strong passwords.
- Encrypt your important data files.

By taking all of the abovementioned standard guidelines and tips for keeping your computer safe from viruses and other malware threats, you can avert big data losses and enjoy smooth Internet browsing without incurring any damage to your computer.

SAMPLE QUESTIONS AND ANSWERS FOR WHAT WE HAVE LEARNED IN CHAPTER 6

Q1. What are the major classes of cybersecurity?

A1: The cybersecurity threat can be classified into the following:

- Computer security
- Network security
- Data security

Q2. What is a firewall software?

A2: Firewall is the first line of defense for a computer, when it is connected through the Internet or other networks. A firewall is a type of security software that is able to check and monitor traffic coming from certain sources and leaving for a certain port or destination.

Firewall software is used as the first line of defense for any kind of security threat originating from the external sources in a connected environment. It is also the last security checkpost for any traffic originating from your computer. There is a hardware version of firewall as well.

Q3. What is antivirus?

A3: Antivirus is one of the fundamental security tools that are recommended for every computer whether that is connected to the external world through Internet or even it operates in stand-alone position or in the silos. Antivirus software is a security software utility that is able to detect different types of viruses and malware programs on computers. It is also able to remove, delete, and quarantine a virus that has already affected the computer.

Q4. What is spam email and spamming?

A4: Spamming is one of the major sources of spreading malware programs on the Internet. Many spammers send malicious code, such as spyware, malware, and viruses, through different kinds of unsolicited emails from different sources. The first spam email is considered to have been delivered through digital communication system about 40 years ago, in 1978 or so.

Email spamming remedies date back to the middle of the 1990s when it became nastier for the companies and email users to sort out the good and bad emails. A huge time was consumed on reading those unsolicited emails, which caused a huge loss to the company productivity. At that time, two IT engineers started working on this problem by sorting out the IP addresses, servers, locations, company names, and other information from where the spamming emails were originating. That list was later used on the routers to filter the spamming emails through the Border Gateway Protocol (BGP) on the Internet. They named it as the Mail Abuse Prevention System (MAPS). The name was a bit difficult, so they reversed the order of the words to make it SPAM.

Q5. Note a few steps and measures to keep your browser safe.

A5: The main settings of the browser to keep one's computer safe from any malicious attempt are as follows:

- Set privacy settings to high level.
- Use separate strong password-based user groups.
- Do not save passwords on browsers.
- Do not login as an administrator unless you really need it.
- Activate the safe browsing settings on the browser.
- Your browsing traffic should be attached with "Do Not Track" request.
- Activate SSL and HTTPS settings.
- All pop-ups, plugins, and other activities should be denied or asked to get permission from the computer admin.
- Computer resources and content access settings should be very strong.
- Always check for harmful software installed on your browser or computer.

SOURCES

https://www.mobt3ath.com/uplode/book/book-26247.pdf
https://www.fbi.gov/wanted/cyber
https://www.mcafee.com/enterprise/en-us/solutions/lp/economics-cybercrime.html
https://www.researchgate.net/publication/252195165_CYBER_TERRORISM-_GLOBAL_
    SECURITY_THREAT
https://www.ndi.org/sites/default/files/Security%20In-a-Box%20How%20To%20Booklet.pdf
https://oag.ca.gov/sites/all/files/agweb/pdfs/privacy/CIS_12_Computer_protection_DOJ.pdf
https://www.techradar.com/news/best-firewall

https://geekflare.com/free-pc-antivirus/

https://www.safetydetective.com/blog/the-best-anti-spyware-software/

http://intosaiitaudit.org/intoit_articles/19_03_Hacking.pdf

https://www.spamtitan.com/anti-spam-software/

https://blog.comodo.com/antispam/what-is-anti-spam-software/

https://www.capterra.com/anti-spam-software/

https://www.digitaltrends.com/computing/spam-making-comeback/

https://us.norton.com/internetsecurity-how-to-the-importance-of-general-software-updates-and-patches.html

https://portal.msrc.microsoft.com/en-us/

http://johnjay.jjay.cuny.edu/files/IT_Security_Guide-101410.pdf

https://www.clearbooks.co.uk/themes/revo/media/white-paper/how-to-prevent-computer-viruses.pdf

https://www4.ntu.ac.uk/information_systems/document_uploads/96800.pdf

https://www.chicagoitsolutions.com/blog/11-ways-to-protect-your-computer-from-viruses/

https://home.bt.com/tech-gadgets/computing/tips-protect-your-pc-hackers-malware-11363942012065

https://www.cypherix.com/docs/cryptainer_information_week.pdf

Thakur, K., Shan, J., and Pathan, A.-S.K., "Innovations of Phishing Defense: The Mechanism, Measurement and Defense Strategies," International Journal of Communication Networks and Information Security, Vol. 10, No. 1, April 2018, pp. 19–27.

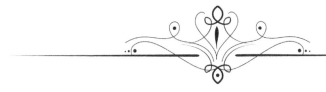

Password Management

7

7.1 INTRODUCTION

According to the information published in Symantec Norton report, there were more than 34% of the people in 2017 who suffered losses due to password hacking. The total cost of hacking was about US$172 billion, which impacted more than 978 million people worldwide with an average loss of about US$142 per user. A user also lost the productivity and peace of mind for over 24 hours on an average to deal with this hacking mess.

The major components of this entire loss in 2017 included virus infection (53%), scam purchases (33%), and personal financial frauds (32%). The email phishing was also one of the major components in this fraud of stealing the personal information and account passwords.

This report also found that more than 20% of the users use the same password (Figure 7.1) on multiple accounts, which is considered to be very dangerous practice for personal account security. And more than 58% of the users have shared their passwords with other people for once at least. The ratio of the users of the fingerprint passwords was about 44%, and those who use the patterns as security measure were about 22% of the people surveyed in the report.

FIGURE 7.1   Password for login system.

A large number of users – more than 70% – do not follow the password management's standard guidelines and recommendations, which is a big gray area for the online users exploited by the malicious cybercriminals. This gray area is badly exploited by the hackers to hack on the accounts, personal information, digital access, and many other cybercrimes. This trend of not following the standard guidelines in the millennial users is much higher than the older users.

In light of these startling statistics, it is very imperative that the basics of password management should be adopted in all level of users across the globe irrespective of their nature of Internet use. The failure to adhere with the basics of the password management may result in huge losses to the Internet users in all parts of the world.

According to the Verizon Data Breach Investigations Report (DBIR) 2017, more than 80% of the hacking activities related to data theft are caused by either stolen passwords or very weak passwords. These passwords are extensively exploited in attempting distributed denial-of-service (DDoS) attacks by using the armies of botnet from multiple locations.

When an army of cyber bots equipped with the stolen passwords attempt to login and request for accessing on any particular website from multiple locations with multiple attempts, the system becomes fully overwhelmed with the malicious traffic and succumbs to the pressure of traffic. Thus, the denial-of-service (DoS) attack on a particular website becomes successful and outage of the service occurs.

The password management is very critical in avoiding password theft and subsequently the DoS attacks as well as other cybercrimes.

7.2 BASICS OF PASSWORDS

The basic objective of using a password is to authenticate your authority to access certain resources. The technique of code word to verify a certain authenticity of person, event, or any other activity was used between two communicators in the old ages.

FIGURE 7.2   Basics of passwords.

The concept of password can be divided into two major eras: the traditional era and the digital era (Figure 7.2).

In the history of Europe, the use of password can be traced back in the biblical book of Judges. Chapter 12 describes an event known as the "Shibboleth Event". The term "Shibboleth" was used by the Gileadite soldiers to identify their enemies in the war against Ephraim tribes. The pronunciation of *shibboleth* made by the Ephraim tribal people was different from that made by Gilead tribal people due to their unique accent. So, it was very easy for the Gilead soldiers to identify the Ephraim tribes in the war.

From that point, the password evolved to code words and then to hard keys and tokens. The physical passwords were also introduced in the locks to get access to certain physical resources. This evolution of password continued in different forms and formats in the traditional era of physical world.

With the advent of modern digital era, the use of password changes drastically in terms of their shapes, sizes, and the ways of using them. The use of password in the digital era, especially in the computing field, was introduced in 1961 at the Massachusetts Institute of Technology (MIT). This time domain-based password first ever in the digital history was introduced as the Compatible Time Sharing System (CTSS) project, which allowed the multiple users to use the computer power at different time slots. This system was a UNIX operating system-based project.

From that point of time, the digital or cyber password has evolved to a very complex and comprehensive security level today. The present forms of the passwords are very strong, reliable, and sophisticated. The ways of using passwords have also changed tremendously.

The modern passwords are used for restricting unauthorized access to the computing machines such as PCs, tablets, mobiles, routers, switches, and many other configurable devices. Moreover, passwords are also used to access the online digital services connected through Internet.

There are different types and forms of passwords used in the modern world. The following are a few among them.

- Conventional password
- Biometric passwords
- Two-factor authentication
- Multi-factor authentication
- Social media logins
- Email logins
- One-time password (OTP)
- Smart keys and physical tokens

The modern passwords consist of minimum length of 8 characters and maximum of 64 characters in certain cases. The strength of password increases with the number of characters because the possibility of guessing and decoding the hash through computer power will be near to impossible in case of strong 64-character passwords.

Let us expand upon more aspects of a modern digital password used in the field of computer and information technology.

7.2.1 Threats to Passwords

The major threat to your password is the user sluggishness, which often discourages the user from following the password management guidelines. The password theft is one of the major reasons of the DDoS attacks and many other data theft, and financial frauds.

According to the latest research conducted in 2018, it was found that a large number of the people use very generic passwords such as 123456, 12345678, and abc123. These passwords are very easy to guess and snoop while you input the password.

The WatchGuard security survey Q2 2018 found that more than 1,700 people working in governmental and military organizations of Australia used "123456" password! Other weak passwords used by those government employees included "password" (544 people), "linkedin" (405 people), and "12345678" (120 people). All these passwords are the most unreliable and easy-to-guess passwords in the world. Many organizations and security companies have already blacklisted these passwords to be used.

The use of weak passwords is highly prone to the risk of being stolen easily. So, easy passwords should never be used. The plain text passwords are even more prone to theft.

The major threats to the password theft include the following:

- Eavesdropping
- Guessing of password
- Cracking passwords through computing software

- Offline cracking of hashes
- Password recovery or reset cyberattack techniques
- Same password use on multiple accounts
- Using default passwords of the system
- Malicious software on your computer such as sniffers and keyloggers
- Backdoor exploit
- Malicious plugins
- Phishing

How to tackle these threats? You can make your passwords secure and safe by following the standard guidelines and recommended software tools to make your software secure from external and internal threats.

7.2.2 Good and Bad about Passwords

After having discussed the suspected threats to the passwords, let us now talk about what is good and what is bad about a password. People are more careless and lazy about remembering hard and strong passwords; so they prefer to use simple and easy-to-remember passwords. That is not a good idea about a good password.

A good password should have the following features:

- Should be longer in a range of 10–15 characters.
- Should not include any plain text, which is easy to guess.
- Should include the combination of lowercase and uppercase characters.
- Should include at least one or more special symbols/characters at random place.
- Should include at least one or more numbers at different places.
- Never use your personal information, which is easy to guess.
- Do not ever share your password with others.
- Always change the password pattern.
- Always change your password regularly.

If you follow these instructions, you will remain more protected and secure in this highly risky environment of Internet.

Now, the main points of a bad password could be as follows:

- Plain text passwords
- Short passwords
- No combination of different types of characters
- No use of upper and lower cases randomly
- Reusing of the same password
- Using meaningful words
- Using meaningful word and adding just one digit like "mango1"
- Reusing the same word twice in the password like "fishfish1"
- Using a word in reverse order like "elppa" for apple

- Using garble word like "0" for o and "3" for E and so on; example includes (z3r0)
- Using the same passwords as their usernames or computer account name and similar.

All of the above mistakes should never be made while choosing a password. Those mistakes can lead you to hacking of your account by different means.

7.2.3 How Do Bad Guys Hack Your Password?

The cybercriminals are highly skilled and qualified people with negative thinking, so they are very creative thinkers in devising strategies and methods to steal the usernames and passwords of the genuine users. They can use any new and innovative technology to get hold on your password, but a few very important techniques are explained below:

1. **Over-the-Shoulder Technique:** This is a traditional way to steal any critical information like password. The bad guys try to steal your password when you enter it into the system or online service. This technique is also useful when you write your password on some diary or paper. The hackers try to peep over to see your passwords in different forms in this method.
2. **Dictionary Hacking Technique:** In this form of exploitation, the hackers try to use the words available in the dictionaries of different major languages. They use different combinations and roots with the help of certain software tools to crack the passwords of the users. This is more sophisticated and effective method to hack the passwords.
3. **Password Guessing Technique:** This is one of the traditional forms of password guessing. The hackers make guesses to crack the passwords. Those guesses are influenced by psychology, gender, mental approach, background, and other factors of the user. Many studies suggest that a majority of the passwords used by the female users include the names of their children, husband, or boyfriends. The hackers take advantage of this trend in women to hack their passwords.
4. **Brute-Force Attack Technique:** This basically means trying all possibilities to break a system. You have already read about the cryptocurrency mining by using the computer processor to decrypt the transaction and verify it. Similar type of technique can also be employed by the hackers to guess your password through a password guessing software. This software uses the combinations of different options and words to guess the password. A simple Pentium 100 computer is able to process more than 20 thousands of combinations in just 1 second. So you can easily understand how dangerous this technique can be in modern technological environment.

The modern hackers are very creative, experienced, and skilled. They can use an out-of-the-box idea to crack the passwords at any time. So, always take care of your passwords to maintain their sanctity and integrity.

7.3 EFFECTIVE PASSWORD MANAGEMENT TIPS

An effective password management plays a vital role in maintaining higher level of security at work as well as at home. Password management is the combination of the procedures and activities that should be accomplished on a regular basis as set forth by the security manager, security management agencies, and industry guidelines (Figure 7.3).

The latest figures regarding the identity theft released by different cybersecurity and news agencies suggest that the number of identity theft is much larger than we considered before. There were more than 6.64% of the online consumers who became the victim of identity theft in 2017. That means 1 in every 15 users of the online services has become the victim of the identity theft.

The number of identity theft in 2017 increased by over 1 million as compared to the identity theft figures in 2016. One user becomes victim of the identity theft in every 2 seconds in our present connected environment.

According to the Credential Spill Report 2017, there were more than 3 billion passwords, which were either stolen or compromised in the year 2016 only. This huge number of stolen passwords was used for different types of DDoS attacks and other cybercriminal activities. This huge number of stolen passwords was misused by the hackers to create more than 90% of the total traffic related to login attempts. Thus, you can imagine how your password is prone to exploitation in the cybercriminal environment.

After creating a strong password, a user has to take different steps to maintain the power and effectiveness of the password. That means, creating a strong password is not sufficient for maintaining a strong cybersecurity. You will have to keep a close look at the security and effectiveness of the password after you created a strong password.

You should consider the below-mentioned steps and follow the guidelines set forth by the security experts and industry standards to maintain the effectiveness of your system and online accounts.

- Always choose longer passwords ranging from 12 to 20 or even more characters.
- Password is a completely private property; so, do not share it with anybody.
- Never create same password for multiple accounts or services.

FIGURE 7.3   Effective password management tips.

- Never write down your password on paper or copy.
- Never save your password on your computer.
- Change your password after 3–4 months.
- Always use different patterns for every password so that it cannot be easily cracked.
- Never use single number at the end of the password.
- Try to use biometric password if available.
- Consider using the two-factor authentication.
- Always enable multi-factor authentication on your account if supported.
- Encrypt the files and data that contain password-related information.
- Do not save your critical passwords on browsers.
- Always try to use a good password manager for managing your password more effectively and efficiently.
- Always type your password fast so that no one can guess it.
- Always remember password so that you do not refer to any paper or file for the same.
- Try to generate strong passwords with the help of password-generating software.
- Never reuse the password over and over again after changing it.
- Never send or save your password in emails because they are not fully secure.
- Always take note of surroundings when you input your password.
- Always choose the strong passwords, but those passwords should be easy to remember for you.

If you take care of all of the abovementioned tips, you would remain fully protected from the identity theft and other hacking activities. Thus, you would be able to manage your passwords more effectively and efficiently.

7.4 CREATING AND MANAGING SECURE PASSWORDS

In the present-day online environment, our business as well as our social life is highly dependent on the computers, Internet, software applications, and online services. We use username and passwords for accessing those services and resources of the computer devices.

Passwords are very critical and valuable for every online user because our personal, business, social, and many other types of data and information are directly linked with the online services and the Internet. If any hacker gets hold on our password, we will become so prone to many types of losses incurred by the breach of data integrity, privacy, and availability of digital resources.

So, the passwords are the lifeline of our online existence (Figure 7.4, conceptual image). If our passwords are compromised, we will lose control over our valuable digital assets.

FIGURE 7.4   Creating and managing secure passwords.

The hackers and cybercriminals are becoming very advanced, and they use the latest, high-tech, and sophisticated techniques to carry out cyberattacks. The password theft is one of the major objectives of the cybercriminals to inflict serious damage to the common users as well as to the businesses and government organizations.

The solution to this problem is the use of strong password and allied services so that the chances of your passwords to have been compromised are reduced. For that purpose, we should use not only strong passwords but also the password strength complementary services. Among such complementary measures to make your password even more reliable, strong, and effective, a few are explained in the following subsections.

7.4.1 Strong Password

The first step towards having a secure and reliable password is to create a very strong password. The qualities and features of a strong password include the following:

- Non-guessable
- Longer length
- Complex pattern of characters
- Complex combination of characters
- Based on the out-of-the-box ideas
- Not influenced with the personal behaviors and information
- Better password management

All of the above features should be taken into consideration while creating a strong password. You can use a creative idea or expression and then, choose random characters from that idea or expression. For example, you think that working in a government organization is so boring. Then, you can make an expression like *I get bored with a government job*. This expression will provide you clue on how to remember your password. Then you can choose letters, numbers, and symbols from this expression to create a strong password.

For example, you take "I", "ge", "bo", "w", "a", "gv", and "j" characters from the above expression. Now you organize them in such a way that they create a strong password. Let us then reduce this expression to "Ig3b0W@gV!" to form a strong password.

Now what you have to remember is that you used zero (0) instead of "o", 3 instead of "e", @ instead of "a", and '!' instead of "j". The capital letters were chosen randomly to make the password even stronger.

Thus, you created a very strong password with an innovative expression that only you know about. It will become very easy for you to remember because you linked your expression and the characters that you chose with certain situations and symbols.

7.4.2 Use of Biometrics

The use of biometrics (Figure 7.5) is becoming a new standard for the passwords. There are many security experts and security companies that advocate the replacement of traditional passwords with the biometric passwords. The use of biometrics makes your passwords more secure and reliable.

As we know, the fingerprints are unique in the world; therefore, there would be no alternative to the fingerprints. Meanwhile, the facial recognition is another important aspect of biometric identification. Again, with the advancement in the artificial intelligence in the software development, the facial recognition is becoming an important standard for the biometric access to the devices and applications.

Moreover, many research works are already in progress to use the walking patterns, body gestures, body movement, shapes of body parts, body odors, and even vein patterns of a hand for this purpose. The use of complete hand scans has become one of the most important identification standards for the governments in passports, immigration, and other governmental procedures.

FIGURE 7.5 Use of biometrics.

Many computers, tablets, mobile devices, and other access control equipment have already been enabled with the biometric support. A large number of mobile applications, desktop applications, and online tracking applications have also been developed to use the biometric authentication in a better way.

In mobile devices, the combination of biometric and traditional passwords or even drawing patterns makes the security of a device more comprehensive and reliable. The improvement in the effectiveness and accuracy of the biometric scanning system is continuously happening, which may lead to its use in the more precise and mission-critical applications extensively.

The scope of biometric identification is very high, but there are some very real concerns pertaining to the privacy of the people. The data of the people can easily be accessed through the use of biometric scans at public places as well as at the other places. But the benefits that the biometric identification offers are tremendously high.

It can effectively be used at public and private places that are highly sensitive in terms of security, military, or even public safety such as airports, malls, hotels, military installations, and many other places. Biometric technology can be used to avert any terrorist activities by identifying the suspected people before they can strike.

7.4.3 Two-Factor Authentication

The traditional form of authentication is single-factor authentication in which you enter your password against your username to access the authorized resources. This method is considered as *low secure* nowadays due to many reasons. One of the main reasons for the low security of single-factor authentication is that it is easy to be compromised if you have to use your password many times a day.

The single layer security is not powered by any additional layer that means if your password is compromised, you will lose the control over your resources and unauthorized cybercriminals can easily break into your resources. The solution to this problem is the two-factor authentication and multi-factor authentication.

The two-factor authentication (Figure 7.6) is also known as dual-factor and two-step authentication. In this process, you get one additional layer of security to access

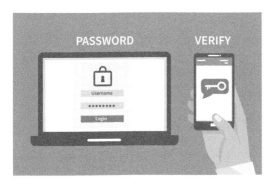

FIGURE 7.6 Two-factor authentication.

your resources. When you enter username and password, you will be prompted to enter the passcode. The passcode is normally sent through a text message or automated call on your mobile phone.

The passcode is normally an auto-generated unique code by the designated server. It is only one-time-use code. That code is also time sensitive which means that the code expires after certain time. This way your code cannot be compromised by any malicious user.

In the latest passcode generating technology, codes can be generated and sent out through emails, text, automated call, web links, and other ways. In the two-factor authentication facial expression, biometric input or other body gestures can also be used. Thus, the access to your resources becomes highly secure and uncompromised by adopting two-factor authentication.

The two-factor authentication is offered by the major public platforms such as Google, Facebook, and many others on their services to make them fully secure and robust. But if you have small- or medium-size business and want to implement two-factor authentication, you can either install/run your own service or hire services offered by two-factor authentication service provider companies available in the market.

To enable the two-factor authentication, you will need to add phone number to the server for receiving the passcode. Normally, the following steps are involved in enabling the two-factor authentication:

- Add your mobile number and alternate phone number.
- Choose the way you want to receive the passcode – either automated voice call or text message.
- The test verification code is sent by server to your phone number.
- The code is inserted into the field to verify the same.
- Two-factor authentication is enabled now.

If you have enabled the two-factor authentication on your any service or account login, you will have to receive a security code on your mobile phone and then, insert it in the security code field to verify your authenticity.

The two-factor authentication depends upon different types of factors used as the second layer of the security factor. A few important second layer of the security factors are listed below:

- Possession factor
- Inheritance factor
- Knowledge factor
- Location factor
- Time factor
- Hardware tokens

Two-factor authentication has become one of the most powerful security layers for password protection from the cybercriminals. Such type of authentication also offers the feature to enable the capability of remembering your device on the second login attempt.

You can choose the *remember my device* option to avoid inconvenience of inserting security code on the same device again and again. But for the most critical data, it is not recommended to use this feature to avoid any mishap or data theft. Always use the security code for every login to secure you critical data and information.

In some of the important security cases of the passwords, the biometric or the facial recognition input is used as the second factor of the security code. Two-factor security is also known as the security based on what you know and what you are.

The security codes can also be received through mobile apps or secure emails. You get either a passcode or a link which you can click to verify that you are the authorized person to access certain resources.

7.4.4 Multi-Factor Authentication

The two-factor authentication improves the security of resource access, but still the level of security that a critical data needs is not sufficient yet. Some important issues were found associated with the security of the two-factor authentication. For example, in 2011, the RAS security company announced that a huge number of important two-factor accounts have been compromised. In that attack, the secure ID authentication tokens were hacked by cybercriminals.

So, the security of the two-factor system offered by the service provider companies is again prone to attack if the security of the company's system is compromised. The process of recovery of the accounts can also be threatened because it uses account setting resets. So, there are certain issues with the two-factor authentication. To further improve the security of the access authentication, multi-factor authentication system is used. This system consists of multi-stage authentication factors as shown in Figure 7.7.

Multi-factor authentication is based on three or more factors. The major three factors used are known as:

- What you know
- What you are
- What you have

FIGURE 7.7 Multi-factor authentication.

7.4.4.1 What you know

This category of the multi-factor authentication deals with the information or factors that a user knows about. For example, password, pin code, or other security code either provided by the service provider company or created by the user. This category of authentication factors is also known as the knowledge factors in the field of computer security.

7.4.4.2 What you are

This category consists of the factors that relate to the personal information such as facial recognition, biometrics, retina scan, and other factors. These factors are also classified as the inheritance factors in some books and technical writings. These are very unique biological characteristics or factors for every individual person. Thus, it makes the multi-factor authentication more robust.

7.4.4.3 What you have

This group of factors is also referred to as possession factors in the field of computer security. In this category, the major factors of authentication include the components such as key fob, digital key, or mobile device with the software application to scan. These factors are extensively used in the modern multi-factor authentication, especially in the industrial and business security systems. To clarify here, a fob, which is commonly called a *key fob*, is a small security hardware device with built-in authentication system which is used to control and secure access to mobile devices, computer systems, and network services and data. It displays a randomly generated access code, which changes periodically – usually every 30–60 seconds.

In the multi-factor authentication, a new category of authentication factors is emerging on the marketplace. This is known as the location-based authentication factor. This code is used for adding another layer of security while accessing the network from the remote locations other than the specified locations saved on the security servers.

When some employee wants to access the corporate network from the location other the local offices, then a soft token will be required to grant the access, but in normal conditions, the user can access by using other authentication factors only.

In some conditions, time window is also used as a layer of security for accessing some particular resources. A user is allowed for a certain time window to access the certain resources. At any time other than the specified window, the access to the resources will be denied despite the fact that the user has full and right credentials.

7.4.5 One-Time Password (OTP)

One-time password (Figure 7.8) is commonly referred to as OTP in the field of software security. This is extensively used by the banks and other financial institutes. Normally, passwords can be classified into two categories:

- Static passwords
- Dynamic passwords

FIGURE 7.8   One-time password (OTP).

The static passwords are the codes saved on the server and used repeatedly for accessing the desired resources or getting the physical access. On the other hand, the dynamic passwords are created, used, and discarded. They are not saved as the valid information for re-login. It is used just for one time to access the resources.

The example of dynamic password is the one-time PIN (also, OTP or OPIN) used in the modern financial systems for online transactions.

One-time PIN is created when you need to accomplish some online transactions on your bank account or any other online resources. You login to your bank account, but every transaction regarding the movement of the funds is associated with the one-time pin or password.

So, the OTP or OPIN is a type of dynamic password, which is valid for only one transaction or session of the login. OTPs offer numerous advantages, which help you improve the security of critical online transactions.

One of the most important benefits of using the OTP is that it cannot be reused for cyberattacks or any other malicious activities. Hence, tracking the OTP numbers will not be harmful for your account security. Even if all the past OTP generated by you are exposed to the cyber hackers, that will not make any difference at all! The attacker would still be clueless.

The OTPs are very difficult to be intercepted during the creation and use of those passwords. Thus, the use of OTPs reduces the amount of attacks. Due to these advantages, OTPs are extensively used in mission-critical systems and financial accounts in banks and other financial institutes such as insurance companies, and other similar kinds of institutes.

7.4.6 Using Password Managers

In the present online environment, we use hundreds of websites, web services, applications, and resources through Internet. The access to the resources is validated through passwords. So, you have to remember hundreds of passwords for accessing those websites smoothly.

FIGURE 7.9   Using password managers.

If you use the same password on all websites, that means your data and personal information are at great danger for sure. The identity theft is one of the major components of the hacking attacks carried out by the cybercriminals on the Internet. Millions of accounts and passwords are being compromised annually.

Two main issues with a user regarding his/her password include the creation of strong password and then managing the password to access the resources smoothly. Normally, a huge majority of the users create weak passwords and follow the non-recommended ways for creating their passwords, which puts them at risk of cyberattack.

Another major problem that the users face is to remember and manage a large number of passwords that they use for getting registered with different services and applications. A good password manager (Figure 7.9, conceptual image) is able to solve both of those issues of a normal user.

A password manager is a software application that offers the services to create a strong password and manage all those passwords in encrypted format so that they are not prone to compromise. A good password manager allows the user to save the encrypted password either in the cloud or on the local drives. Online storage of passwords in the cloud is easy to access it from anywhere in the world, but the passwords saved locally are a bit difficult to access from other locations.

You can create multiple passwords for multiple websites and applications on the password manager that you use, but you have to remember just one password, which is known as the master password. You can also save and carry the saved passwords in the flash drive with you.

There are password manager-like features in the major browsers such as Chrome, Firefox, and Internet Explorer, but majority of them save the passwords in plain text format, not in the encrypted format, which is dangerous for you and your data. These passwords are not usable on the cross platforms like passwords saved on the Windows are not supported on the Linux.

So, using a good password manager may be a suitable solution for an online user in today's environment of the Internet.

7.4.6.1 Main reasons to use a password manager

The major reasons for using a good password manager include the following:

- Generating strong passwords
- No need to remember multiple passwords
- No need to worry about password theft
- Passwords are stored in fully encrypted formats
- Options to save passwords locally and in the cloud
- Easy to access passwords

You can create and save your passwords on password manager software tools. They save your passwords in an encrypted format and they retrieve in the normal state when requested. The hackers will not be able to decrypt your passwords saved on the password managers.

You can easily access your passwords saved in the cloud. If you want to save them on your local computer, you can do that very easily. In that case, the online access of the passwords will be a bit difficult. It is recommended by the security experts to use good password managers to avert any identity theft and related cyberattacks.

It is very important to note what level of encryption a password manager uses before you decide to use any one of them. A good password manager should use at least 256-bit or even more level of encryption. Normally, 256-bit encryption is considered as a suitable format for data files to keep them secure. So, the password data file should be encrypted with 256-bit or higher level of encryption.

7.5 PASSWORD MANAGER TOOLS

Password managers are the major components in the computer and data security of our modern IT world. There are hundreds of great password managers available in the marketplace. You can choose any one of those password manager tools based on the features, capabilities, and design.

You should also consider the security guidelines and recommendations for data security in your own country. In the United States, the National Security Agency (NSA) issues guidelines for the critical data security in the country.

Let us know about the top five password manager tools extensively used in the marketplace.

7.5.1 Dashlane

Dashlane (Figures 7.10 and 7.11) is one of the most popular and password manager tools on the Internet. It is available in FREE as well as paid version. It is very easy to use. The free version supports up to 50 passwords to create, store, and use. You can create

FIGURE 7.10   Dashlane logo.

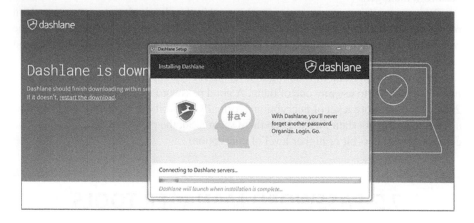

FIGURE 7.11   Dashlane installation.

and store your passwords with strong encryption protocols and access from anywhere around the world.

It supports multiple browsers such as Firefox, Chrome, and Internet Explorer. It also supports the mobile wallets and payment gateway password protection. There are more than 10,000 enterprise customers using this tool for their password security.

The other main features of Dashlane password manager include the following:

- It is very smooth, clean, and clutter-free software tool
- Supports auto-fill and auto-login capabilities
- Stores and transmits password data in secure form to access
- Generates strong passwords for any new registration of service
- Uses strong AES-256 encryption protocol
- Supports multiple passwords on a same website
- Offers you access through web from anywhere
- Supports Android and iOS, PC, and Mac platforms
- Supports local as well as cloud storage

- One-click support to change your existing password
- Supports password migration from other services
- Allows categorization of the passwords according to critical levels
- Intuitive web interface
- Supports Chrome OS, MS Edge, and Linux
- Supports two-factor authentication
- Additional features of credit monitoring and data backup
- Supports identity theft insurance and identity restoration help
- Supports instant dark web alerts
- Supports password group share for business users
- You can save personal information, IDs, receipts and payments information
- Your data is unknown to even the company employees and owners

You can choose from multiple options and plans to use the Dashlane password manager, such as free, monthly plans, annual plans, and business plans.

7.5.2 LastPass

LastPass (Figure 7.12) password manager is one of the leading names in the password security field. It is trusted by more than 43,000 enterprise customers and over 16.5 million personal users. This is an easy-to-use tool that offers high level of security of data, privacy of personal information, and fully encrypted storage of the entire information.

The interface of this password manager is very intuitive to learn without referring to any procedural documents. It offers numerous features and capabilities; a few very important features are listed below:

- Available in both free and paid versions
- Multiple plans suitable for different segments of users
- Offers secure password vaults
- Multi-platform support such as Android, iOS, Mac, PC, and Windows
- Smooth password access on all types of devices
- Offers auto-fill and saving options
- Offers strong password generation capabilities

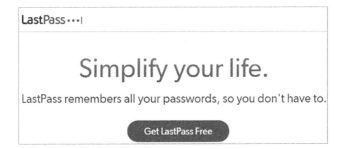

FIGURE 7.12   LastPass.

- Additional feature of authenticator
- Supports multi-factor authentication
- Allows to create secure notes
- Supports secure sharing
- Data file storage up to 1 GB
- Supports emergency access function
- Fully cloud-based service easy to register
- TRUSTe (a privacy compliance technology company) certified for privacy
- Supports many popular web browsers
- Supports Chrome OS and Linux
- Offers a few options for master password reset
- Easy and intuitive interface to manage and access your passwords
- Password strength alerts along with the strength scores
- Offers two-factor authentication
- Supports automatic password change
- Multiple plans available in both personal and enterprise categories
- Supports auto-fill feature
- Offers capability of generating strong passwords
- Supports username-generating features, too
- Supports zero-knowledge standard, which means company does not know about your information and passwords
- Auto-fill shopping form makes your shopping experience great
- Supports storing credit card information, personal information, payment wallets, and Wi-Fi information
- Offers great customer support

You can get multiple options and plans of using the LastPass password manager.

7.5.3 ZOHO Vault

ZOHO is one of the major providers of wide range of software-based cloud services that include customer resource management, sales, marketing, communication and collaboration, finance, and many others. ZOHO vault is one of those services for personal as well as for the enterprise users. It was initially started as a free service for all. At this time, ZOHO vault (Figure 7.13) is offered not only as a free service, but also in different paid plans, which are very affordable for all types of users.

ZOHO vault offers enterprise grade password management services through its password manager known as ZOHO vault. It offers great features and capabilities that make it one of the popular password managers in the marketplace.

The main features of ZOHO Vault password manager are listed below:

- Easy to access and manage your passwords
- Powered by the strongest AES-256 encryption standard
- Supports zero-knowledge architecture

FIGURE 7.13   ZOHO vault.

- Easy sharing within the group of users
- Supports auto-login feature for the saved websites
- Supports different roles and levels for your password
- Single logout feature for a centralized control
- Options to easily import and export the passwords
- Centralized password management for enterprises
- You can access your passwords from anywhere and anytime
- Supports mobiles and PCs equally
- Supports multiple web browsers commonly used in the marketplace
- Supports multiple operating systems including Windows, Linux, Android, Mac, iOS, Chrome OS, and others
- Available in multiple plans that fit for all types of users
- A lifetime free plan is available
- Easy to set up and use tool
- Supports two-factor authentication
- It is lightweight service through both cloud- and browser-based plugins
- Offers the features to save your personal information, social security, passport, credit card, and other information
- Supports auto form-filling capability
- Offers the features of creating different chambers to categorize different level of security of your information and passwords
- Supports sharing of password to external users through a link and secret key
- Supports the transmission of data in SSL connection

The integration of ZOHO vault with many other services offered makes it a better choice for the users of the ZOHO services. The low pricing plans are very attractive for normal users.

7.5.4 KeePass

KeyPass (Figures 7.14 and 7.15) is a lightweight password manager tool, which is open source and free to use for managing your multiple passwords in a secure, private, and reliable environment. It has been released under GNU license for free of cost. It is very useful in generating strong passwords for your different accounts and managing those passwords in highly secure environment.

It is a multi-platform and multi-device software tool that offers highly featured and reliable password security services to the personal as well as the business user. It is known for the rich features that it offers.

FIGURE 7.14   KeePass icon.

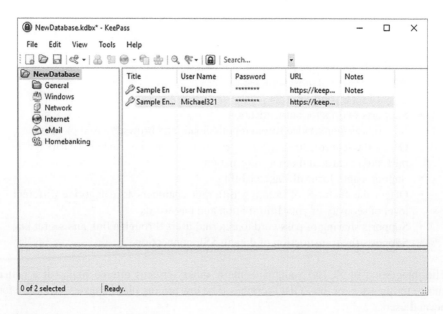

FIGURE 7.15   KeePass window.

The main features of this enterprise-grade password manager are listed below:

- Open-source software released under GNU license for free
- Supports multiple platforms such as Windows, Linux, Mac, iOS, and Android
- Supports both online and local storage of data
- Offers option to categorize the passwords in multiple folders
- Offers the feature to take password data in portable storages
- Supports password strength check and alerts
- Supports import and export data from other password managers
- Supports importing the data from the supported web browsers
- Offers data editing options to update the information
- Uses the high level of security standards such as AES-256 protocol and Twofish
- Offers password-generating capabilities to generate strong passwords
- Offers advanced features that make the database security even stronger
- Powerful keylogger protection
- Uses SHA-256 for hashing the master key components
- It is hard for the brute-force attacks to affect KeePass security
- Offers full control over the source code
- Very simple and intuitive interface
- Easy to use software
- Fully customizable software
- Stores data files locally
- Supports multiple files for import and export of data
- Supports global auto-type hot key features
- Offers drag-and-drop capability for data transfer
- Plugin-based architecture
- Available in more than 40 languages

This is not so fancy in terms of outlook and interface, but very simple, professional, and intuitive. It offers great level of security to your data and passwords.

There are certain downsides of this password manager tool. For example, this software does not support automated entries of usernames and passwords for any new website or any other online service. You need to add every entry manually; this may be a bit annoying for many users.

7.5.5 RoboForm

RoboForm (Figure 7.16) is a highly secure and reliable password manager software tool. It is available with multiple plans to match with your password security requirements. It offers services for both personal and enterprise users through different plans.

It is considered as one of the rich-featured password manager tools in the marketplace. It is able to store personal info, credit card information, passwords, contacts, identities, notes, and other critical information in different folders. It synchronizes all the bookmarks on your current browsers with the applications.

FIGURE 7.16   RoboForm.

A few very important features of RoboForm password manager are mentioned below:

- It is a highly secure and rich-featured software tool.
- It is a cross-platform software that runs efficiently on all major operating systems.
- It offers apps to run on mobile devices.
- Supports both cloud and local storage.
- Uses AES-256-bit encryption along with BPKDF2 SHA-256 protocol.
- Supports one-click capability to fill up the forms.
- Stores your personal and billing information for auto-fill feature.
- Secures sharing of login information through email.
- Offers password generator tool for creating strong passwords.
- Supports single-click option to save passwords in the database.
- Offers multiple plans for personal as well as business users.
- Free subscription is available for lifetime with limited features.
- One-click database synch option.
- Option to enter your passwords manually or automatically.
- Offers account data backup.
- Allows database access from anywhere at anytime.
- Offers powerful password and personal information management options.
- Very easy and fast to install.
- Extensions available for all major browsers.
- Supports importing and exporting of passwords to major password managers.
- Offers two-factor authentication.
- Allows emergency access capability.
- Supports both web and window app passwords.
- Offers the feature of safe notes for secure storage of your personal notes.
- Highly user-friendly interface.
- Zero-knowledge-based business architecture.
- Offers good customer support.

If we look at the main features and capabilities of RoboForm, we will be able to decide that it is one of the best password manager tools in the marketplace.

SAMPLE QUESTIONS AND ANSWERS FOR WHAT WE HAVE LEARNED IN CHAPTER 7

Q1. What is the main objective of a password?

A1: The basic objective of using a password is to authenticate your authority to access certain resources. The technique of code word to verify a certain authenticity of person, event, or any other activity was used between two communicators in the old ages. The concept of password can be divided into two major eras: the traditional era and the digital era.

Q2. Name different forms of modern-day passwords.

A2: There are different types and forms of passwords used in the modern world. The following are a few among them.

- Conventional password
- Biometric passwords
- Two-factor authentication
- Multi-factor authentication
- Social media logins
- Email logins
- One-time password (OTP)
- Smart keys and physical tokens

Q3. What are the major threats to passwords theft?

A3: The major threats to the password theft include the following:

- Eavesdropping
- Guessing of password
- Cracking passwords through computing software
- Offline cracking of hashes
- Password recovery or reset cyberattack techniques
- Same password used on multiple accounts
- Using default passwords of the system
- Malicious software on your computer such as sniffers and keyloggers
- Backdoor exploit
- Malicious plugins
- Phishing

Q4. What is over-the-shoulder technique of hacking password?

A4: This is a traditional way to steal any critical information like password. The bad guys try to steal your password when you enter it into the system or online service. This technique is also useful when you write your password on some diary or paper. The hackers try to peep over to see your passwords in different forms in this method.

Q5. What are the qualities and features of a strong password?

A5: The qualities and features of a strong password include the following:

- Non-guessable
- Longer length
- Complex pattern of characters
- Complex combination of characters
- Based on the out-of-the-box ideas
- Not influenced with the personal behaviors and information
- Better password management

SOURCES

https://www.montclair.edu/media/montclairedu/oit/policies/password-management-policy-1.2.pdf

https://www.infosec.gov.hk/english/technical/files/password.pdf

https://www.symantec.com/content/dam/symantec/docs/about/2017-ncsir-global-results-en.pdf

https://www.cso.com.au/mediareleases/29642/hacked-passwords-cause-81-of-data-breaches/

https://www.verizondigitalmedia.com/blog/2017/07/2017-verizon-data-breach-investigations-report/

https://searchsecurity.techtarget.com/definition/password

http://theconversation.com/the-long-history-and-short-future-of-the-password-76690

https://www.eurodns.com/blog/password-management-data-security

https://www.watchguard.com/wgrd-resource-center/security-report-q3-2018

https://www.connectsafely.org/tips-to-create-and-manage-strong-passwords/

https://insights.samsung.com/2017/04/13/six-password-management-tips-for-work-and-life/

https://www.wired.com/story/7-steps-to-password-perfection/

http://info.shapesecurity.com/rs/935-ZAM-778/images/Shape-2017-Credential-Spill-Report.pdf

https://www.identityforce.com/blog/identity-theft-odds-identity-theft-statistics

https://usa.kaspersky.com/resource-center/definitions/biometrics

https://searchsecurity.techtarget.com/definition/two-factor-authentication

https://www.fidelity.com/security/how-two-factor-authentication-works

https://whatis.techtarget.com/definition/RSA-Security

https://en.wikipedia.org/wiki/Multi-factor_authentication

https://searchsecurity.techtarget.com/feature/The-fundamentals-of-MFA-Multifactor-authentication-in-the-enterprise

https://www.researchgate.net/publication/268585556_Generation_of_Secure_One-Time_Password_Based_on_Image_Authentication

https://www.researchgate.net/publication/264155414_A_REVIEW_OF_ONE_TIME_PASSWORD_MOBILE_VERIFICATION

https://en.wikipedia.org/wiki/One-time_password

https://www.howtogeek.com/141500/why-you-should-use-a-password-manager-and-how-to-get-started/

https://www.webopedia.com/TERM/P/password-manager.html

https://lifehacker.com/the-five-best-password-managers-5529133

https://www.cnet.com/news/the-best-password-managers-directory/

https://www.pcmag.com/article2/0,2817,2407168,00.asp

https://www.techradar.com/news/software/applications/the-best-password-manager-1325845

https://www.pcworld.com/article/2043301/review-dashlane-is-a-robust-password-manager-
    with-a-gorgeous-interface.html
https://www.tomsguide.com/us/dashlane,review-3767.html
https://www.dashlane.com/
https://me.pcmag.com/lastpass
https://www.tomsguide.com/us/lastpass,review-3775.html
https://www.lastpass.com/
https://www.tomsguide.com/us/zoho-vault,review-4979.html
https://www.cloudwards.net/zoho-vault-review/
https://www.zoho.com/vault/online-password-manager-features.html
https://keepass.info/features.html
https://www.ghacks.net/2018/05/28/keepass-password-safe-review/
https://www.tomsguide.com/us/keepass,review-3768.html
https://www.cloudwards.net/roboform-review/
https://www.roboform.com/

Prevention from Cyberattacks

8

8.1 INTRODUCTION

Cyberattacks cost billions of dollars to the businesses, government organizations, defense institutes, and many other sectors that directly impact on our day-to-day lives. The cyberattacks are becoming more and more sophisticated and advanced in technology and ideology. New techniques and patterns are being utilized to launch these attacks on the networks, data, and services to disrupt the genuine processes and systems all around the globe.

The prevention from cyberattacks needs superior thought process than that of the cybercriminals (to counter them), but often, we see that the cybercriminals win in the thought race. Indeed, the cybercriminals are often found to be more creative and diverse in their thoughts. But the main components that they use for launching the cyberattacks include the exploitations of the weaknesses in your computers, web pages, networks, databases, and lack of awareness about the security threats among the users of the Internet and computer technologies.

Cybersecurity to prevent or reduce the impact of cyberattacks (conceptual image in Figure 8.1) is the name of continuous practice of security measures and standards.

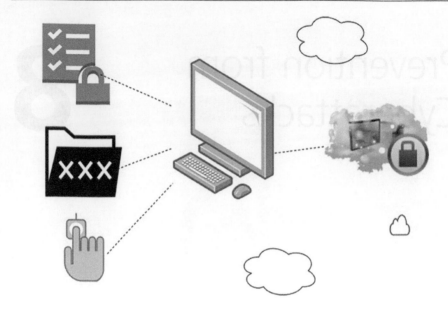

FIGURE 8.1   Preventing cyberattacks (conceptual image).

So, the fundamental component to prevent your IT system from cyberattacks is the *security awareness* of the users of the IT systems. The awareness of the cybersecurity will include the following important factors:

- Continuously educate the people about cybersecurity.
- Make the users realize the importance of password security.
- Train about keeping the software updated.
- Provide guidelines on how to deal with unknown emails.
- Train for the potential social engineering ways that exploit the innocence of people.
- Implement proper system logout and monitoring mechanism.

The awareness and implementation of the standard guidelines in the people creates a strong shield against the cyberattacks. According to the Small Biz Trends research, more than 52% of the cyberattacks on small businesses take place due to the human errors, system failures, and other factors, while 48% of the attacks are done deliberately for fulfilling the malicious intentions.

From these figures, it is very clear that small businesses are normally short of money to purchase and train the staff for cybersecurity. That is why some of the serious attacks take place on the small businesses on a regular basis. According to the report, more than 43% of the global cyberattacks are focused on the small businesses because the success rate of cyberattacks on small businesses is comparatively high. An interesting issue that some security experts jokingly mention sometimes is that a system may be made somewhat "full-proof", i.e., involving no risk or harm, or never-failing, but it is extremely difficult to make any system "foolproof", i.e., the system would still work even if a fool were operating it. This is because lack of awareness of the situation, or proper working method, or lack of knowledge about security or system-related issues may cause any system to go wrong. Correct knowledge of the users about the system is indeed the first line of prevention.

The cyberattack prevention measures can be classified into two major categories:

- Cyberattack preventive measures
- Cyberattack corrective measures

The cyberattack preventive measures include the following major activities:

- Stick to the company security guidelines.
- Never underestimate the hackers.
- Keep all software and tools updated.
- Always back up your data.
- Keep your backup data encrypted and protected.
- Follow the password management policies strictly.
- Follow email use policy strictly.
- Use intrusion detection and intrusion prevention systems (IDS/IPS).
- Implement antivirus software and firewalls.

On the other hand, the corrective measures are normally taken when some cyberattacks have broken into the system and there is an urgent need for immediate and befitting response to reduce the negative impact of the cyberattacks.

- Block the suspected IDs and Internet Protocols (IPs) but often blocking is not the solution because legitimate nodes can be behind those IDs or IPs.
- Isolate the affected or targeted system from the other network.
- Rerouting of the traffic should be done.
- Block the malicious and suspected traffic.
- Implement the disaster recovery mechanism.
- Assess the depth of the attack and consequent damages.
- Inform the concerned security and law enforcement agencies.
- Use the backed up data to restore the services.

As we all know, the prevention of cyberattack is a complex matter owing to many reasons and causes of cyberattacks coming from unknown users, terrain, and time zones. Hence, the cyberattack prevention is a multipronged field.

If we constitute steps of activities after the cyberattack has hit and also has been detected, see the list below:

- **Survey**: Survey the attack to know about vulnerability, damage, and attackers.
- **Limit**: Limit the attack by blocking, diverting, and isolating the system and traffic.
- **Record**: Record the impact by recording effects, levels, and disruptions.
- **Engage**: Engage with concerned agencies and authorities.

- **Notify**: Notify the affected users and seek legal counseling.
- **Learn**: Learn a lesson from the attack and prepare for better preventive steps.

Now, let us discuss the main techniques, systems, and guidelines used for the prevention of cyberattacks today.

8.2 ALGORITHMS AND TECHNIQUES

This is very important to know that our online as well as offline digital resources are not at all 100% safe, though many great security methods, policies, techniques, and modern algorithms (Figure 8.2 shows a conceptual image) have designed and implemented in the cybersecurity field. The cyberattack prevention is a wide field, which encompasses the detection of the problems, predictions of the threats, and prevention of the same. Some of the security experts add the response to the threats also as the fourth component of the cyberattack prevention methodology.

Let us divide the cyberattack prevention with its major components and then dig into the techniques used in those components to achieve the desired goals. The approach of prevention of cyberattacks falls in the three major activities as listed below:

- Detection of cyberattacks
- Prediction of cyberattacks
- Prevention of cyberattacks

Prevention and prediction can be considered together. Every approach takes different algorithms for the prevention of the cyberattacks. Figure 8.3 depicts the different approaches and their algorithms.

Two approaches mentioned in the diagram shown in Figure 8.3 – cyberattack detection and predictions – commonly use similar types of algorithms. Those

FIGURE 8.2   Algorithms and techniques (conceptual image).

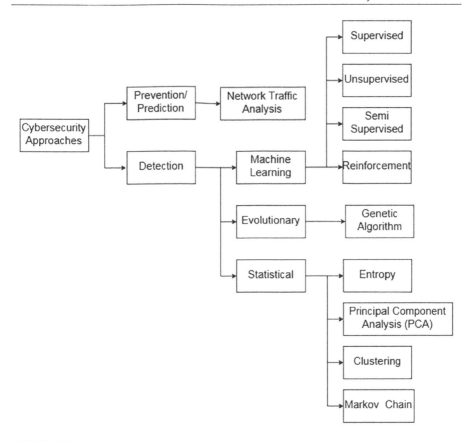

FIGURE 8.3 Cyberattack detection and prevention approaches.

algorithms include the evolutionary, statistical, and machine learning, while the cyber-attack prevention approach uses the network traffic analysis algorithms to achieve the desired objectives.

8.2.1 Cyberattack Detection

Cyberattack (Figure 8.4) detection approach is very fundamental in ensuring the security of the IT resources including the computers, servers, networks, and databases. The cyberattack detection approach builds foundation of the cybersecurity. Other actions related to the prevention of the cyberattacks are taken on the basis of the findings of the detection approach.

The cyberattack detection uses three major types of algorithms as mentioned below:

- Machine learning algorithms
- Evolutionary algorithms
- Statistical algorithms

FIGURE 8.4   Cyberattacks (conceptual image).

Machine learning is one of the most important domains in the field of information technology. Many software and gadgets have been developed that work on the basis of machine learning principles. Those software tools help in learning the traffic patterns, plain language learning, code detection, behavior detection, body gesture detection, biometrics, facial recognition, and many other processes.

All these algorithms are now applied in the detection of the cyberattacks launched on any network, databases, or other digital properties. As we know, machine learning is further divided into different categories and types, such as supervised, semi-supervised, unsupervised, and reinforcement machine learning types.

All those types of machine learning are implemented in the processes of cyberattack detection as the algorithms that help detect the malicious or suspicious activities on the IT systems. The automated and unsupervised algorithms are extensively used in the modern techniques for detecting and predicting the suspicious movements in the cyber networks.

The example of such algorithms to detect the cyberattacks is known as intrusion detection systems or commonly referred to as IDS. This process uses further algorithms to profile the network's usage patterns and compares any suspicious activity if it is not as per preset traffic profiles. The details of the other algorithms used in IDS will be discussed in the IDS topic later.

The evolutionary algorithms of cyberattack detections are based on the genetic approach. In the genetic algorithm, precisely referred to as (GA), the metaheuristics are defined with the help of natural selection process. To clarify here, *metaheuristic* is a higher-level procedure or heuristic designed to find, generate, or select a heuristic (partial search algorithm) that may provide a sufficiently good solution to an optimization problem. The genetic approach is able to identify various forms of cyberattacks based on the evolutionary theory. This algorithm is mostly used in optimizing both the constrained and unconstrained problems, which are based on the natural selection.

A generic flowchart of evolutionary algorithm is shown in Figure 8.5.

Another important approach for the detection of the cyberattack is known as statistical approach. This approach uses different algorithms for detecting the

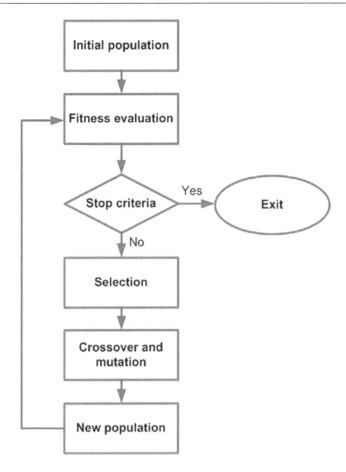

FIGURE 8.5   A generic flowchart of evolutionary algorithm.

cyberattacks or malicious activity on the network and on the cyber infrastructures. In this approach, different algorithms, namely, principal component analysis (PCA), entropy analysis (EA), and Markovian models are extensively used. These algorithms can also be used with the evolutionary algorithms to improve the efficiency and accuracy of the combined algorithms.

In the modern cyberattack detection systems – for example IDS – hybrid algorithms and combination of multiple algorithms are used for the purpose of generating high level of accuracy in the results.

8.2.2 Cyberattack Prediction

The main objective of the cyberattack prediction (Figure 8.6) approach is to improve the security system and enhance the security preemptive power of the cyber systems. This approach is based on different approaches as used in the cyberattack detection system. Both the cyberattack detection and prevention work almost on the same algorithms.

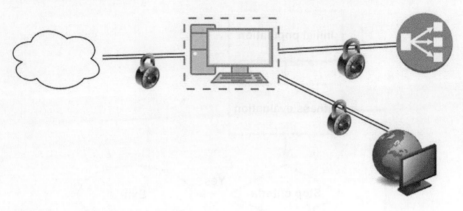

FIGURE 8.6   Cyberattack prediction (concept).

The major algorithms used in the security prediction system include the following:

- Machine learning-based algorithms
- Genetic algorithms
- Data analysis statistics algorithms

The main difference between cyberattack detection and prediction is that detection normally takes place once the attack has already been launched. But the prediction of the cyberattack approach uses and analyzes the vulnerabilities and possible loopholes in the security system from where the attacks can be launched. The analysis of the cyber threat environment is also done to predict the possibilities of cyberattacks on the available vulnerabilities in the cyber environments.

In cyberattack prediction approach, different algorithms are used in a combination to construct a cyberattack tree. This attack tree is constructed based on the critical episodes that overran the episode window. This model of cyberattack prediction generates very efficient results. On an average, the accuracy of this model was measured as about 95%.

Normally, the attack tree simulates the decision-making process that a cyberattacker will like to take in the certain given conditions. That cyberattack tree is very easy to understand for the security professional because it uses many easy-to-understand steps in the modeling of the attack tree.

A large number of new cyberattack prediction models and even tools have emerged in the market that can be used for this purpose of detecting the probability of the cyberattacks on your digital environment.

8.2.3 Cyberattack Prevention

The prevention of cyberattacks (thematic image in Figure 8.7) is the most critical aspect of the cybersecurity, which includes the detection, prediction, and disaster recovery activities. But the most important of all is the cyberattack prevention. This is a proactive process in which the security system and the concerned security professional preempt the possibility of cyberattacks.

FIGURE 8.7 Cyberattack prevention.

In the modern cybersecurity field, many cyberattack prevention systems have already been introduced. The IPS is one of the most important tools to name among such cyberattack prevention mechanisms.

Other than the software systems installed to prevent any cyberattack before it can inflict substantial damage, the security professionals and the entrepreneurs should also take their proactive responsibilities and implement the standard cyberattack prevention measures effectively. Among such preemptive measures, the important ones are listed below:

- Follow security guidelines strictly.
- Update all software applications and tools.
- Keep a close eye on the internal and external threats.
- Always backup the critical data and store safely.
- Make an emergency plan to cope with any disastrous situation.

The most important algorithm used in the cyberattack prevention approach is the sniffing and analysis of the incoming traffic from different sources. The close monitoring of the traffic patterns, traffic type, and other characteristics of the traffic will help you detect the intention of the traffic. Once the traffic nature is known, the system can take the predefined actions to prevent the attackers to succeed in their malicious activities.

In this approach of cyberattack prevention, the suspected traffic once found is either blocked or redirected to the other dummy servers. The traffic analysis is a very powerful component for the security professionals as well as for the operations team to monitor the quality, condition, and performance of the communication.

Many software programs are used for sniffing the traffic packets to know about the details of the traffic. These packets are analyzed for the origination, destination, and content of the traffic. Other than these three major components, the sniffers also investigate different attributes of the packets such as port numbers, payload size, and other factors. If any traffic is coming from a suspicious destination or terminating at unauthorized point in the network, the traffic is either diverted or stopped.

This type of security measure is mostly taken through IPSs and other sniffer software tools, which monitor the traffic and analyze it as per preconfigured criteria and actions. This approach is widely used in the modern cyberattack prevention mechanisms.

8.3 FIREWALLS

We talked about the basics of firewalls in Chapter 1, and the firewall settings were discussed in Chapter 6. In this section, some practical tips will be mentioned for activating a firewall. Also, some related issues will be discussed that are imperative for a network security professional or enthusiast to know. As we know, firewall (Figure 8.8) is the most important and first layer of defense for any online network. It has been used extensively in the cybersecurity field for over 25 years now. A firewall basically acts as the filter for the traffic, both incoming and outgoing.

A firewall checks and monitors the traffic continuously before the traffic enters into the network. It monitors and analyzes the incoming traffic to avoid any attack originating from the external untrusted sources. Similarly, it monitors the patterns and parameters of the traffic originating from the internal networks and going out to certain networks.

FIGURE 8.8 Firewalls (thematic image).

Firewalls can either be a software program installed on the servers, computers, or routers to safeguard any computer, server, or even the entire system, or be a dedicated hardware device loaded with the dedicated firewall software on it. In our daily use, for PCs and mobile devices, we use the software firewalls installed on those devices to protect us from external deliberate attacks by the hackers.

Big networks, such as enterprise networks, corporate networks, service providers, data centers, and government departments normally use the dedicated firewall devices with specialized firewall programs running on those devices. The terminating traffic enters the network through firewall.

The firewall checks the traffic as per its configurations that were set earlier. If the firewall finds any kinds of problem or threat in the incoming traffic, it will not allow entering the network by either redirecting or blocking the traffic.

Normally, there are many advanced settings and features in the firewalls, which can be activated, customized, and configured so that the high level of network security can be achieved. But using all features and capabilities creates communication delays and performance issues due to heavy use of resources for detailed analysis of the traffic.

Therefore, the main and very important features are configured so that the performance of the communication services can be maintained.

Let us have a look at how to activate and configure software firewalls on different computers.

8.3.1 Activating Windows Firewall

All the latest Windows operating systems come with integrated software of firewalls. You can easily turn on the Windows firewall software and configure as per your requirements. The newer versions such as Windows 10, Windows 8, and Windows 7 have two types of firewalls installed on the systems. So you need to enable both of them as per your required security level.

8.3.1.1 Windows 10 firewall

Windows 10 comes with two types of firewalls. They are listed below:

- Windows Firewall
- Windows Defender Firewall

It is highly recommended to configure both of the firewalls so that your computer and any network lying behind your computer remains safe from any malicious attack originated from the untrusted resources. Windows Firewall should be enabled by default to protect your computer on Windows 10, and you should also configure the Windows Defender Firewall by taking the following steps:

- Click the **Start ⊞** button.
- Choose the **Settings ⚙** option.

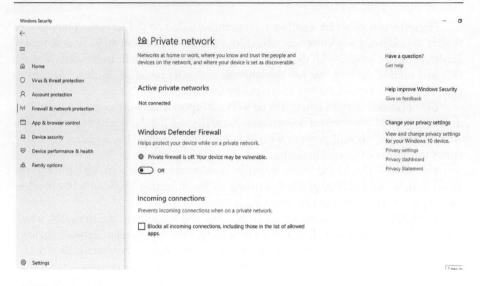

FIGURE 8.9   Windows security page.

- Choose **Update and Security** option.
- Select **Windows Security.** Windows security page appears (Figure 8.9).
- Finally choose **Firewall & Network Protection** option.
- Turn the button to **On** position.

You can configure other parameters by just clicking the links shown in the above figure and then set the required parameters of the traffic or internal device.

8.3.1.2 Windows 7 firewall

Like Windows 10, there are two firewall software embedded in the Windows 7 operating system. It is highly recommended to enable and use both of the firewalls listed below:

- Windows 7 Firewall
- Windows Defender

Let us know how to work with both the firewalls on Windows 7 operating system.

8.3.1.3 Enabling Windows 7 firewall

In Windows 7 operating system, Windows Firewall is enabled by default for both the private and public networks. The private networks include both the home and work networks. We can configure Windows 7 Firewall for exceptional traffic source and other features and capabilities.

To open the Windows 7 Firewall, take the following steps:

- Click the **Start** ⊞ button.

FIGURE 8.10   Windows Firewall settings.

- Choose the **Control Panel** option. All windows configuration options appear.
- Click the **Windows Firewall** link. Windows Firewall settings page appears (Figure 8.10).
- Click the "Allow a program or feature through Windows Firewall" (Figures 8.11 and 8.12) link to add the ports and services through Windows Firewall. You can also unselect the programs and features to set their direct access to the internal network and resources.
- Click the "Change Notification Settings" link to modify the firewall settings for both the private and public networks as shown in Figure 8.13.
- If you have any other program, which is not listed on the above list, but you want to add on the exception list, then click the "Allow another program…" button.
- New pop-up window appears with the list of the other programs installed on your computer
- Choose the desired program that you want to add to the exception list.
- Click the "Browse…" to locate the desired program that does not appear in the list of the programs.
- Locate the desired program and include in the list.
- Finally click the "Add" button. The desired program will show up in the exception list of the Windows 7 Firewall.
- Select that desired program and change the configuration settings by clicking on the "Change Settings" button located at the top of the window.
- For configuring the firewall advanced settings, click the "Advanced Settings" link in the left panel. The advanced settings window appears as shown in Figure 8.14.
- On the advanced settings page, you can configure advance rules such as inbound traffic rules, outbound traffic rules, connection security rules, and monitoring capabilities.

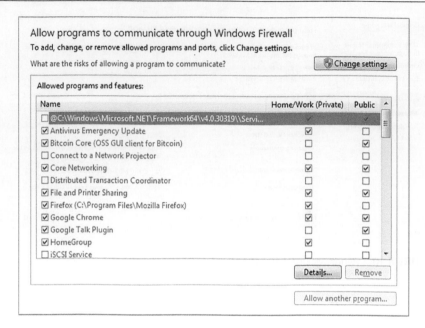

FIGURE 8.11   Allow a program window.

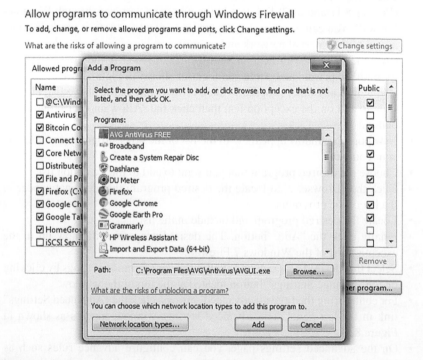

FIGURE 8.12   Pop-up window for allowing programs to communicate through Windows Firewall.

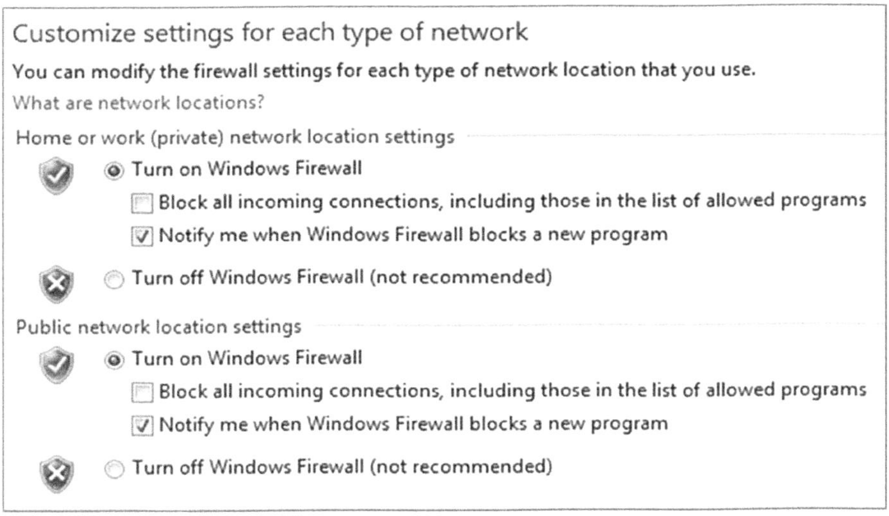

Customize settings for each type of network

You can modify the firewall settings for each type of network location that you use.

What are network locations?

Home or work (private) network location settings

◉ Turn on Windows Firewall

☐ Block all incoming connections, including those in the list of allowed programs

☑ Notify me when Windows Firewall blocks a new program

○ Turn off Windows Firewall (not recommended)

Public network location settings

◉ Turn on Windows Firewall

☐ Block all incoming connections, including those in the list of allowed programs

☑ Notify me when Windows Firewall blocks a new program

○ Turn off Windows Firewall (not recommended)

FIGURE 8.13   Notification option.

FIGURE 8.14   Advanced settings.

- You can add different inbound and outbound profiles to make your network security more advanced and professional.
- If you have already a defined security policy in a text form, you can import that security policy by clicking "import policy" link and following the instructions.
- Click the "export policy" to export the security policy enabled on your computer for backup or using on the other computer.

8.3.1.4 Enabling Windows firewall service

In windows operating system, Windows Firewall is embedded in the system as a service. You can enable it as an automatic or manual service. You can also disable it directly in the windows services panel.

Take the following steps to enable the Windows Firewall service:

- Click the **Start** ▦ button
- Search for services in the search bar, and click the **Services** link (Figure 8.15).
- Locate the **Windows Firewall** service (Figure 8.16) from the list.
- Right click on the firewall service and choose the desired option that includes start, stop, properties, and other options.

FIGURE 8.15 Searching "Services".

FIGURE 8.16 Windows Firewall.

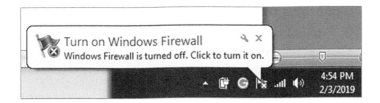

FIGURE 8.17   Windows Firewall turned off warning.

Note: If you turn off the Windows Firewall, the computer will warn you that the firewall is turned off (Figure 8.17) and your computer might be at risk.

You can also turn on the firewall by directly clicking on the pop-up message and choosing the "firewall turn-on" option.

8.3.2 Traffic Issues

8.3.2.1 What are traffic rules?

Traffic rules define the criteria for the traffic – both inbound and outbound – to pass through the firewall. In the traffic rules, different parameters are used to define the authorization of the traffic either to pass through or to stop at the security firewall. The traffic rules are classified into two types:

- Inbound traffic rules
- Outbound traffic rules

The inbound traffic rules apply to the traffic coming from the other networks or hosts to the computer on which the firewall is configured. The outbound traffic rule applies to the traffic that originates from the device on which the firewall is installed. The rules are defined based on the port numbers, users, programs, services, and protocols.

Then the rule is applied to different user profiles, network adopters, and service profiles. Multiple rules for inbound and outbound traffic can be created. The created rules can easily be modified and removed if needed. You can enable and disable the rules used by the Windows Firewall. Any rule that is green in the list is active or enabled, while any rule that is gray is disabled. You can change the status of the rules whenever you like to do so.

To know about the rules, you need to right click the rule >> click the **Properties** option. The details of the rules appear as shown below

- Click **Protocol and Ports** tab to know about the port and protocol details.
- Similarly, for services and program traffic profile, click **Program and Services** tab.

8.3.2.2 *Creating a new inbound rule*

You can create four different types of inbound security rules on your firewall by using the advanced settings (Figure 8.18). These four types of rules are listed below:

- Program connection rule
- Port connection rule
- Predefined connection rule for windows experience
- Custom connection rules

As an example, let us create one inbound connection rule. For creating an inbound rule, take the following steps:

- Open Control Panel on your computer.
- Click the **Windows Firewall** link on the control panel list.
- Click the **Advanced Settings** link in the left panel of the firewall window. The Windows Firewall with Advanced Security window appears, as shown in Figure 8.19.
- Click the **Inbound Rules** link in the left pane of the window.
- Click the New Rule link on the right pane of the window, the **New Inbound Rule Wizard** will appear (Figure 8.20).
- Select the type of inbound rule by choosing the desired radio button – program, port, predefined, or custom.
- As an example, click the **Program** radio button to create a rule for the connection that controls a particular program and click the **Next** button.
- Choose the path of the desired connection or select all program option, and click the **Next** button.

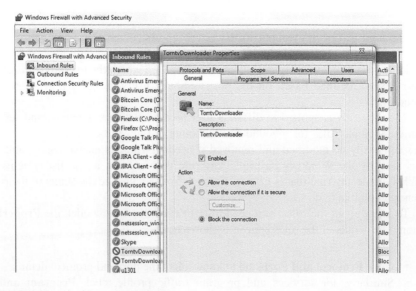

FIGURE 8.18 Blocking connection.

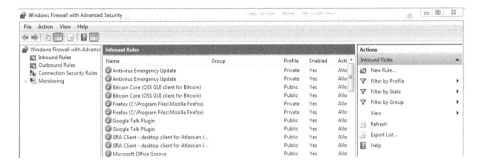

FIGURE 8.19   Advanced security settings window.

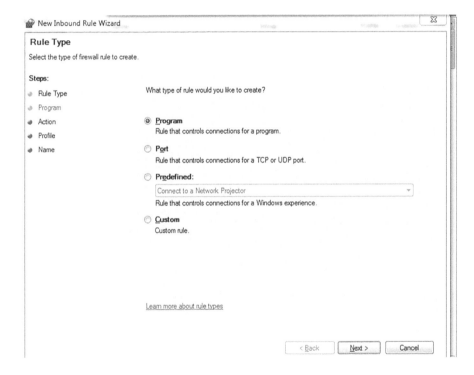

FIGURE 8.20   New Inbound Rule Wizard window.

- Choose any one of the desired options for the connection to take actions. The options to choose through radio buttons include **Allow the connection**, **Allow the connection if it is secure**, and **Block the connection**. Choose **Block the connection** option in our example.
- Click the **Next** button.
- Choose the desired profile from the available list of three profiles – **Domain**, **Private**, and **Public**. In our case, we choose the **Public** option and click the **Next** button.

- Add the suitable name for this rule along with the description in the respective fields as shown in Figure 8.21. In our case, it is "Inbound 1" rule name.
- Click the **Finish** button. The inbound rule has been created, and it appears in the right pane of the Advanced Security window as shown in Figure 8.22.

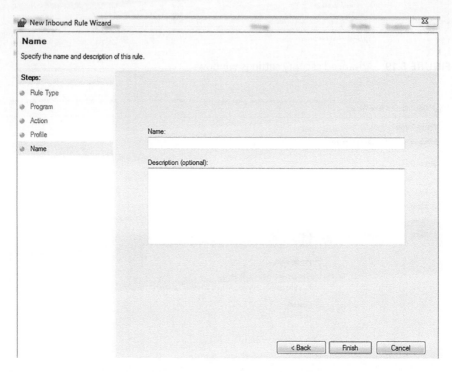

FIGURE 8.21   Adding name for rule.

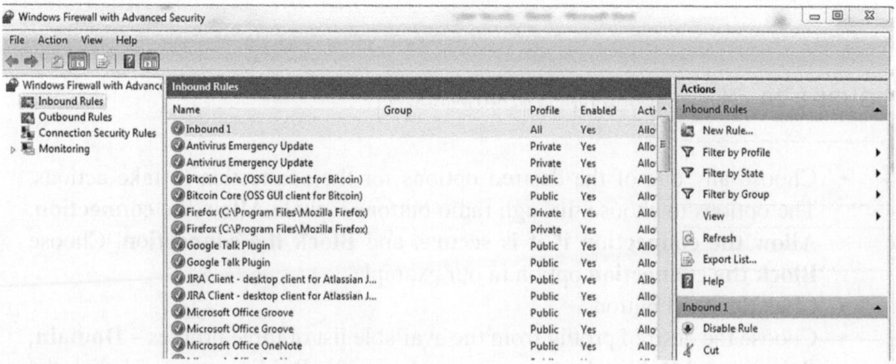

FIGURE 8.22   After finishing the procedure of setting rules.

Similarly, you can create other types of rules by using the same steps and varying the parameters as per your own security requirements on your firewall.

8.3.2.3 Creating outbound rule

Like inbound rules, you can also create four types of outbound rules to control the connections of the traffic. To create the outbound rule, take the following steps:

- Click the **Outbound Rules** in the left pane of the Advanced Security window.
- Click the New Rule… link in the right pane. The **New Outbound Rule Wizard** appears.
- Choose the desired type of rule and click the **Next** button.
- Choose the program path and click the **Next** button.
- Choose the desired action to take through this rule and click the **Next** button.
- Select the desired profile of the outbound rule and click the **Next** button.
- Choose the desired name and description of the outbound rule and click the **Finish** button.
- The desired outbound rule has been created successfully, and it appears in the right pane of the window.

8.3.2.4 Creating connection security rule

Unlike the inbound and outbound security rules, which apply only to the computer itself for the traffic security, the connection security rule applies to the whole connection connecting two computers on a computer network. The connection rule defines the security of the communication between the two computers, such as how the data will travel, what encryption, and other security measures will be taken.

For using the benefits of this feature of the Windows Firewall, you need to define the same connection rules on the two computers that communicate with each other. If one computer has this rule, while the other computer in communication does not have this rule, you cannot benefit from this feature of firewall's advanced security.

Let us have a look at how to create a connection security rule on a network.

- On the **Windows Firewall with Advanced Security** window, click the **Connection Security Rules** link (Figure 8.23) on the left page of the window.

FIGURE 8.23   Connection security rules.

- Click the **New Rule...** link in the right pane of the window as shown above. The **New Connection Security Rule Wizard** appears as shown in Figure 8.24.
- Choose the desired type of rule. There are five types of rules on the options' list (Figure 8.24).
- In our case, choose the **Server-to-Server** type and click the **Next** button.
- Add single or multiple IPs used on the both end points of the connection as shown in Figure 8.25 and click the **Next** button.
- Choose any desired option on the requirement window and click the **Next** button. In our case, we choose **require authentication for inbound and outbound connections** option.
- Select the authentication method. You have two options – computer certificate and advanced. Choose **computer certificate** in our example (Figure 8.26).
- Click the **Browse...** button to locate and select the desired computer certificate as shown in the following figure.
- Click the **Next** button.
- Select the desired profile of the connection security rule from the available three categories – public, private, and domain. Click the **Next** button.
- Finally, enter the name of the connection security rule and its descriptions.

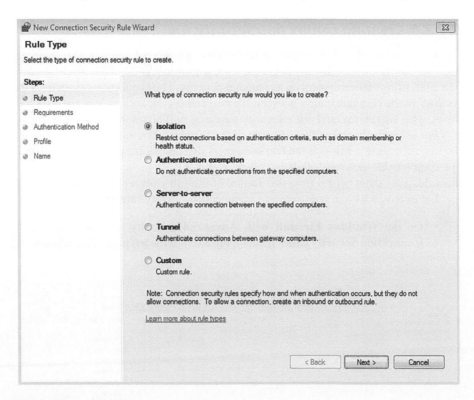

FIGURE 8.24   Rule type.

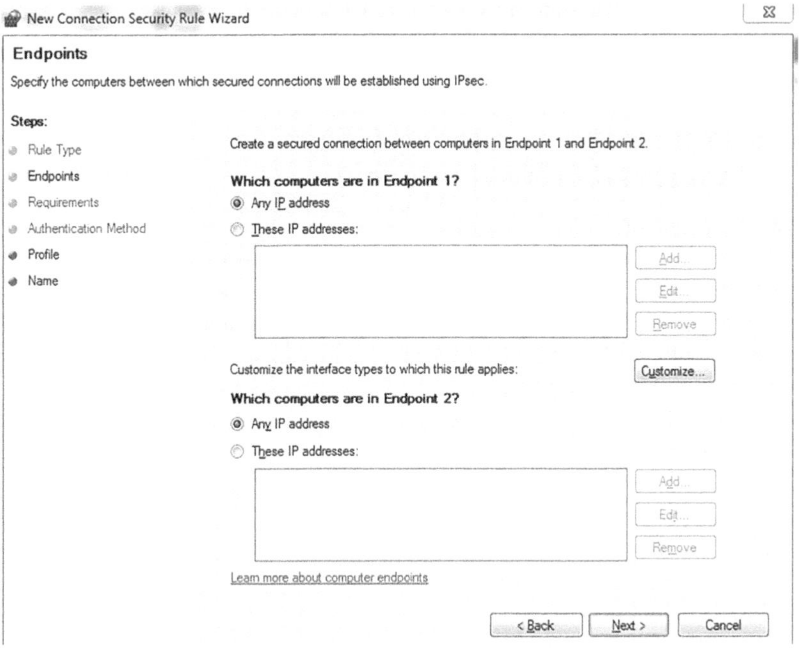

FIGURE 8.25   New Connection Security Rule Wizard. IP address adding.

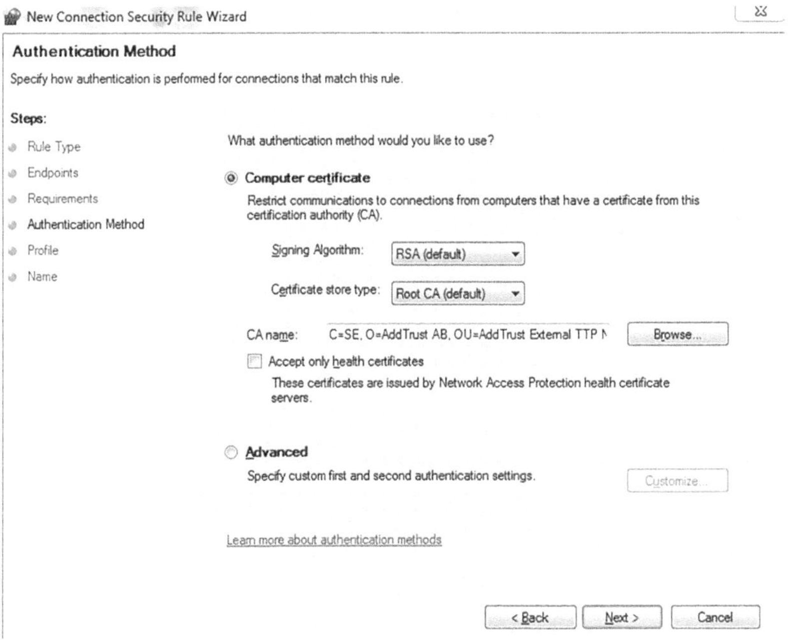

FIGURE 8.26   Choosing computer certificate.

- Click the **Finish** button. The desired connection security rule has been created successfully, and it appears in the right pane of the advanced firewall settings window.

8.3.2.5 What is the monitoring feature on advanced firewall settings?

Windows Firewall offers the capabilities of monitoring of the security rules on any particular profile. You can see security monitoring on different active connections, rules, and other security associations active on your computer.

Monitoring displays only active inbound, outbound, and firewall rules. So, you cannot see any other rules and security features enabled on any other network profile, if that is not active at the time of viewing the monitoring status of the firewall.

The pictorial view of the monitoring features on an active network connection is shown in Figure 8.27.

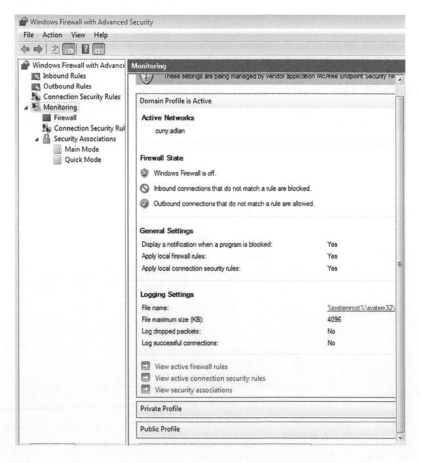

FIGURE 8.27   Monitoring features on an active network connection.

You can also view the status of all active connections, and you can also monitor the general settings, firewall state, and logging settings through this feature. The active firewall and connection rules can also be monitored from this window.

8.4 INTRUSION DETECTION/ PREVENTION SYSTEMS

IDS and IPS are the most effective ways of the modern security systems on the networks as well as on computer host. Let us dive a bit deeper in both of these systems separately.

8.4.1 Intrusion Detection System (IDS)

IDS is a combined system of devices or sensors and the software application. Intrusion detection system device is also known as IDS sensor.

An IDS system monitors the malicious activities and events on the network as well as on the host operating system and its major registry files. It works on the basis of certain algorithms defined for detecting the malicious activities.

Machine learning is used as one of the most important parts of this entire system for detecting the malicious activities. And, many other algorithms and approaches are also used in determining the malicious activities. There are three major IDS systems:

- Network intrusion detection system, NIDS
- Host intrusion detection system, HIDS
- Application-based detection system

The network-based IDS monitors and analyzes the traffic patterns and other parameters on the network traffic. If any anomaly in the traffic is found, it immediately alerts the network administrator or the security information and event management system (SIEM) for the corrective measures to safeguard the data and take the effective measures to avert any cyberattack. SIEM is a centralized security management system equipped with the security policy, alarm management, and many features related to network and system security.

The position of the IDS for the internal as well as external traffic is shown in Figure 8.28.

The host-based IDS system monitors and analyzes the files and events on the operating system for detecting any malicious activity. Two major detection methods are commonly used in the IDS systems; they are as follows:

- Anomaly-based detection
- Signature-based detection

It is very important to note that IDS is also capable of identifying and detecting the hacking attacks from within the system along with the external intrusion detection.

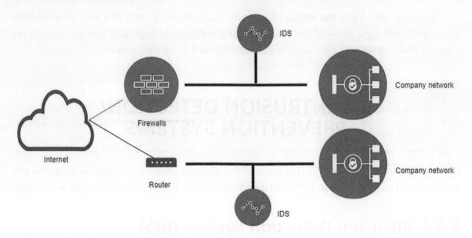

FIGURE 8.28   Intrusion detection system, IDS.

Host-based IDS takes images of the file frequently and compares them with the previous one. If any anomaly is found, it alerts the network administration or centralized security system for the subsequent actions.

The network-based IDS systems monitor and analyze the data packets passing through the network. You can install the data sensor at any point in the network – internal or external network sides. Application-based IDS is precisely referred to as AppIDS. This is developed for a particular application that may include content management system, database system, or accounting system.

The major functions of a good IDS include the following in the real-world sequential order:

- Data collection
- Feature selection
- Analysis of data
- Action

The security of networks and servers is becoming a big challenge not only for the security professionals but also for the enterprises and corporations. The newer security technologies are emerging, and the IPS is the advanced system for detecting and preventing the cyber threats on the network.

8.4.2 Intrusion Prevention System (IPS)

Firewall and intrusion detection are two major components of a security system in a network or on a host. But they have their own shortcomings that do not make them a perfect security tool. For instance, firewall is only able to block the traffic that uses the port numbers that are not configured for the authorized traffic in the system; that means, it is able to block any port that is not in use for the genuine traffic. But a security firewall is unable to stop the malicious traffic that is passing through the allowed port. If hackers exploit the vulnerabilities of the allowed ports, firewall can easily be deceived.

On the other hand, the IDS is capable enough to analyze and detect the malicious traffic passing through the allowed ports, but still not able to take any appropriate action against that breach. So, the security people needed an advanced system that could automatically take actions against the intrusion into the system. Hence, IPS was introduced that has advanced capabilities to detect, analyze, and prompt an appropriate action against any intrusion (Figure 8.29). Figure 8.30 shows the picture of a Cisco IPS 4240 Sensor.

The main advantages of the IPS system include the following:

- Offers a comprehensive network security.
- Offers robust protection against viruses or even any other traffic designed for attacking any network or web service.
- Offers details of the origination of the cyberattack.
- Automated response to the attacks and proper event recording.
- Provides instant alerts and preemptive actions.
- Stops access to email contacts

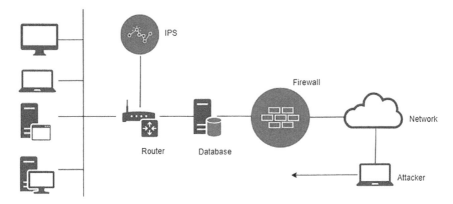

FIGURE 8.29   Intrusion prevention system (IPS) – advanced IDS.

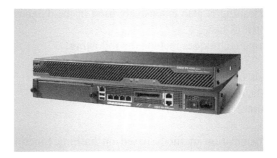

FIGURE 8.30   Cisco IPS 4240 sensor.

- Prevents reversal of the system directories.
- Protects all resources of the system and network.

Like IDS systems, there are two main types of IPS systems, which are given below:

- Host-based intrusion prevention system (HIPS)
- Network-based intrusion prevention system (NIPS)

The HIPSs are normally software-based IPS systems, but not all the time. Similarly, the NIPSs are normally appliance-based systems, but not every time. The main approaches and algorithms used by both the HIPSs and NIPSs are listed below.

- Protocol anomaly detection approach
- Detection of state-full signature approach
- Kernel-based approach
- Sandbox analysis approach
- Software-based heuristic approach
- Combined or hybrid approach

The latest IPSs mostly rely on multiple approaches used in an effective combination so that the threats can be detected, analyzed, and preempted more effectively and comprehensively.

8.5 AUTHENTICATION USING HASH

Hashing (Figure 8.31) is a type of computer process in which certain information in plain language is transformed into fixed-length short codes that are not understandable for a normal reader without any help of computer and processing through the hashing function. The hashing is used for the security and integrity of the messages transported over the Internet.

Authentication using hash is a type of authentication of the message to make sure that the data has not been altered and the sender is the person that the receiver wants to receive data from. Hashing is also extensively used in the databases for indexing and retrieving the data strings fast.

The major hashing techniques include the following:

- Cryptographic hash functions (CHFs)
- Message authentication code (MAC)
- Digital signature (DS)

Many kinds of authentication methods based on hashing functions are used for the integrity and security of the messages sent over the Internet. A few of them are listed below:

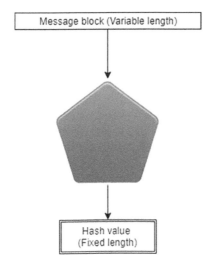

FIGURE 8.31   Schematic diagram of hashing process.

- Message Digest 2 (MD2)
- Message Digest 4 (MD4)
- Message Digest 5 (MD5)
- Secure Hash Algorithm (SHA)

In the abovementioned hashing methods, the MAC and DS use the private key for the authentication of the message at the receiving end. But the CHFs do not require private or secret key for the authentication of messages.

Cryptographic functions do not use the secret key over the Secure Sockets Layer (SSL) encrypted connection for the transportation of the information or messages. The most commonly used cryptographic functions on SSL presently are: MD5 and SHA.

8.5.1 Message Digest 5

MD5 is a hashing algorithm most extensively used in the SSL encryption protocol. It is a one-way hashing function that takes the message of any length as an input and returns a fixed length of encrypted code (i.e., which is fixed in length). This code is used for the authentication of the message to check its originality and integrity of the content.

The MD5 algorithm is governed by the Internet Engineering Task Force via RFC 1321. The fixed output generated by the MD5 encryption algorithm is 128-bit message digest. At present, for high-tech cybersecurity field, 128-bit encryption is not considered as the high level of security anymore. It is recommended to use at least 256-bit or higher level of encryption methods. This series of encryption functions starting from MD2, MD4, and MD5 have been designed by Ronald Rivest. The latest version in the market is MD6, which is 256-bit based encryption.

8.5.2 Secure Hash Algorithm

SHA is a hashing algorithm. It has multiple versions in the series, such as SHA0, SHA1, SHA2, and SHA3 with different capabilities and features. This algorithm was developed by the US National Security Agency (NSA).

SHAs are published and governed by the National Institute of Standards and Technology (NIST), which is a US standard organization. The latest standard SHA3 is capable of encrypting the data with 224-bit, 256-bit, 384-bit, and 512-bit encryption. But the most commonly used SHA algorithm is SHA3 with 256-bit encryption.

8.6 MULTI-FACTOR AUTHENTICATION

Multi-factor authentication (as we discussed previously in Chapters 1 and 7) is another very useful and effective way to prevent the threats of cyberattacks. It is highly recommended in the modern field of cybersecurity that your passwords should not only be strong, but should also be powered by the multi-factor authentication process so that the malicious activities to steal your passwords can be averted easily.

In multi-factor authentication, the access to the digital resources such as computer system, web account, cloud service, or any other digital access is not granted through just one credential like password. But you have to provide more credentials other than the password.

The additional factors other than username/password can be generalized in three categories as shown in Figure 8.32.

One factor should be the knowledge question, which relates to some knowledge that only you know, and the other factor is referred to as biometric, which is unique and only you can be that. The third category of multi-factor authentication is referred to as one-time password (OTP), which only you can have through email, mobile, or you already have it as a hard key.

Those credentials are normally one-time-use codes to access the digital resources. Among such second factor for the authentication may include the following factors:

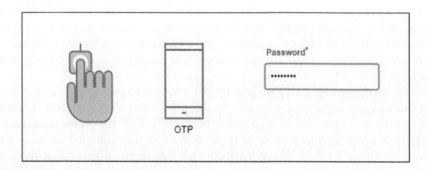

FIGURE 8.32 Multi-factor authentication.

- Short code sent through mobile phone
- A user-generated pin on the system
- One-time password (OTP)
- Digital signature
- Fingerprints
- Key fobs
- Digital card swiping

The computer processors have become very fast with the advent of advanced computing systems such as general-purpose graphics processing unit or GPGPU and other techniques of processing. It has become comparatively easy to break the password through brute force attacks. So, you need multiple factors to make your digital resources secure.

For instance, some hacker has succeeded in breaking your password through super-processing devices, and he wants to access your resources. He can easily access your account and hack your account if you do not have the multi-factor authentication activated. But if you have activated the multi-factor authentication on your digital account, the hacker will be asked to enter the other authentication factors that you have enabled on your account such as fingerprints, card swipe, OTP, or mobile code.

The hacker has no control over your phone number or other data. Thus, he/she will not be able to get access to your account despite the fact that he has stolen your legitimate password.

The multi-factor authentication will also alert you that someone has attempted to sign into your account by sending you the second factor code to enter. Thus, that will also be your alert to change the password again.

So, the multi-factor authentication is a very useful tool in maintaining a high level of security of your digital accounts and resources. The most commonly used multi-factor authentication method in the present days is the two-factor authentication through mobile or email.

This method uses your mobile phone or email to send you a one-time-use code to enter whenever you login to your account. Thus, your accounts remain safe and your password becomes a strong factor of your digital account security.

8.6.1 Activating Two-Factor Authentication

As discussed before, two-factor authentication is one of the most popular methods of multi-factor authentication system. It is extensively used by the private as well as public companies for the security of the passwords. The major cloud-based services offer the capabilities of two-factor authentication; among such services, Google, Yahoo, Hotmail, Facebook, and YouTube are a few to name.

Many private organizations either install or purchase the two-factor authentication service for their employees to use the higher level of security. Let us have a look at the step-by-step procedure to enable a two-factor authentication on the most commonly used cloud service by Google.

Take the following steps, to activate the two-factor authentication on Google account:

Step #1: Login to your Google account by entering your username and password. Or, click on the thumbnail image of your account located at the right corner of your Gmail account (Figure 8.33). Whatever the interface is, more or less the steps would remain the same.

Step #2: Click the **Google Account** button. The Google account settings page appears as shown in Figure 8.34. Here on this page, you can configure activation and different features and capabilities along with enabling the two-factor authentication service offered by the Google.

Step #3: Click the **Security** link on the left page of the Google account settings page. The **Signing in to Google** option appears on the page.

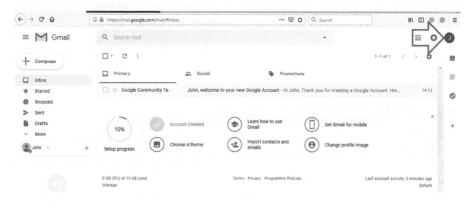

FIGURE 8.33   Gmail window.

FIGURE 8.34   Google account settings page.

Step #4: Click the **2-Step Verification** link located in the signing in to Google block as shown in Figure 8.34. The 2-Step Verification page appears (Figure 8.35).

Step #5: Click the **Get Started** button. The account login verification page appears requiring you to enter your active and valid password of the account. Enter the password to proceed. The 2-Step Verification wizard appears as shown in Figure 8.36.

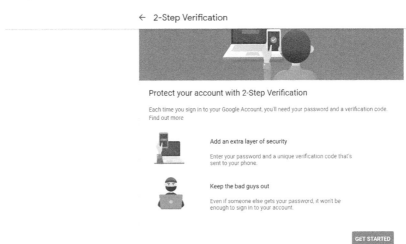

FIGURE 8.35   Two-step verification page.

Google Account

← 2-Step Verification

Let's set up your phone

What phone number do you want to use?

🇨 ▾   +92

Google will only use this number for account security.
Don't use a Google Voice number.
Message and data rates may apply.

How do you want to get codes?

◉ Text message   ○ Phone call

Don't want to use text message or voice call?
Choose another option

Step 1 of 3   NEXT

FIGURE 8.36   Two-step verification wizard start.

Step #6: Select the country and enter the valid phone number that you want to use to receive the text message from Google server. Also select the way you want to be contacted for the second factor security code. Google offers two options – text message and phone call. Click the **NEXT** link.

Step #7: A five-digit random code will be sent to your mobile for one-time use. You need to enter that code in **Enter the Code** field as shown in Figure 8.37, and click the **NEXT** link. The confirmation page will appear as shown in Figure 8.38.

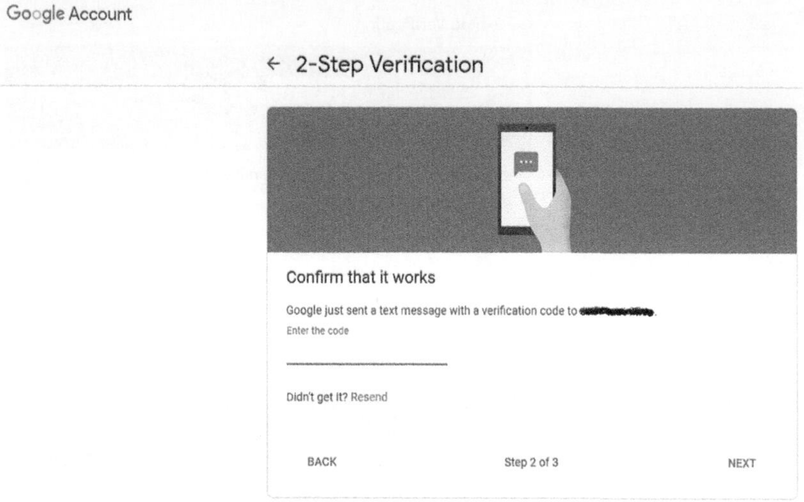

Google Account

← 2-Step Verification

Confirm that it works

Google just sent a text message with a verification code to ▓▓▓▓▓▓▓▓.
Enter the code

_____

Didn't get it? Resend

BACK   Step 2 of 3   NEXT

FIGURE 8.37   Confirming the code sent via phone number.

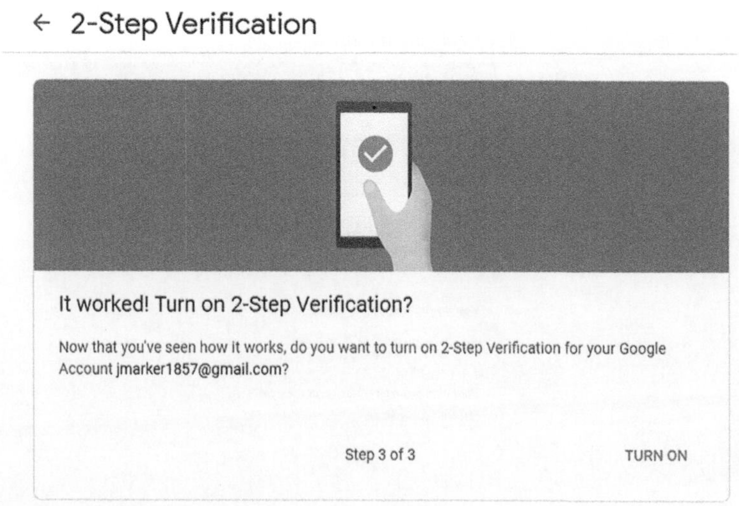

← 2-Step Verification

It worked! Turn on 2-Step Verification?

Now that you've seen how it works, do you want to turn on 2-Step Verification for your Google Account jmarker1857@gmail.com?

Step 3 of 3   TURN ON

FIGURE 8.38   Confirmation window.

Step #8: Click the **TURN ON** link to confirm your selections. The desired two-factor authentication on your Google account has been succeeded. You can modify your information or turn off the two-factor authentication, if you want as shown in Figure 8.39.

Step #9: You can also choose to inform Google to login to your account without typing in the code by adding the **ADD GOOGLE PROMPT** option. The pop-up window appears (Figure 8.40).

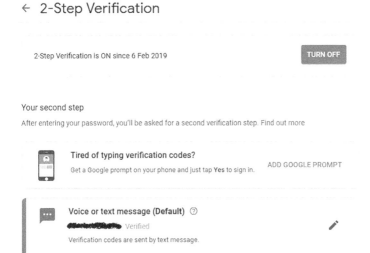

FIGURE 8.39 Turn off option window.

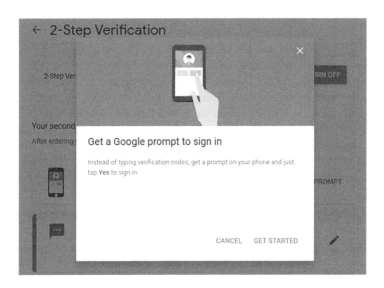

FIGURE 8.40 Google prompt sign in.

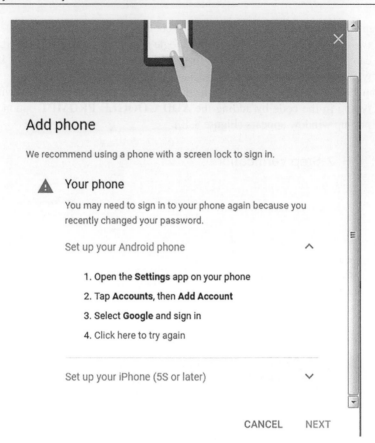

FIGURE 8.41   Adding phone number.

Step #10: Click the **GET STARTED** link on the pop-up message. The Add Phone option appears (Figure 8.41). Google supports adding Android and iPhone for this service. Go to your desired phone and set your phone for the Google **Yes** to login option. The phone that you added will automatically appear; if not, you need to click the "Click here to try again" link.

Step #11: Click the **NEXT** link. And you will be asked to enter the code you received on your mobile. Go to the mobile phone and click the "Yes" push notification that you received from the Google server. You will be automatically logged into your account without typing the code in your Google account.

8.6.2 Creating Application Specific Passwords

Google offers great security with two-factor authentication on your devices. Google also offers the high security on using third-party applications on your mobiles. When you use any third-party application on your mobile device with your Google account, you will need to generate an application-specific password from the Google account.

To generate an application-specific password, take the following steps:

- Login to your Google account (Figure 8.42).
- Click the **Avatar** button and then choose the **Google Account** option. The account settings page appears.
- Click the **Security** link on the left pane of the page. The security settings appear.
- Click the **App Passwords** link. Google asks to verify your password.
- Enter your valid password (Figure 8.43) and click the **Next** button. The **App Password** page appears as shown in Figure 8.44.
- Select the desired app and the device type that you use from the drop-down arrows as shown in Figure 8.45.

FIGURE 8.42   Google account log in.

FIGURE 8.43   Entering password.

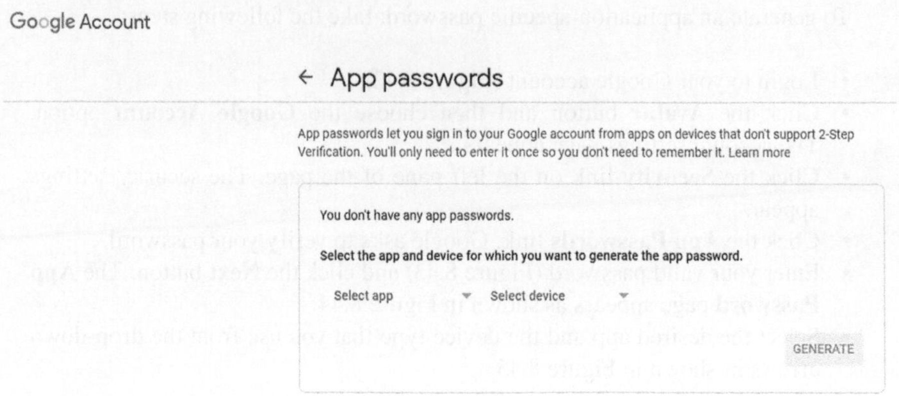

Google Account

← App passwords

App passwords let you sign in to your Google account from apps on devices that don't support 2-Step Verification. You'll only need to enter it once so you don't need to remember it. Learn more

You don't have any app passwords.

Select the app and device for which you want to generate the app password.

Select app   ▼   Select device   ▼

GENERATE

FIGURE 8.44   App password window.

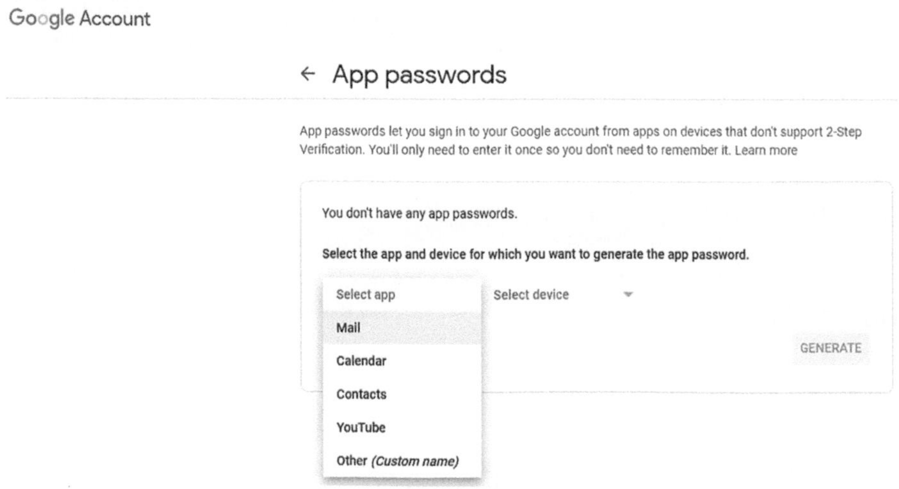

Google Account

← App passwords

App passwords let you sign in to your Google account from apps on devices that don't support 2-Step Verification. You'll only need to enter it once so you don't need to remember it. Learn more

You don't have any app passwords.

Select the app and device for which you want to generate the app password.

Select app   Select device   ▼

Mail

Calendar   GENERATE

Contacts

YouTube

Other *(Custom name)*

FIGURE 8.45   Selecting app.

- Click the **GENERATE** button. The app password will be generated as shown in Figure 8.46.
- A full details of how to use the application-specific password is also described.
- Copy this application-specific password.
- Open the application on the selected device that you want to link with your Google account for using the applications.
- Enter the application-specific password in the application and click the login button to login to that particular application.
- All these app-specific passwords are saved for future use of that password on that particular application.
- You can create passwords for other applications by following the same procedure.

Generated app password

Your app password

anxn bmio lmnp fcci

Email

securesally@gmail.com

Password

•••••••••••

How to use it

Go to the settings for your Google Account in the application or device you are trying to set up. Replace your password with the 16-character password shown above.
Just like your normal password, this app password grants complete access to your Google Account. You won't need to remember it, so don't write it down or share it with anyone.

DONE

FIGURE 8.46   Generating app password.

8.6.3 What If Your Phone with All Apps Enabled Is Lost?

Google offers a robust security for all your devices, but you have to be proactive enough to follow the security measures in case you lose your mobile. First of all, you should revoke the application-specific passwords on any of your device. To do so, take the following steps:

- Go to your account settings and click the Security link on the left pane (Figure 8.47).
- Click the App Passwords link. The existing application-specific passwords will appear (Figure 8.48).
- Click the 🗑 icon to delete the application-specific passwords.
- Your applications will logout on your mobile device that you lost. You can create new application-specific password on your new device.
- Change the password of your Google account and its backup numbers.
- It is always recommended to add backup phone number so that you can recover your Google account in case of losing mobile device with the primary phone number.
- Another option is to save the codes that you generated on your computer.

FIGURE 8.47   Security option.

← App passwords

App passwords let you sign in to your Google account from apps on devices that don't support 2-Step Verification. You'll only need to enter it once so you don't need to remember it. Learn more

Your app passwords

Name	Created	Last used	
YouTube on my iPhone	14:10	–	🗑
Mail on my iPhone	14:10	–	🗑

Select the app and device for which you want to generate the app password.

Select app   ▼   Select device   ▼

GENERATE

FIGURE 8.48   App passwords option.

8.7 MAC COMPUTER FIREWALL CONFIGURATION

Mac computers are brand names of Apple Inc. Mac computer runs on operating systems called OS X and macOS. The Apple computers' operating system evolved from its OS X 10 beta release in 2000. From there on, the OS X 10 releases continued till OS X 10.11 commonly known as El Capitan (Gala), which was released in the month of September, 2015.

Afterward, the OS X name was changed to macOS. The first version was named as macOS 10.12 Sierra. The latest version of Apple computer operating system is macOS 10.14 released in September 2018.

The firewall functionalities are inbuilt in the macOS operating systems (Figure 8.49). By default, the firewall blocks any traffic terminating on the unused ports. The open ports are normally exploited to scan the security and other settings of your computer by the hackers. So, you should enable the firewall on your Apple computer to keep the hackers at bay.

You can configure and activate the exceptions on the enabled ports by taking the following step-by-step procedure.

- Open the **Apple Menu** and choose the **System Preference** option. The system preference window will open as shown in Figure 8.50.

FIGURE 8.49   Mac computer firewall configuration.

FIGURE 8.50   Mac system preferences.

- Click the **Security & Privacy** icon. The security and privacy window appears as in Figure 8.51.
- Choose the **Firewall** tab on the security and privacy window. The details of firewall will appear.
- Click the **Lock** icon at the bottom of the window. Enter the valid administrator password. You are now logged in as administrator to make the desired changes in the Firewall and other security settings. All inactive buttons will activate.
- Click the **Turn Off Firewall** button (Figure 8.52), if you want to disable the firewall. Click the "Start" option to turn on the firewall appears, if you turn off the firewall.

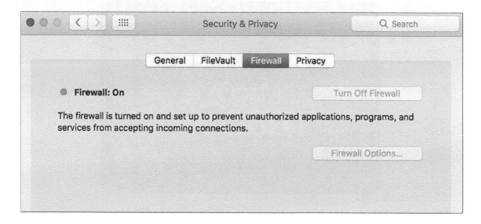

FIGURE 8.51   Security and privacy window.

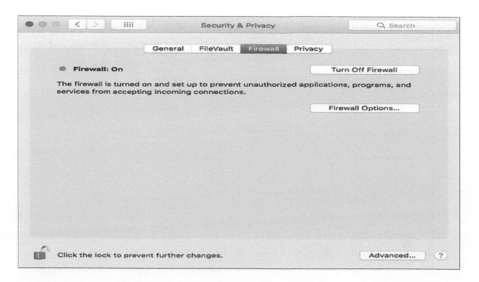

FIGURE 8.52   Firewall options.

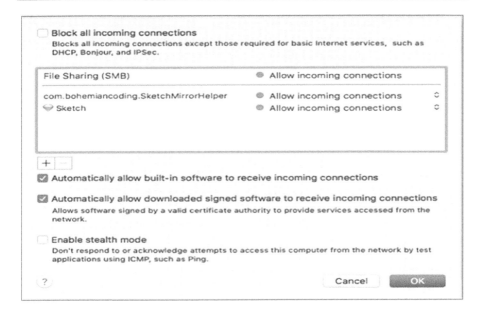

FIGURE 8.53 Application-related connections.

- Click the Firewall Options… button. The list of applications will appear as shown in the screenshot image in Figure 8.53.
- Select any application shown in the list and then click the (–) sign, if you want to remove from the list.
- Click on the (+) sign and choose the desired application that you want add into the list.
- Click the **Enable Stealth Mode** checkbox to enable the stealth mode for the hacker to respond to the probing activities on the computer.
- Choose the **Block all incoming connections** checkbox to stop traffic to any port on your computer.
- Similarly, select/deselect the Automatically allow built-in software to receive incoming connections checkbox to activate and deactivate this option on the firewall of Apple macOS computers.
- Click the **OK** button to enable the desired firewall settings.
- Close the firewall, privacy & security window to take effect the newly configured settings of the firewall.

8.7.1 Important Note

The firewall is designed to block the Internet-based incoming connections; so, some connections that use different protocols at the transport layer may not be affected by the firewall settings on Apple computers. This is the downside of the Apple firewall. The connection like AppleTalk, which uses a proprietary protocol, is not affected by the firewall settings on the Apple computers.

And, ICMP (Internet Control Message Protocol) pings are blocked by enabling the stealth mode, which does not allow the external probing that mostly use the ping command to check the status of the ports and applications.

8.8 CHOOSING THE RIGHT BROWSER

A secure, reliable, and fast browser makes your Internet experience great. Any old version or bad browser can expose you to the security threats because the browser is the basic component that you sail on to surf the world of Internet. So, always choose the right browser that is 100% fit for your requirements, system configuration, and security level.

For choosing the right browser for your computer, you should have clear knowledge about the following things:

- Your system information
- Your browsing activities on Internet
- Level of security you need

Once you have this information on paper, you can easily take the following steps to choose the right browser for you and your computer.

- First of all, check the configuration of your computer so that you can find the most suitable browser that is fully fit with the computer resources.
- Click 🪟 button and choose **Control Panel** option. The control panel window appears.
- Click the **System** option on the control panel. The details of your computer system appear (Figure 8.54).
- Write down the information regarding operating system, service pack, RAM, system type, and processor information.
- You need to search for the best browsers suitable for your computer operating system. This is important to note that there are many browsers for different operating systems available in the market.
- Go to Internet and Google the best Internet browsers as shown in Figure 8.55.
- Google will return you with the top rated browsers suitable for the operating system you are using on your computer (Figure 8.56).
- Search for the top ten reviews in the Google.
- Click the toptenreviews.com website to research about the features and capabilities of the browsers (Figure 8.57).
- Scroll down to the comparative properties on this website as shown in Figure 8.58.
- Scroll the comparison table to the right to see more features. This compares many features, performance factors, required system configuration, prices,

FIGURE 8.54   Systems window.

FIGURE 8.55   Google search for best browser.

FIGURE 8.56   Best browser search.

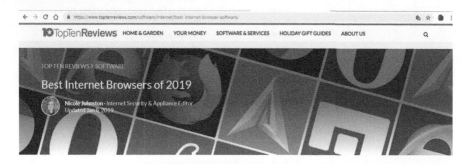

FIGURE 8.57   TopTenReviews website.

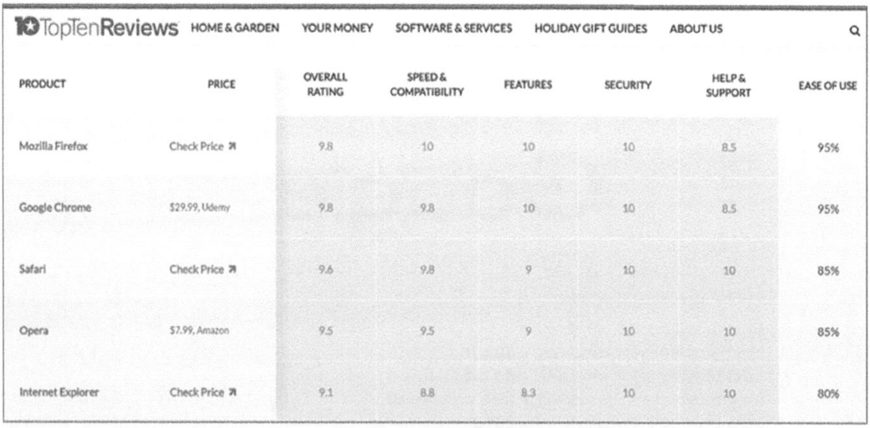

PRODUCT	PRICE	OVERALL RATING	SPEED & COMPATIBILITY	FEATURES	SECURITY	HELP & SUPPORT	EASE OF USE
Mozilla Firefox	Check Price ⌐	9.8	10	10	10	8.5	95%
Google Chrome	$29.99, Udemy	9.8	9.8	10	10	8.5	95%
Safari	Check Price ⌐	9.6	9.8	9	10	10	85%
Opera	$7.99, Amazon	9.5	9.5	9	10	10	85%
Internet Explorer	Check Price ⌐	9.1	8.8	8.3	10	10	80%

FIGURE 8.58   Comparative properties of different browsers.

and much more. To know more, scroll to the right for information as in the image in Figure 8.59.

- If you are looking for fast performance with the basic features of bookmarks and search bars, you would like to use browsers Midori, Vivaldi, Torch, and similar.

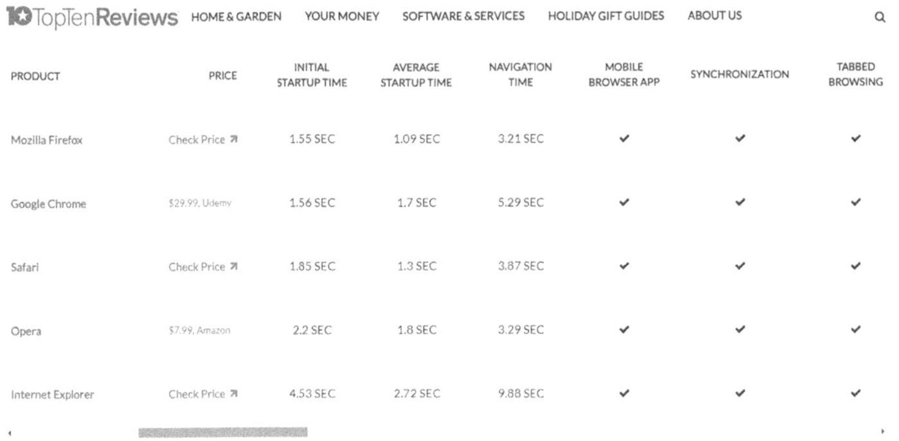

8 • Prevention from Cyberattacks   193

10TopTenReviews   HOME & GARDEN   YOUR MONEY   SOFTWARE & SERVICES   HOLIDAY GIFT GUIDES   ABOUT US   Q

PRODUCT	PRICE	INITIAL STARTUP TIME	AVERAGE STARTUP TIME	NAVIGATION TIME	MOBILE BROWSER APP	SYNCHRONIZATION	TABBED BROWSING
Mozilla Firefox	Check Price ↗	1.55 SEC	1.09 SEC	3.21 SEC	✓	✓	✓
Google Chrome	$29.99, Udemy	1.56 SEC	1.7 SEC	5.29 SEC	✓	✓	✓
Safari	Check Price ↗	1.85 SEC	1.3 SEC	3.87 SEC	✓	✓	✓
Opera	$7.99, Amazon	2.2 SEC	1.8 SEC	3.29 SEC	✓	✓	✓
Internet Explorer	Check Price ↗	4.53 SEC	2.72 SEC	9.88 SEC	✓	✓	✓

FIGURE 8.59   More properties.

- For the performance, reliability and features, you can choose Google Chrome or Mozilla Firefox for your Windows 7 OS.
- If you have a slow Internet connection and want to use the faster than fastest browsers, then use the text-based browsers.
- The top examples of text-based browsers include Elinks, WebIE, Lynx, Labnol.
- If you want to use different types of plugins and other third-party apps, then choose either Mozilla Firefox or Google Chrome browsers. They are easy to use with a wide range of plugins.
- Download the browser of your choice once you decided the best fit for you.
- Install the browser and go surfing the Internet.

8.9 SECURE SOCKETS LAYER

SSL is a type of security protocol for secure data transfer from web server to the browser and vice versa. The SSL is a recognized and standard security protocol that establishes a secure and encrypted link between the web server and the browser so that the transactions of data between the client and the server are fully secure and reliable (Figure 8.60).

FIGURE 8.60   Secure Sockets Layer.

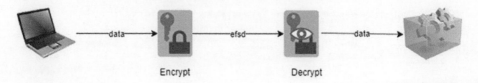

FIGURE 8.61 Symmetric encryption.

There are two most commonly used types of data encryption methods. They are given below:

- Symmetric encryption
- Asymmetric encryption

Symmetric encryption uses the same key for the encryption and decryption of the data as shown in Figure 8.61.

On the other hand, the asymmetric encryption uses two separate keys for encryption and decryption, respectively. Asymmetric encryption uses 2,048-bit keys nowadays. Previously, it also used the 1,024-bit key, but now, it is not considered as very safe encryption. Figure 8.62 shows the asymmetric encryption, which uses two separate keys for encryption and decryption.

SSL protocol works on certain data encryption algorithms. The most commonly used public and private key-based encryption uses the following encryption algorithms:

- Rivest, Shamir, Adleman (RSA) algorithm
- Elliptic Curve Cryptography (ECC) algorithm

The SSL encryption is based on the SSL certificate, which is normally installed on the web server. The SSL certificate is purchased from the issuing authorities commonly known as Certificate Authority (CA) after proper verification of the business and websites.

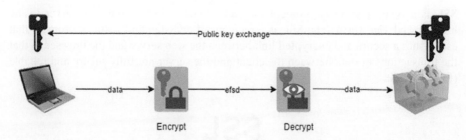

FIGURE 8.62 Asymmetric encryption.

First of all, you need to generate a certificate signing request (CSR) via local browser on the web server. This report is a file of data, which includes web server information and private key. This CSR is submitted to the certificate authorities for issuance of certificate. The web administrator and developer request for SSL certificate. When it is received from the issuing authorities, it is installed on the web server.

When the SSL certificate is installed, the communication between browser and the server will take place on a secure and encrypted link. On that link, the data travels in the encrypted form and hackers will not be able to breach the integrity of the data while in transit over the secure link.

To establish a secure socket connection between server and web browser, the following steps take place.

- Browser sends the secure connection request through the "HTTPS" request through the https://websiteURL.
- The web server receives the request and responds with the SSL certificate to the browser that requested for the certificate.
- The web browser authenticates and verifies that the SSL certificate is valid. This process is referred to as "SSL handshake".
- When the browser verifies the SSL certificate, a padlock icon appears in the address bar of the browser as shown in Figure 8.63.
- A secure connection is established between browser and web server. Now, the communication over the link is fully encrypted and secure.

The workflow of SSL link establishment is given in Figure 8.64.

A secure website is the new security standard of safe browsing. It is highly recommended not to visit the websites that are not SSL enabled. The secure websites increase the trust of the visitors and subsequently increase the conversion rate.

The increase in traffic to your website is another important effect of having your website a digital certificate for SSL communication link.

FIGURE 8.63   Padlock icon in the address bar.

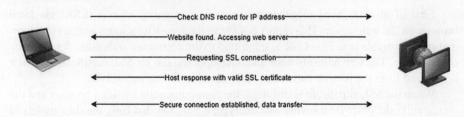

FIGURE 8.64   Workflow of SSL link establishment.

8.10 VIRTUAL PRIVATE NETWORK

Virtual private network or VPN is a type of communication tunnel that is highly secure for private services and communication over the Internet. It is also known as tunneling protocol on the public networks.

The main characteristics of a VPN connection include the following:

- Secure, private, and anonymous routing through tunnel
- Encapsulation of one protocol over the other is done to hide the details of the origination and termination of the communication
- Routing of your communication through a proxy server
- It hides your Internet activities from other external interceptions
- Your IP address is masked with the VPN number/address
- History is fully hidden from even service providers
- Hides your location
- Hides your device identity
- It is a complete connection from device to network

In the normal communication over the Internet, hackers can intercept your data packets and decrypt to know about your communication. But the communication over VPN is completely hidden, private, and secure passing through a private tunnel, which is created on the public network. The communication over the VPN connection is near to impossible to intercept and interpret.

VPN service is extensively used by the corporations and government organizations for remote work so that the communication remains private and secure from the external interceptions. Two major types of VPN connections are commonly used in our modern Internet services; they are as follows:

- Site-to-site VPN connections
- Remote-access VPN connections

The site-to-site connections are normally used to connect multiple sites and locations of a corporation or governmental organization through VPN connections.

These connections are created over the public Internet via private proxy servers or the proxy servers of the service providers.

The remote-access VPN connections are normally used for remote work. Any employee who is traveling can access the corporate or other private networks through a VPN connection over the Internet. His/her communication with the corporate network remains private for the other Internet users.

VPN uses encryption to encrypt the data before transporting over the private tunnel. It also uses other techniques and mechanism to hide the data from any breach. Then, the original communication protocol is masked with the VPN protocol and transported over the secure tunnel created between proxy server and the VPN-enabled device.

The original packet of information is encrypted at the network layer to disguise it from being identified, and then the entire encrypted packet is repacked into an IP envelop to travel over the Internet. Thus, the packet data and the message attributes are disguised in the tunneling process.

The schematic diagram of VPN connectivity on public Internet to connect to the corporate private network is shown in Figure 8.65.

The main advantages of VPN connection include the following:

- Higher level of privacy
- Greater data security
- Better reliability
- Anonymity
- Reduced cost of connection

All of the abovementioned features help you maintain high level of cybersecurity that helps you prevent any kind of cyberattack on your data and communications.

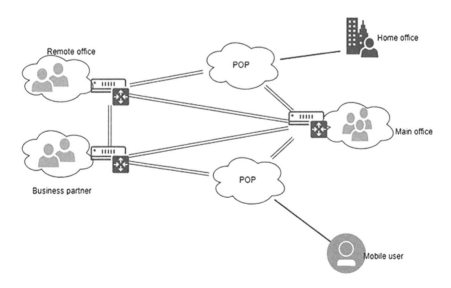

FIGURE 8.65 Virtual private network.

SAMPLE QUESTIONS AND ANSWERS FOR WHAT WE HAVE LEARNED IN CHAPTER 8

Q1. What are the key factors for cybersecurity awareness?

A1: The awareness of the cybersecurity includes the following important factors:

- Continuously educate the people about cybersecurity.
- Make the users realize the importance of password security.
- Train about keeping the software updated.
- Provide guidelines on how to deal with unknown emails.
- Train for the potential social engineering ways that exploit the innocence of people.
- Implement proper system logout and monitoring mechanism.

Q2. If we constitute steps of activities after a cyberattack has hit, what those will be?

A2: If we constitute steps of activities after the cyberattack has hit and also has been detected, we need to do these:

- **Survey**: Survey the attack to know about vulnerability, damage, and attackers.
- **Limit**: Limit the attack by blocking, diverting, and isolating the system and traffic.
- **Record**: Record the impact by recording effects, levels, and disruptions.
- **Engage**: Engage with concerned agencies and authorities.
- **Notify**: Notify the affected users and seek legal counseling.
- **Learn**: Learn a lesson from the attack and prepare for better preventive steps.

Q3. What are the main three tasks for cyberattack prevention?

A3: The approach of prevention of cyberattacks falls in the three major activities as listed below:

- Detection of cyberattacks
- Prediction of cyberattacks
- Prevention of cyberattacks.

Q4. What is Metaheuristic?

A4: Metaheuristic is a higher-level procedure or heuristic designed to find, generate, or select a heuristic (partial search algorithm) that may provide a sufficiently good solution to an optimization problem.

Q5. What are the main firewall types?

A5: Firewalls can be either a software program installed on the servers, computers, or routers to safeguard any computer, server, or even the entire system or it can be a dedicated hardware device loaded with the dedicated firewall software on it. In our daily use, for PCs, and mobile devices, we use the software firewalls installed on those devices to protect us from external deliberate attacks by the hackers.

SOURCES

https://perspectives.tieto.com/blog/2015/04/4-steps-to-combat-cyber-attacks-in-a-digitalised-world/

https://smallbiztrends.com/2017/01/cyber-security-statistics-small-business.html

https://www.securitymagazine.com/articles/88375-preventative-corrective-detective-ways-to-protect-your-data-after-the-equifax-breach

https://www.american.edu/kogod/research/cybergov/upload/what-to-do.pdf

https://www.researchgate.net/publication/326698342_A_Survey_of_Cyber_Security_Approaches_for_Attack_Detection_Prediction_and_Prevention

https://pdfs.semanticscholar.org/5d9a/7c4efe43c76a6cb6f2ab760bb7e83cb76c6b.pdf

https://www.csoonline.com/article/3153707/security/top-cybersecurity-facts-figures-and-statistics.html

https://perspectives.tieto.com/blog/2015/04/4-steps-to-combat-cyber-attacks-in-a-digitalised-world/

https://waset.org/publications/10000665/quick-reference-cyber-attacks-awareness-and-prevention-method-for-home-users

https://support.microsoft.com/en-au/help/4028544/windows-10-turn-windows-defender-firewall-on-or-off

https://www.researchgate.net/publication/316599266_INTRUSION_DETECTION_SYSTEM

https://www.utica.edu/faculty_staff/qma/ids.pdf

https://www.sans.org/reading-room/whitepapers/detection/intrusion-prevention-systems-securitys-silver-bullet-366

https://www.researchgate.net/publication/281120779_INTRUSION_PREVENTION_SYSTEM

https://searchsqlserver.techtarget.com/definition/hashing

https://www.ibm.com/support/knowledgecenter/en/SSYKE2_7.0.0/com.ibm.java.security.component.70.doc/security-component/jsse2Docs/cryptographichashetc.html

http://web.cse.ohio-state.edu/~lai.1/651/6.hash-MAC.pdf

https://searchsecurity.techtarget.com/definition/MD5

https://searchsecurity.techtarget.com/definition/multifactor-authentication-MFA

https://www.eff.org/deeplinks/2016/12/how-enable-two-factor-authentication-gmail-and-google

https://blink.ucsd.edu/technology/security/user-guides/firewall/mac-snow.html#2.-Activate-the-firewall

https://www.instantssl.com/ssl.html

https://www.comodo.com/resources/small-business/about-ssl.php

https://httpd.apache.org/docs/2.4/ssl/ssl_intro.html

https://www.digicert.com/ssl-cryptography.htm

https://www.cisco.com/c/en/us/support/docs/security-vpn/ipsec-negotiation-ike-protocols/14106-how-vpn-works.pdf

https://www.wiley.com/legacy/compbooks/press/0471348201_09.pdf

Wireless Network Security　9

9.1 INTRODUCTION

Wireless networks have got vast grounds in our network communication during the past couple of decades. Being comparatively new technology, wireless security (Figure 9.1) is more prone to threats than the wired networks. Wireless network security is a part of computer network security in which the wireless access points (APs) and wireless

FIGURE 9.1　Wireless security conceptual image.

cards are used as the points to secure through the latest security protocols, techniques, and algorithms.

Securing your computers, data, and other digital resources that are connected through wireless connections is commonly referred to as wireless network security. Wireless is a medium on which data transfer and computer communication occur. The protocols that handle the wireless communication such as 802.11b, 802.11g, 802.11n, and others normally deal with the physical and data link layers of the Open Systems Interconnection (OSI) model. The upper layers of the communication protocols are almost same with a little variation in the modern wireless technologies.

The protocol stack of IEEE 802.11 is shown in the Figure 9.2.

It is very important to note that anybody that is in range of the wireless field can access the signals easily. That means your network is physically exposed to the hackers. Now, you have to make sure that your network is logically secure. Normally, the security of the wireless network starts from the network layer, which is third in OSI layer model.

The use of medium access control (MAC) address of the device is also used for the static configuration of the MAC binding. But in other cases, the security of the network takes place at the third layer of the OSI model commonly known as network layer.

The gravity of the security problems with the wireless networks can easily be assessed from this fact that you do not need a wire to connect to the organization network. You can sit in the parking of the company and can have access to the data layer level of the network.

Any wireless network-enabled computer connected to the company network through wire can also behave like a point for the hacker to intrude into your network. Thus, the wireless network is more prone to security threats as compared to the wired networks.

The major threat points vulnerable to security breach in a wireless network include the following:

- Bluetooth connection
- ZigBee connection
- Bluetooth Low Energy (BLE)
- Wireless access point
- Wireless network cards

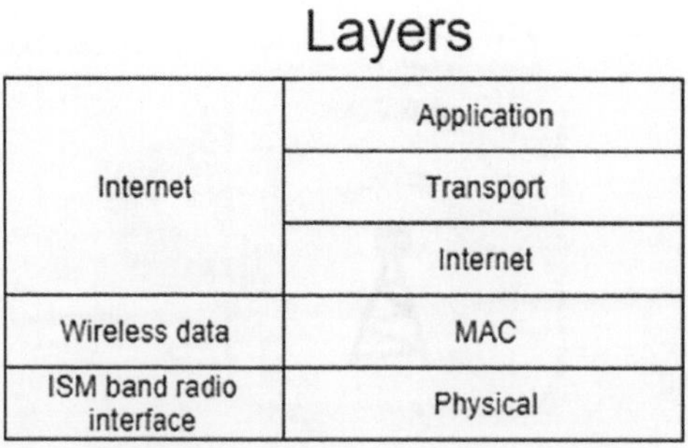

Layers

	Application
Internet	Transport
	Internet
Wireless data	MAC
ISM band radio interface	Physical

FIGURE 9.2   IEEE 802.11 protocol stack. (ISM means industrial, scientific, and medical).

The security protocols dealing with the security of the wireless networks are also less mature as compared to those dealing with the wired networks. The authentication and encryption protocols are evolving rapidly due to the increased use of wireless networks in our day-to-day life. The Internet of Things (IoT) is driving the wireless security market extensively.

The major data encryption and security protocols used by the wireless networks are listed below:

- Wired Equivalent Privacy (WEP)
- Wi-Fi Protected Access (WPA)
- Wi-Fi Protected Access v2 (WPA2)
- Wi-Fi Protected Access v3 (WPA3)

Before we deep dive into the security protocol-related wireless security and other mechanisms used for securing the valuable data and networks from external threats, let us have a look at the major vulnerabilities of a wireless network.

We explain wireless network vulnerabilities in terms of local area network (LAN) and wide area network (WAN) vulnerabilities in the following sections.

9.2 LAN VULNERABILITIES

Wireless local area network (WLAN) is more prone to threats (conceptual image is in Figure 9.3) as compared to the wired local area network because wireless network uses open air as the medium, which is easily available to anyone located within the range of

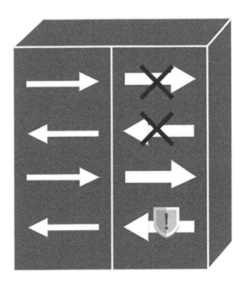

FIGURE 9.3   LAN vulnerabilities (conceptual image).

the wireless radius. A hacker can easily connect to the network as far as the medium of communication is concerned. This is a big downside of wireless network as far as the security of the wireless networks is concerned.

Like wired network, the wireless networks are prone to the following types of major attacks:

- Passive attacks
- Active attacks

In passive attacks, the hackers only try to intrude into the wireless network communication to steal the information about the network and passwords. They do not try to damage the digital resources or take any materialist advantage. But they take the information, which can be used for the active attacks in the future. In passive attacks, a hacker just listens to the inbound and outbound traffic of the wireless communication. The main objective of the hacker in passive attack is just to gather sensitive information, which is useful for carrying out active cyberattacks on the wireless networks.

The passive attacks are the types of attacks that target the network system and the wireless network to harm the digital resources on the network. The active attacks are normally done through worms, viruses, Trojan horses, and the similar methods.

The other major types of cyberattacks that are unleashed on the wireless network may include the following:

- Distributed attacks
- Phishing attacks
- Password attacks
- Insider attacks
- Hijack attacks
- Close-in attacks

These attacks are normally carried out by exploiting the vulnerabilities and security loopholes in the wireless network and its security mechanisms. The major vulnerabilities of a wireless security may include the following:

- Reconnaissance or lack of physical security vulnerability
- Resource stealing and invasion
- Rogue APs
- STA (Station) and AP plain text transaction
- Denial of service (DoS)
- Default AP configuration
- Rogue insiders
- Protocol vulnerabilities
- Ad hoc network mode security problems

Let us discuss all of the above vulnerabilities one by one.

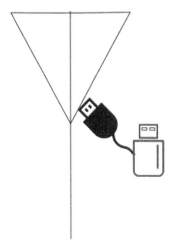

FIGURE 9.4   Reconnaissance vulnerability – antenna.

9.2.1 Reconnaissance Vulnerability

The reconnaissance vulnerability is one of the most critical vulnerabilities in the WLAN security system. The wireless router of the WLAN transmits the signals within the rated radius. The signals are easily catchable by any hacker that is present in the field of active range of the wireless signals. The signals of the wireless network can also be enhanced and caught through very powerful antennas used by hackers to access the wireless signals of a remote network.

The image of a powerful antenna to boost the wireless signals is shown in Figure 9.4.

By using high-power Wi-Fi antennas, you can boost the strength of signals and increase the coverage area of wireless local network. Thus, the reconnaissance vulnerability of the WLAN increases with the increased strength of Wi-Fi signals and, subsequently, the coverage area of the wireless signals.

9.2.2 Resource Stealing and Invasion

In this type of vulnerabilities, the hackers use the main devices of the wireless network such as wireless router that offers the first layer of the security and the computer devices that have wireless cards.

The routers maintain a routing table and intelligent algorithm for fast routing. The routing table is manipulated by using some techniques like Internet Protocol (IP) spoofing and similar; consequently, the device is invaded and befooled to do what the hacker wants to do.

The devices that are connected to the switch through network cables will act as wireless device too due to their wireless-enabled cards. This vulnerability is exploited by the hackers very easily to intrude into the security system and steal the useful data that can be used for the lethal cyberattacks on the network of systems.

9.2.3 Rogue Access Points (APs)

The rogue AP is one of the major vulnerabilities that are exploited by the hackers for man-in-the-middle (MITM) attacks. The rogue APs are those wireless devices that are connected to the network, but have very weak security features or the configuration is done by the physical intruder to access the network in the future.

Such APs are normally configured at the edge of the wireless network or away from the security surveillance. First, these APs are used for passive attacks to steal the information of the network and then, the stolen information is used for bigger and more lethal cyberattacks (Figure 9.5).

The legitimate users connect to the rogue AP, which is not authorized to work in the network, but it connects the users and routes the traffic through it. The traffic is intercepted and analyzed for the useful data that can help unleash a lethal cyberattack on the network.

These kinds of rogue APs become very nasty in certain cases because the network administrator is fully unaware of the activities of rogue APs that are monitoring the traffic and compromising the network security of the WLAN.

Rogue APs can also be installed on the network by getting physical access to the organization network and placing the AP at some hidden place and connected to the company network switch through a wire.

The physical access is normally achieved by either compromising the physical security or getting help from the accomplice that have access to the physical area of the

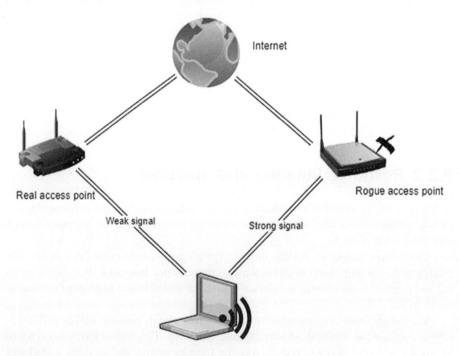

FIGURE 9.5   Rogue access point (AP).

organization. If a rogue AP is installed in the legitimate wireless network, the security of the network is at a high risk.

Sometimes, the employees or other legitimate users bring and insert the AP with standard configuration to extend the coverage area within the work area. The default configuration or somewhat security features-enabled AP falls a prey to the hackers easily, and they use it as rogue AP for network attacks.

9.2.4 STA and AP Plain Text Transaction

The traffic redirection is done by exploiting different vulnerabilities in the network. The main exploits that enable the traffic redirect attack include phishing and session hijacking through MAC spoofing. It is very important to note that the first communication step between AP and the legitimate stations commonly referred to as STA takes place in plain text due to encryption/decryption protocols' inability at that point.

The plain text information is interrupted by the hackers, and thus, the information about the MAC address of AP as well as legitimate user can be achieved. Once the information about the MAC address is achieved, the hacker can spoof the MAC address and intrude into the network. Once the session is established, the network security can easily be compromised.

9.2.5 Denial of Service (DoS)

The DoS attacks are easier to carry out in wireless networks because of the following factors:

- Easy access to the wireless medium
- Availability of powerful radio devices like wireless cards
- Wireless jammers

We talked about general DoS before. Now, let us know more in wireless environment. In the DoS attack, one or multiple legitimate users can be prevented from getting access to the network by spoofing the authentication and association sessions. The client joins the network once the AP is authenticated and associated with the client or the STA. The authentication and association messages can be spoofed as non-legitimate messages, and thus, the users could be pushed out of the services. Thus, the DoS attacks in wireless networks are much easier to exploit than that of the other wired networks.

9.2.6 Default AP Configuration

The default configuration of any AP is a big vulnerability that can put your entire network at a very high risk of cyberattacks. Normally, the default settings of APs manufactured by any vendor in the world have the known username and password.

For example, the wireless routers manufactured by the Cisco Systems have the username as Cisco and the password as Cisco. The other manufacturers have the similar types of default standards. The access to the router is free without any password by default. And, many other security features such as encryption and other standards are by default not configured; so, the default configuration can be very dangerous for the security of the wireless network.

In many cases, it has been observed that the small organizations where the standard security mechanism or policy is not available, the users configure the APs with very normal security configurations. Thus, the APs with less security features enabled become a big point of exploitation for attacking the wireless network.

9.2.7 Rogue Insiders

The rogue insiders are also a big threat for the security of the wireless as well as wired network, but for the wireless network, they can be very risky. Hackers can easily exploit the activities of the rogue insiders to compromise the security of the network.

A rogue employee can leak the data of the wireless network as well as connect his/her laptop to the network through a wire and provide access to the hackers through wireless card of the computer. The rogue insider can exploit the wireless network very badly.

9.2.8 Protocol Vulnerabilities

As mentioned in the earlier topics, STA and AP start authentication and association through plain text conversation. This is the first vulnerability of the protocol, which can be exploited by the hackers. By exploiting this vulnerability, the hackers can establish a control over the session and then carry out other malicious activities when they are on the wireless network.

Similarly, the encryption protocols used by the WLAN include WEP, WPA, and WPA2, and there are certain vulnerabilities in those protocols, which can be exploited by the hackers. For instance, any wireless network using WEP protocol is very insecure. The hackers can break the encryption of WEP within just a one minute time. It has been marked as expired in the marketplace, but if anybody is using this, he/she is at very high risk.

The WPA uses the pre-shared key, which is also vulnerable in the modern security scenario. It uses message integrity checks and Temporal Key Integrity Protocol (TKIP). The International Consortium for Advancement of Cybersecurity on the Internet (ICASI) has already warned of a few vulnerabilities even in the WPA and WPA2. The organization termed the vulnerabilities as Key Reinstallation Attack (KRACK).

By using these vulnerabilities, the hackers can inject some of the specially-crafted packets during the course of authentication handshake. That data packet will force the system to install a key, which is actually controlled by the hackers. Thus, the wireless network using the WPA protocols can also be compromised.

The major vulnerabilities of WPA protocol are summarized in the following list:

• It uses encryption RC4, which is vulnerable to DoS attacks.
• It uses the MIC (Message Integrity Code) value in the EAPoL (Extensible Authentication Protocol (EAP) over LAN) message in plain text, which is easy for the hackers to attack and break.

Similarly, the main vulnerabilities of WPA2 protocol are listed below:

• The "hole196" is one of the most known vulnerabilities.
• The CCM Mode Protocol (CCMP) protocol used in WPA2 encryption mechanism is vulnerable to Time-Memory-Trade pre-computation attack.

ICASI suggested some guidelines for the manufacturers as well users to avoid the exploitation of those WPA-enabled security protocols to avoid any compromise on your WLAN security.

9.2.9 Ad Hoc Network Mode Security Problems

The use of ad hoc networking is supported by many operating systems including the Windows operating system. By using ad hoc network, every host in the network can communicate with the other network based on agreed SSID (Service Set Identifier). This type of wireless network is very vulnerable in terms of security because there is no firewall behind this network (Figure 9.6).

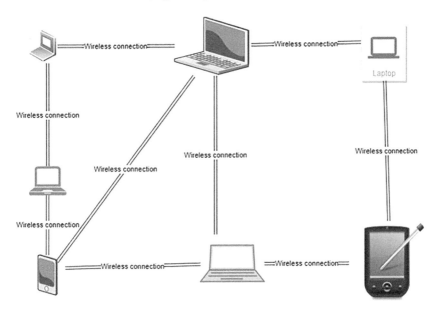

FIGURE 9.6   Ad hoc network mode security problems.

Every node in the network connects with its peer without any security firewall or other network security measures. In such conditions, any virus, worm, or other malware available on any one node can easily travel to the other node without any security cover by the network firewall.

9.3 WIRELESS WAN VULNERABILITIES

The wireless wide area network (WWAN) is the wireless network spread over large area of operation. The main examples of WWANs include the 2G, 3G, 4G, and 5G networks. All mobile broadband networks are the examples of wide area networks. The WWANs can be classified into two sections as listed below:

- Circuit-switched data network
- Packet-switched data network

The security of the WAN is implemented by the Internet Service Providers commonly known as the ISPs. The security of those WWAN is mostly implemented at the protocol, system backbone, and base stations of the network. The main protocols used in the circuit-switched data networks for the authentication of the users include, PAP (Password Authentication Protocol), CHAP (Challenge-Handshake Authentication Protocol), and SPAP (Shiva Password Authentication Protocol). These protocols have their own pros and cons in terms of their security and other features.

There are certain WWAN vulnerabilities that are given below:

- PAP is normally used for authentication, which uses the plain text messages without any encryption for getting the username and passwords for authentication.
- Circuit-switched network uses public network prone to cyber threats.

The other form of WWAN is based on the packet switching. This network uses the packet routing that takes place from multiple routers and always from the different paths. The data transfer is also encrypted. The schematic diagram of a packet-switched WAN powered by wireless technology is shown in Figure 9.7.

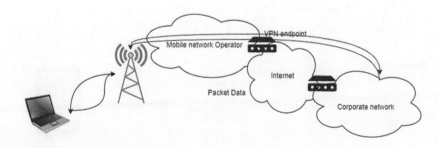

FIGURE 9.7   WWAN vulnerabilities.

The security of this network is much stronger than the previous types of WAN. This type of network uses the point-to-point virtual private network (VPN) connection, and hence, the security of the data is much higher than the other forms.

9.4 IoT VULNERABILITIES

IoT is a type of networking technology, which is in the market for quite a few years now. It is a network of IP-enabled devices all connected in a networked environment and controlled through a centralized control unit. The examples of IP-enabled devices include all the main appliances and machines that we use in our day-to-day life. For example, printer, door lock, fridge, AC, heater, water tank, cooker, microwave oven, and many others.

According to the Statista predictions, the total number of connected devices worldwide will cross 75.44 billion by 2025. The number of IoT connected devices worldwide was about 26.66 billion in 2019.

The major driver of this technology is the centralized wireless network that connects the devices altogether at office, home, shopping mall, and even in the industry. The centralized unit and the other nodes in an office or home connect to the central control unit through wireless networks that include the following wireless networks:

- Low-power wide area networks (LPWANs)
- BLE and Bluetooth networks
- Cellular technologies such as 5G, 4G, 3G, and others
- Radio frequency identity (RFID)
- Wi-Fi network
- ZigBee network
- Z-wave

According to the latest research conducted by the Hewlett & Packard, more than 70% of the connected devices in an IoT network have serious security vulnerabilities. Those vulnerabilities combined altogether form a complex set of security vulnerabilities in an IoT network.

The vulnerabilities in the IoT network are the combination of all vulnerabilities that are associated with a particular technology used in the IoT network. It is a very complex and highly vulnerable system to manage to make it a fully secure environment (Figure 9.8). Many automated operations and security management software tools are used to manage the entire connected network of IoT.

The main challenges related to the security of IoT network include the following:

- Securing the wireless-enabled connected devices
- Updating the firmware and software of the devices
- Securing communication between the nodes

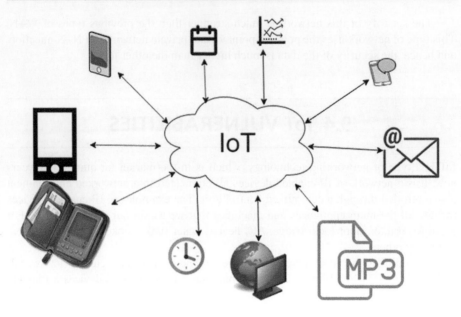

FIGURE 9.8   IoT vulnerabilities.

- Detecting vulnerabilities at different levels of the network
- Securing the authentication and authorization process of connected devices
- Security of mobile and web applications used in managing the network
- Wireless connectivity security
- Ensuring the data integrity and privacy
- Security of cloud applications
- Maintaining stability of a complex network

Due to its complexity, IoT requires high level of precision and accuracy in managing the entire network to make sure that network remains secure and available for round the clock.

9.5 WIRELESS NETWORK SECURITY MEASURES

Wireless networks are more prone to risks as compared to the wired networks owing to their signals going out of the boundaries of your home and organization. A hacker can easily catch the wireless signals and use the sophisticated techniques to intrude into your wireless network.

FIGURE 9.9   Wireless network security measures (conceptual image).

You need to consider the level of security that you require for your data and other resources on your network. If you are running a business and have business information on your network, you should consider developing a proper security policy so that you can manage your security at higher level. If you want to secure your home network with less important data on the network, you can take general guidelines and security measures that can help you secure your home network (conceptual image is in Figure 9.9).

Now, let us learn about the major security measures that can help you secure your home or office wireless networks.

9.5.1 Modify Default Configuration

The default settings of your wireless router or other nodes of your wireless network are common and known to everybody with a little technical knowledge. You should modify all major default configurations to new ones. The configuration interface of most commonly used Linksys router is shown in Figure 9.10.

You should use unique names, numbers, and passwords that are strong and difficult for the other people to guess. You should also add new data for the following parameters of your wireless router:

- Service Set Identifier (SSID)
- Administrator username and passwords
- Remote access feature
- Enable stealth mode
- Network partitions
- WPA2 password
- Enable stronger encryption

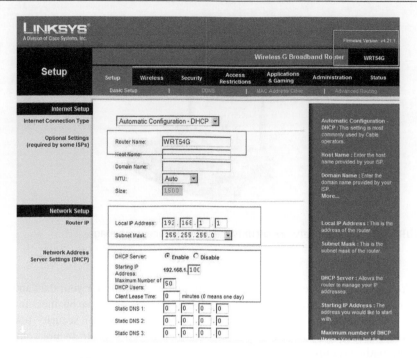

FIGURE 9.10   Modify default configuration.

9.5.2 Wireless Router Location

The location/placement of the router either in office or home is very important. The location of the router affects the wireless network performance as well as the security of the network. The Wi-Fi router should be placed at the centralized location where the signals of good strength could reach to all legitimate users, but outsiders may not get signals strong enough to connect. Thus, you will lay strong foundation for the network security by placing the router at a very suitable location in the office or home.

9.5.3 Update Router Software

All manufacturers of Wi-Fi routers and other networking devices always release new software patches and software updates. Those updates are developed to remove any bug or vulnerability in the software. In a wireless network, you should always make sure that your routers as well as other networking devices are updated regularly.

It is highly recommended to check for any new updates in the administration interface of the router and download to install the new patches or versions of the software. This will prevent your wireless network from any cyber threat. Many routers update automatically, if you set the configuration to automatic update. This will prevent from regular checking for the software updates.

9.5.4 Stronger Encryption Algorithms

Encryption is the method to scramble the data and communication messages into fixed codes so that the hackers are not able to decode those messages. Wireless network routers support different types of encryption algorithms, which make them secure according to their features and capabilities. Among such encryption algorithms, WEP, WPA, WPA2, and WPA3 are a few important algorithms that are supported by the modern wireless routers.

To make your wireless network's security stronger, use the latest encryption method such as WPA2 or WPA3 so that your network remains secure from any attack on data integrity.

9.5.5 MAC Address Filtering

MAC address filtering is a process in which Wi-Fi router checks and verifies the MAC address of the device that sends connection request whether to allow it to connect or not. This task is normally done manually to add the MACs of the devices that you want to allow connecting to the wireless network. By doing this, your Wi-Fi router will not allow any device to connect other than the devices whose MAC addresses are already added on the allowed list.

In Linksys router, you can enable wireless MAC filter feature on the **Wireless MAC Filter** tab of the **Wireless** configuration menu as shown in Figure 9.11. To modify the MAC address in the list, click the **Edit MAC Filter List** button and make the desired changes on the list.

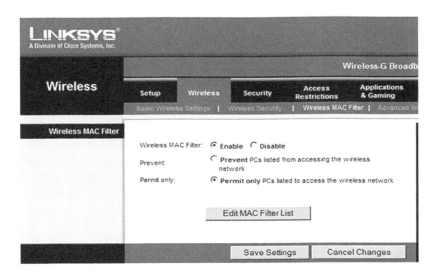

FIGURE 9.11 MAC address filtering.

9.6 USEFUL TIPS ON SAFE USE OF WIRELESS NETWORK

Wireless network is more vulnerable as compared to the other wired networks; so, it is highly recommended to follow the standard and industry guidelines while using the wireless networks either at home or at office.

Many security experts, standards' organizations, and regulators agree upon the following main tips for using the wireless network securely:

- Always change the default settings of your router and other networking devices.
- Use very strong admin and passcode passwords that are longer and include capital letters, lowercase letters, numbers, and symbols.
- Always keep your wireless router in stealth mode so that your router does not broadcast the SSID on the air interface.
- The SSID should be longer and more robust to maintain high security.
- Turn on strong encryption mechanism like WPA2 or more advanced algorithms, such as Advanced Encryption Standard (AES).
- Disable the Wi-Fi Protected Setup (WPS) feature.
- Always keep the Universal Plug N Play (uPnP) feature disabled.
- Always configure manual MAC address binding with Internet connection on your router so that no other device can connect to your network.
- Disable the auto-connection feature on all your network and computer devices so that they don't connect to the routers of the neighbors and insecure hotspots.
- Always search for the rogue routers (APs) on your network coverage area. If you find rogue AP, remove it and take the security steps to avoid such things in the future.
- Always use security firewalls on your network so that it can block any external threat.
- Use static IPs for the devices that you use. This is a bit cumbersome to configure static IPs manually, but offer great security.
- Turn off the network elements, if not in use for longer periods.
- Change the default IP address of your router and configure other IP address.
- Never enable the remote administrator access to your router, this will increase the risk of cyberattacks on your router.
- The software on your router and other nodes should be always up to date. It is a good idea to enable auto-update option on your network devices so that any new patch or software release is automatically installed.
- Always configure a separate network with limited authority for the guest users to avoid any intentional and unintentional malicious activity on the network.
- If possible, use a VPN connection for secure, private, and anonymous browsing.

- Always use the Ethernet cable to access the control panel of the wireless router and try to avoid the use of wireless connectivity to access the control panel.
- Locate your wireless router at the central location of your place so that the signals are contained within the boundaries of your place.
- Turn off the wireless router, if not in use.
- All of the above guidelines should be implemented on time without any delay. If you put today's task on tomorrow in wireless network environment, your network security is at risk.

SAMPLE QUESTIONS AND ANSWERS FOR WHAT WE HAVE LEARNED IN CHAPTER 9

Q1. Draw the IEEE 802.11 protocol stack.

A1: The protocol stack of IEEE 802.11 is shown below:

Layers

	Application
Internet	Transport
	Internet
Wireless data	MAC
ISM band radio interface	Physical

Q2. What are the main threat points of vulnerability in a wireless network?

A2: The major threat points vulnerable to security breach in a wireless network include the following:

- Bluetooth connection
- ZigBee connection
- Bluetooth Low Energy (BLE)
- Wireless access point
- Wireless network cards

Q3. Name the major data encryption and security protocols used by the wireless networks.

A3: The major data encryption and security protocols used by the wireless networks are listed below:

- Wired Equivalent Privacy (WEP)
- Wi-Fi Protected Access (WPA)
- Wi-Fi Protected Access v2 (WPA2)
- Wi-Fi Protected Access v3 (WPA3)

Q4. What is passive attack?

A4: In passive attacks, the hackers only try to intrude into the wireless network communication to steal the information about the network and passwords. They do not try to damage the digital resources or take any materialist advantage. But they take the information, which can be used for the active attacks in the future. In passive attacks, a hacker just listens to the inbound and outbound traffic of the wireless communication. The main objective of the hacker in passive attack is just to gather sensitive information, which is useful for carrying out active cyberattacks on the wireless networks.

Q5. Write about the major vulnerabilities of WPA protocol and WPA2 protocol.

A5: The major vulnerabilities of WPA protocol are summarized in the following list:

- It uses encryption RC4, which is vulnerable to DoS attacks.
- It uses the MIC value in the EAPoL message in plain text, which is easy for the hackers to attack and break.

Similarly, the main vulnerabilities of WPA2 protocol are as follows:

- The "hole196" is one of the most known vulnerabilities.
- The CCMP protocol used in WPA2 encryption mechanism is vulnerable to Time-Memory-Trade pre-computation attack.

SOURCES

Boubiche, D.E., Pathan, A.-S.K., Lloret, J., Zhou, Hong S., Amin, S.O., and Feki, M.A., "Advanced Industrial Wireless Sensor Networks and Intelligent IoT", Guest Editorial of the Special Issue of IEEE Communications Magazine, February 2018, pp. 14–15.
https://www.engineersgarage.com/Articles/Data-Link-Protocols-Computers
https://en.wikipedia.org/wiki/Wireless_security
https://www.infosec.gov.hk/english/technical/files/wireless.pdf
https://www.youtube.com/watch?v=sxJSbAG_3nQ
http://h20331.www2.hp.com/Hpsub/downloads/WWAN-Security.pdf
http://etutorials.org/Networking/Wireless+lan+security/Chapter+6.+Wireless+Vulnerabilities/
https://www.techopedia.com/2/28536/networks/wireless/top-3-wi-fi-security-vulnerabilities
http://www.valencynetworks.com/articles/cyber-attacks-device-evasions.html
https://pdfs.semanticscholar.org/cabd/a6b52dfd269e5e478ddeaa86220ef3abe4ef.pdf
https://www.watchguard.com/wgrd-blog/wpa-and-wpa2-vulnerabilities-update
https://dzone.com/articles/iot-security-challenges-and-5-effective-ways-to-ha-1
https://behrtechnologies.com/blog/6-leading-types-of-iot-wireless-tech-and-their-best-use-cases/
https://developer.ibm.com/articles/iot-top-10-iot-security-challenges/
https://ieeexplore.ieee.org/document/7522219
https://www.researchgate.net/publication/326579980_Security_in_Internet_of_Things_Issues_Challenges_and_Solutions
https://www.researchgate.net/publication/326579980_Security_in_Internet_of_Things_Issues_Challenges_and_Solutions#pf9

https://kb.iu.edu/d/avat

https://www.techradar.com/news/networking/wi-fi/five-tips-for-a-secure-wireless-network-1161225

https://heimdalsecurity.com/blog/home-wireless-network-security/

https://www.lifewire.com/wireless-home-network-security-tips-818355

https://www.kaspersky.com/resource-center/preemptive-safety/wireless-network-security-simple-tips

https://www.makeuseof.com/tag/7-tips-make-wireless-network-secure/

Pathan, A.,-S.K., *Securing Cyber-Physical Systems.* ISBN: 9781498700986, CRC Press, Taylor & Francis Group, Boca Raton, FL, 2015.

Secure Online Shopping and Internet Browsing

10

10.1 INTRODUCTION

Total global sales through e-commerce amounted to as much as US$2.84 trillion in 2018, according to the Statista information. It is expected to cross the US$4.48 trillion mark by 2021. The total number of online buyers was about 1.66 billion people in 2017. The increase in the online shopping (Figure 10.1) is gigantic, and it will keep growing for many years to come.

Meanwhile, the number of Internet users has increased tremendously across the globe. There are more than 4.4 billion active users of the Internet globally. The number of social media users is about 3.5 billion people. With this huge digital population of the world, the volume of both risk and opportunity has increased tremendously. The biggest risk for this huge digital population is cybercrime.

It is very important to note that cybercriminals are highly creative, technically sound, and cunning. They exploit every aspect of an online user including the way he/she uses the Internet, types of tools, financial credentials, personal information, and many others things.

FIGURE 10.1 Secure shopping.

According to the FBI Internet Crime Complaint Center, more than 300 thousand complaints were received in 2017 regarding the online crimes. The total cost of those criminal activities amounted to about US$1.4 billion to the complainants in 2017 in the United States only.

So, it is highly recommended to use all necessary measures related to the online shopping and Internet browsing to keep the digital criminals at bay.

The main points that are normally exploited by the cybercriminals include the following:

- Introduction of poisonous links by using the black-hat search engine optimization (SEO)
- Malicious links and emails for phishing purpose
- Text messages and pop-up notifications
- Identity theft techniques
- Social engineering methods
- Software vulnerabilities to send virus, Trojan horse, and worms
- Operating system vulnerabilities
- Vulnerabilities in browsers
- Fake websites and offers
- Exploit your personal information that you provide
- Rogue and public access point vulnerabilities
- Use of weak passwords
- Bad password management
- And yes, your own carelessness

So, always take special care while shopping online or even browsing the Internet and follow the security guidelines to avoid any cyberattack on you. Let us now talk about the major things and activities that will help you enjoy the secure online shopping and Internet browsing.

10.2 HTTP WEBSITES

Initially, the websites used the Hypertext Transfer Protocol (HTTP) for the communication between server and client. The web browsers are normally the clients of HTTP communication, and the web server applications are the server of this communication.

HTTP is considered as insecure nowadays because of the nature of plain text communication between client and server over the Internet. The use of HTTP has been replaced by the HTTPS or HTTP (secure), which include the capabilities of encrypted communication between server and client over the communication link.

HTTP can easily be converted to the HTTPS by adding the Secure Sockets Layer (SSL) encryption protocol. We will describe the step-by-step method on how to install SSL certificate to convert the HTTP to HTTPS on the websites later in this section too. Before that, let us know about the HTTP.

Hypertext Transfer Protocol precisely HTTP is an application-layer communication protocol that is used for establishing the Internet communication between client and server. A client is any software browser that is used to send the request for accessing certain resources located on the web server. The web server has the server part of the HTTP that provides response to the requests originated from the HTTP client.

The schematic diagram of an HTTP communication is given in Figure 10.2.

The communication transactions of HTTP client/server are listed below:

- Client (web browser) sends HTTP request to server.
- Server takes the request and starts app to process HTTP request.
- Generates and sends back the required response requested by the client.
- Client receives the response to display on the browser.

In this request/response communication, the client can request for the website (HTML) page, database, JavaScript file, JPG images, or style sheets. The response of the server would include the HTML, JSON/XML, JS, JPG, or CSS files.

The different methods used for the HTTP communication include the following:

- GET Request Method
- POST Request Method
- DELETE Request Method
- HEAD Request Method

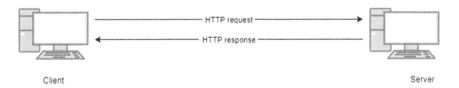

FIGURE 10.2   HTTP websites.

- OPTIONS Request Method
- HEAD Request Method

GET and POST request methods are extensively used in the HTTP server/client communication. They have their own efficient and effective merits and demerits for World Wide Web (WWW) communication.

10.2.1 Hypertext Transfer Protocol Secure (HTTPS)

Numerous data security-related problems exist in the HTTP. HTTP uses plain text data in messages over the communication link that is very easy for the hackers to intercept and know about the data. There is no transport-level encryption of the communication in HTTP.

If you use the HTTP on your website, then the data you receive and send is subject to external threats such as man-in-the-middle (MITM) attacks, eavesdropping of the communication, and credential theft. To prevent your data from hackers in the transit or during transmission, you should use the HTTPS (Figure 10.3), which is almost similar to the HTTP in terms of workflow except that the additional capability of data encryption is available during the exchange of messages.

So, HTTP is considered as unsafe protocol for any transaction that involves your personal information, financial data, or any other valuable information. That information can easily be compromised over the communication link. For secure online shopping and Internet browsing, HTTPS-based websites should be used to prevent any cybercriminal activities.

Initially, HTTPS was introduced for the financial and other critical transactions over the Internet to secure the data while transferring from one place to another one. But now, it is transitioning to become a full standard for online communication over WWW.

Google search engine has started penalizing the HTTP-based websites and rewarding the HTTPS websites. Thus, the websites are transitioning to the HTTPS very fast.

HTTPS

FIGURE 10.3   HTTPS image (conceptual image).

HTTPS uses a digital certificate signed by the certificate authority (CA). The websites purchase those certificates from the CAs for their websites. Normally, two major types of certificates are used in the HTTPS websites, which are listed below:

- Secure Socket Layer (SSL)
- Transport Layer Security (TLS)

The SSL is the most commonly used certificate for HTTPS website. The communication or transaction carried out on the websites using SSL certificates are known as HTTPS over SSL. The advanced version of SSL technology for encryption is known as TLS. TLS is more secure and advanced encryption method than the SSL technology.

Almost all new digital security certificates issued to the websites are TLS-based technology. But in the network security field, the latest digital security certificate is also referred to as SSL security certificate. The security certificate is a file of data with public and private key installed on the website for which the security certificate is purchased.

The data file is installed on the website. The website creates a security socket for the communication on the 443 port. The default port 80 used for the HTTP is not used in HTTPS. In HTTPS, certificate installation port number 443 is used, which is secure for the communication. A socket is created on the port number 443, which is fully encrypted and secure for the communication over the Internet.

The website that uses HTTPS and is secure to surf and shop can be identified by the following marks:

- The address bar shown HTTPS://
- A lock 🔒 sign appears on the address bar before website URL

To know details about the website security, click either lock 🔒 icon in Google Chrome or ⓘ symbol in Mozilla Firefox on the address bar. The details appear as shown in Figure 10.4.

FIGURE 10.4 Secure connection.

10.2.2 Installing Security Certificate on Windows IIS Server

The latest version of Windows Internet Information Service (IIS) web server is v10. You need to purchase a digital security certificate commonly known as SSL certificate from the CA and then install on your web server.

To install an SSL server on your website, take the following steps:

- Click **Start** menu, type **IIS Manager** in search bar, and open IIS manager. IIS Manager page appears.
- In the left-pane connection tree, locate and click the domain name of the web server. The **Server Home** window appears as shown in Figure 10.5.
- Double click the **Server Certificates** icon. The server certificate page with existing list of certificates appears.
- On the right pane, click the **Create Certificate Request...** link. The Request Certificate wizard with the distinguished name properties appears.
- Provide the detailed information about your website, company, or organization's detailed physical address and other information required as shown in Figure 10.6.
- Click the **Next** button when the required fields are filled with the valid information. The Cryptographic Service Provider Properties page appears.
- Fill up the name of the cryptographic service provider and the required SSL security bit length in the respective fields as in Figure 10.7.
- Click the **Next** button. The **File Name** page appears.
- Choose the file name and location where you want to save that CSR file.
- Click the **Finish** button. The CSR file will be created at the desired location.

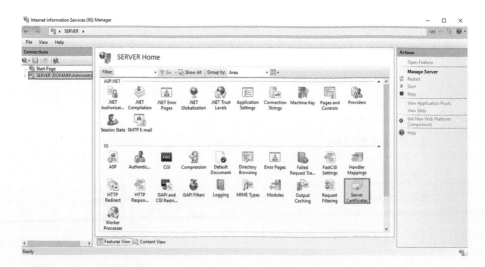

FIGURE 10.5 IIS Manager.

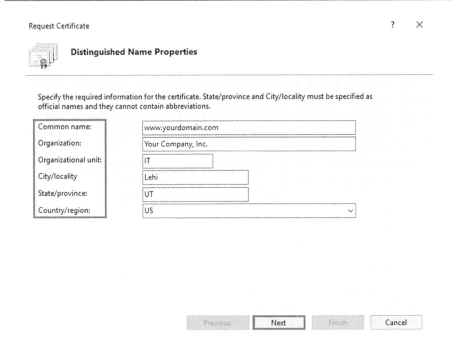

FIGURE 10.6 Distinguished name properties.

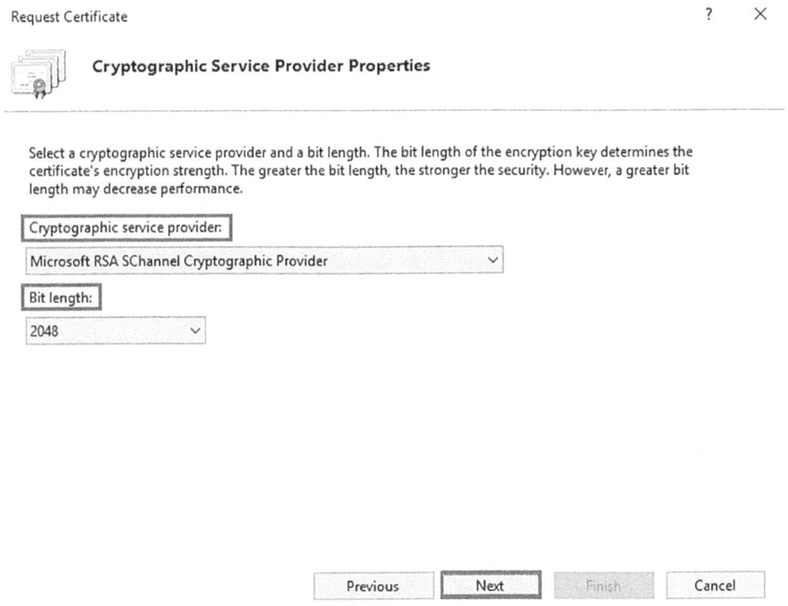

FIGURE 10.7 Cryptographic service provide properties.

- Open the CSR file and copy the entire text file, and use the copied text to place order to the CA website.
- After some verifications, the CA will send you SSL security certificate through email.
- Save the SSL security certificate on your computer.
- Go to the **Server Certificates** page again (Figure 10.8).
- Click the **Complete Certificate Request...** link in the right page (**Action**), as shown in Figure 10.8. The **Specify Certificate Authority Response** page appears (Figure 10.9).
- Enter the domain name of your website, select the hosting provider's name, and locate the certificate file response received from the CA.
- Click the OK button once you are done with entering the required information. The SSL certificate is installed on your server successfully.

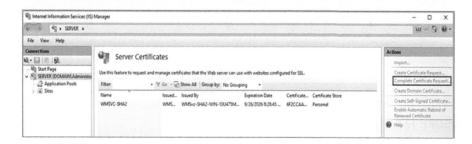

FIGURE 10.8 Server certificates.

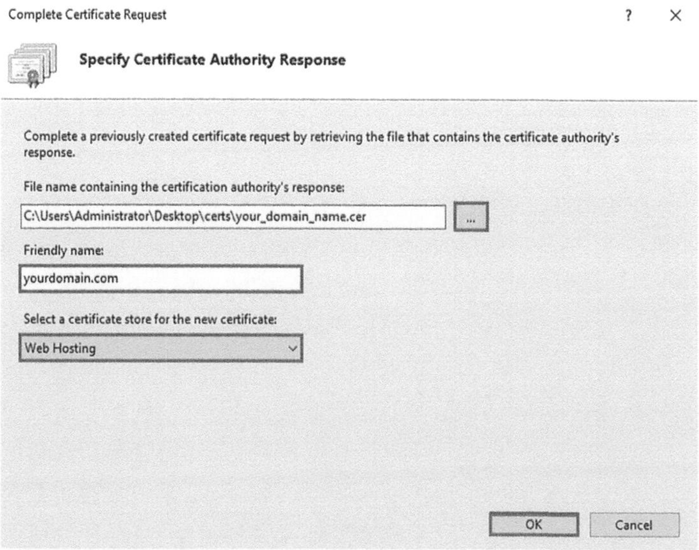

FIGURE 10.9 Specifying certificate authority response.

- Now, you need to assign the newly installed SSL to the desired website.
- On the **Internet Information Service IIS Manager** page, expand the **Server (Domain) Administration** page to locate the **Sites** option.
- Click the **Sites** link in the left page. The list of the existing websites appears.
- Click the desired website. In our example, it is **Default Web Site** option. The home page of the desired website appears as shown in Figure 10.10.
- Click the **Bindings...** under **Edit Site** option in the right pane (**Actions**). The **Site Bindings** window appears.
- Click the Add... button. The Add Site Binding window appears as shown in Figure 10.11.
- Choose **HTTPS** in the type field, the **All Assigned** option in the IP address field, and **443** in the port field.

FIGURE 10.10   Default websites.

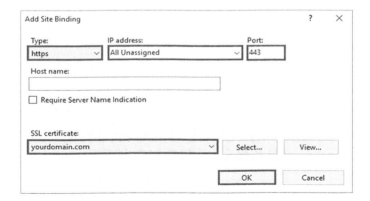

FIGURE 10.11   Add site binding.

- Select the domain name for which you want to bind the SSL certificate in **SSL Certificate** field.
- Click the OK button, when done with the data entry. Your website has been bound with the SSL certificate and you are ready to go.

You can also install multiple SSL certificates on your server and bind them with the multiple domain names of the websites by repeating the same step-by-step process as mentioned above.

10.2.3 How SSL Encryption Works

The domain name bound with the desired certificate will create a socket layer of communication between the supported browsers and the website communication port number 443. The secure communication between a web browser and website through SSL communication socket takes place in the following steps:

- Browser sends the HTTP request to prove the SSL/TLS certificate targeting 443 port on the web server.
- The website server sends response with the certificate chain, which includes the primary, intermediate, and root certificates of the CA.
- All browsers have public keys and related information of all CAs.
- Compares the information with the local SSL information to verify the certificate.
- When the public key of the server is verified in terms of validity and authority, it sends its own public key to the server.
- On the basis of the public key received from the browser and the private key of the server, an encrypted message will be created and sent out through port 443 to the browser.
- The browser decrypts the message with the help of public key.
- Thus, the communication over SSL link starts.

It is important to note that encrypted transmission of data over the Internet is becoming the fundamental requirement for safe browsing of the Internet. Any website without encryption is considered as risky for the security of your data and system.

So, always visit the websites that are secure with the SSL/TLS encryption. This will save your communication from being compromised during the course of transition on the Internet links.

10.3 SECURE ELECTRONIC TRANSACTIONS (SET)

Secure Electronic Transactions (conceptual image is in Figure 10.12) precisely SET is a comprehensive communication protocol for maintaining the full security of the online

FIGURE 10.12   Secure Electronic Transactions (SET) – conceptual image.

payments and financial transactions. As we discussed in the previous topic, the websites that support the encrypted communication over the Internet are very important for the secure browsing of the Internet. Similarly, SET protocol is very critical for the secure and reliable transactions of financial payments.

This protocol was initially adopted by MasterCard and VISA card in 1996. The development of this protocol was accomplished under a consortium named as Secure Electronic Transaction Consortium or SET Consortium. The other companies that joined this project at that time were Netscape, IBM, GTE, Microsoft, and a few others.

The main purpose of developing a new technology for the secure payment was to make sure that the valuable information is not shared with the undesired stakeholders of the transactions and smooth tracing of the transaction can also be done easily. This protocol helps all parties including the buyer, merchant, bank merchant, payment gateway, and any other authority that is involved in the payment process.

The secure, reliable, and stress-free online transactions of your e-commerce orders or any other electronic payment for any other purpose should be performed through this protocol. If you choose your transactions with the company that uses this protocol, you must feel secure and relaxed in terms of your online transaction security.

10.3.1 What Is SET Transaction Flow?

SET is a consolidated online financial transaction protocol to carry out the secure online transactions such as online shopping, online bill payment, money transfer, and others. As we know, there is always a risk of hackers to exploit your online activities and inflict you with substantial financial losses. This secure technology for online transaction will help you make your online experience so good.

The technical flow of SET transactions is shown in Figure 10.13.

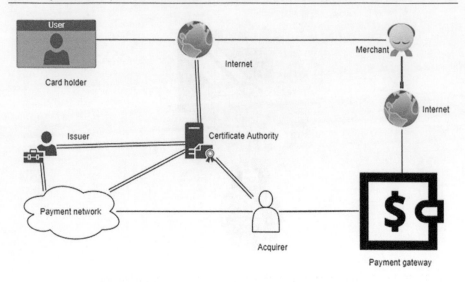

FIGURE 10.13   SET transaction flow.

This protocol requires a digital signature for even the online buyer or cardholder. It uses the dual-signature technology to make your online transactions fully secure, traceable, and reliable. There are nine basic steps that accomplish a secure transaction over the Internet. The steps of activities that take place during the course of an electronic transition are mentioned below:

- The customer browses the Internet and chooses the desired product to purchase.
- The customer places the order to merchant. That order consists of two parts of information: (1) purchase order (PO) information, which is meant for the merchant, and (2) payment information (PI) or card information (CI), which is meant for the merchant's bank only.
- When the second part of the PO is received by the merchant's bank, it forwards that information to the payment authorization issuing authority.
- The card issuer sends the authorization information to the merchant's bank.
- Now, the merchant bank sends the authorized PI to the merchant.
- The merchant completes the order after receiving the confirmed information from the bank and sends the confirmation note to the customer for his/her purchase.
- The merchant takes the payment transaction information from his/her bank.
- The card issuer sends the invoice for the purchase to the cardholder or customer.

Thus, the secure and safe transaction of online shopping completes in the abovementioned nine steps. You can also do the other online transactions by using this protocol. This protocol does not allow the merchant to know details about the customer credit card and other private information. It is directly sent to the bank. The PO details are not sent to the bank because the bank is not supposed to know about the purchased products of the company. Still, the traceable binding codes are maintained so that transactions can be traced and settled in case of any dispute or litigation.

10.3.2 Main Features of SET Technology

SET technology was developed to offer the full security to the valuable data, personal information, and bank authorization. The main features of SET protocol are listed below:

- Maintains high level of personal information confidentiality
- Maintains high-level data integrity
- Incorporates merchant authorization
- Incorporates the authentication of cardholder's account
- Uses dual-signature mechanism for authentication and authorization
- Uses separate message digest (MD) algorithms for order information and PI
- Powered by a large number of financial organizations

For maintaining your online transactions secure, always use the services of those merchants and other stakeholders that implement the SET technology in their backend payment systems. This will make your online transactions more secure and safe.

10.3.3 Key Stakeholders of SET Protocol

The SET technology involves the following stakeholders during the course of online order processing and digital financial transactions (Figure 10.14).

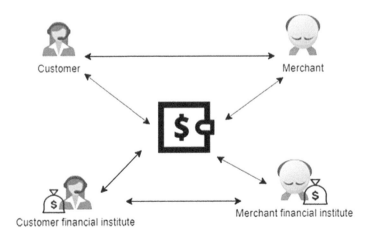

FIGURE 10.14   Key stakeholders of SET protocol.

- Customer or cardholder
- Seller or merchant
- Card issuing authority
- Merchant bank or acquirer
- Electronic payment gateways
- Certification authorities (CAs)

The SET technology uses Microsoft's Secure Transaction Technology (STT) in combination with the Netscape's SSL, which makes your online transactions so secure and you enjoy full freedom of doing your online purchases without any worry.

So, make sure you take note of SET technologies when you do any kind of online financial transactions including online shopping.

10.4 WEB FRAUD DETECTION SYSTEMS

The market size of global e-commerce business is continuously increasing worldwide. According to the latest forecasts, the total revenue of retail e-commerce sales is expected to cross US$4.5 trillion by 2021. The risk of lost revenue on e-commerce is also increasing consistently due to the sophisticated approaches applied by the hackers to walk away with the online transactions.

The latest statistics suggest that the average lost e-commerce revenue in the United States is just below 1% of the total e-commerce market value. Can you imagine how much web frauds account for in the US for market only? The total volume of e-commerce was about US $504.6 billion, according to the Statista information. If we calculate 1% of this amount, it will be around US$5 that is lost due to the web frauds (Figure 10.15) and other cybercrimes.

Numerous security measures have been taken to prevent and reduce these web losses. Among such online security measures, web fraud detection system (WFDS) is very important to note. WFDS is required for all companies that accept the credit card and bank cards for the online transactions. This system is designed to avert the fraudulent transactions commonly referred to as Card Not Present (CNP) transactions.

FIGURE 10.15   Web fraud detection systems (concept).

10.4.1 What Is a Card Not Present Transaction?

"Card Not Present" is a fraudulent transaction, which is performed by the cybercriminals who have got the access to the information of the compromised credit card, such as card number, security code (three digits), and personal information of the cardholder. By using that information, a cybercriminal initiates an unauthorized transaction to purchase some goods.

In this transaction, the genuine owner of the credit card is completely unaware about that fraudulent transaction until the transaction is completed successfully. To avert these kinds of web frauds, web fraud detections and web fraud prevention systems are normally used. The CNP frauds are committed through multiple ways of known cyber methods as listed below:

- Skimming of the credit card
- Phishing technique of transaction
- Carding activity

10.4.2 Workflow of Web Fraud Detection System

WFDS is a software-based system, which uses the latest technologies such as artificial intelligence and the latest scoring methodologies to find out the authenticity of the transaction. The workflow of this system is shown in Figure 10.16.

The main focus of this system remains of the origination of the account, payment frauds, and takeover of the account. The systems dealing with the account takeover and the origination of the account mainly try to root out the transactions that initiate from the suspicious users, who pose themselves as the genuine users. The fraud detection module of the system mainly focuses on checking whether the transactions are being performed with the stolen card or information.

The workflow of the WFDS is based on three major stages. First, the WFDS software collects the data of the web transaction. This information includes the user ID, location of the user, user authentication, user behavior, and other information. This information is later compared with the data attributes with the help of certain algorithms that use artificial intelligence and other technologies.

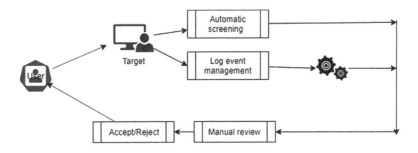

FIGURE 10.16 Workflow of WFDS.

In the third stage, if the transaction is found valid based on the predefined algorithmic results, it is allowed to go ahead; otherwise, the transaction is suspected by the system and an alert is generated to reverse or stop the transaction as malicious or faulty transaction.

10.4.3 What Algorithms Are Used in WFDS?

WFDS is a software system, which uses the latest software technologies for detecting the fraudulent transaction. It uses the scoring system, which scores the transactions with the help of some algorithms known as the scoring algorithms. The main scoring algorithms used by the WFDSs are listed below:

- Predictive Behavioral Scoring Model
- Rule-Based Scoring Model
- Hybrid Scoring Model

These scoring methods use the user behavior, use patterns, or both pattern and behavior collectively to assess the web transactions.

This system is very important from the online merchants' perspective to increase their credibility and customer satisfaction. All kinds of online businesses including small, medium and large businesses should strictly follow these services to avoid any cyber frauds inflicted on the online buyers.

There are many SaaS (Software as a Service) companies that offer the services of WFDS to the small and medium-sized businesses that cannot afford to develop their own platform. The large organizations can have one developed on premises or they can use the web-based services of WFDS service providers available in the marketplace.

As far as the user perspective is concerned, they should choose the companies for their online purchases, which use the latest web transaction detection systems to provide great user experience to their online customers.

10.5 BROWSER CACHE CLEARING

Normally, all types of browsers cache the information about the browsing history, browsing information like forms, data, and other information that you browse through. This is done to save the repetitive downloading time, but this is also associated with some online security risks related to the breach of privacy.

So, it is good idea to clear browsing cache (Figure 10.17) before performing any online financial transactions. The clearing of browser cache helps you improve your privacy and find the fresh data online. The history of the browsing data on a shared computer exposes your privacy and browsing habits, if not cleared.

Similarly, the browsers save certain forms and data retrieved from the online sources. Those forms and offline data are saved in the browser's cache memory load when you visit the related URLs. You can also load those resources offline, if saved for that purpose.

FIGURE 10.17   Browser cache clearing (conceptual image).

The step-by-step procedures for clearing the browser cache of a few popular web browsers are described in the following sections.

10.5.1 Google Chrome

To clear the cache of Google Chrome browser, take the following steps:

- Run the Google Chrome browser.
- Click the ⬚ symbol located at the right corner of the screen. The list of the options appears as in Figure 10.18.
- Click the **Settings** option from the list. The **Setting** page appears.
- Scroll down to the **Advanced** option and click it.
- **Privacy and Security** category appears as shown in Figure 10.19.

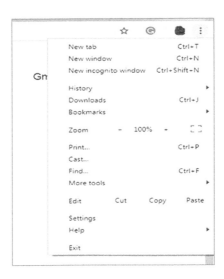

FIGURE 10.18   Google Chrome browser options.

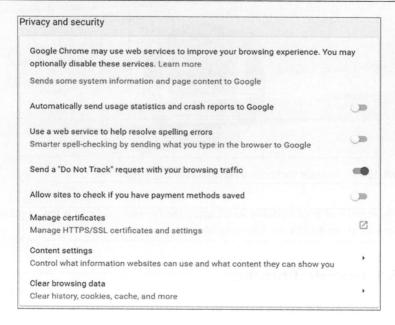

Privacy and security

Google Chrome may use web services to improve your browsing experience. You may optionally disable these services. Learn more
Sends some system information and page content to Google

Automatically send usage statistics and crash reports to Google

Use a web service to help resolve spelling errors
Smarter spell-checking by sending what you type in the browser to Google

Send a "Do Not Track" request with your browsing traffic

Allow sites to check if you have payment methods saved

Manage certificates
Manage HTTPS/SSL certificates and settings

Content settings
Control what information websites can use and what content they can show you

Clear browsing data
Clear history, cookies, cache, and more

FIGURE 10.19   Privacy and security options.

- Scroll down and click to the **Clear browsing data** option. The **Clear Browsing Data** window (Figures 10.20 and 10.21) with different options such as browsing history, cookies and other site data, and cached images and files appears.

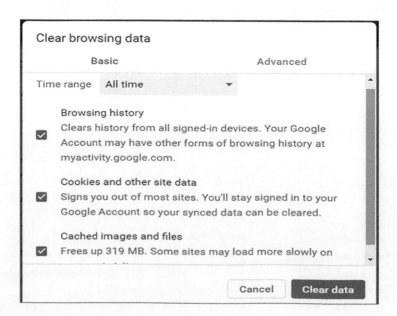

Clear browsing data

Basic   Advanced

Time range   All time

Browsing history
Clears history from all signed-in devices. Your Google Account may have other forms of browsing history at myactivity.google.com.

Cookies and other site data
Signs you out of most sites. You'll stay signed in to your Google Account so your synced data can be cleared.

Cached images and files
Frees up 319 MB. Some sites may load more slowly on

Cancel   Clear data

FIGURE 10.20   Clear browsing data options.

FIGURE 10.21   Time range.

- Select the checkbox against the **Cached images and files** option.
- Click the All Time dropdown arrow to display time range options. The drop-down time options appear as shown in Figure 10.21.
- Choose the desired time range from the dropdown options.
- Click the **Advanced** tab to display more options regarding the browsing history of the synch devices, such as mobile and tablets or any other device.
- Click the **Clear Data** button at the bottom of the window. The cached images and files are cleared successfully on Google Chrome browser.

10.5.2 Mozilla Firefox

To clear cached content on the Mozilla Firefox, take the following steps:

- Run Mozilla Firefox browser.
- Click the ≡ menu option. The list of available options appears (Figure 10.22).
- Click ✿ symbol from the list. The Preference page of Mozilla Firefox appears as shown in Figure 10.23.
- Click the **Privacy & Security** link in the left pane. The **Privacy & Security** page appears.

FIGURE 10.22   Available options.

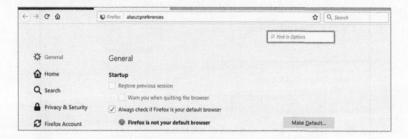

FIGURE 10.23   Preferences in Mozilla Firefox browser.

- Scroll down to the **Cookies & Site Data** section. Different options regarding the cached content, cookies, and browsing history appear as shown in Figure 10.24.
- Click the **Manage Data…** option. The **Clear Data** window (Figure 10.25) will appear.
- Select the **Cached Web Content** checkbox.

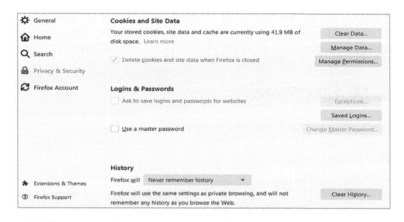

FIGURE 10.24   Cookies and site data option.

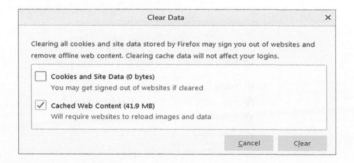

FIGURE 10.25   Clear data option.

- Unselect the **Cookies and Site Data** checkbox.
- Click the **Clear** button, once done with the selection. The cached data will be cleared successfully.

10.5.3 Internet Explorer

To clear the cached content in the Internet Explorer, take the following steps:

- Run the **Internet Explorer** browser.
- Click the **Tools** dropdown arrow. The list of the options appears.
- Select the **Internet Options** from the list. The **Internet Options** window with multiple tabs of options appears as shown in Figure 10.26.
- Click the **General** tab.
- Click the **Delete...** button. The **Delete Browsing History** page (Figure 10.27) with multiple options for clearing data on the Internet Explorer browser appears.
- Select the Temporary Internet Files checkbox.
- Unselect the Preserve Favorite Website Data checkbox.
- Click the **Delete** button, once done with your desired selection. The cashed data will be deleted from the Internet Explorer successfully.

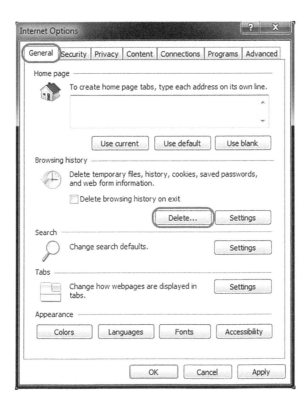

FIGURE 10.26   Internet options for Internet Explorer browser.

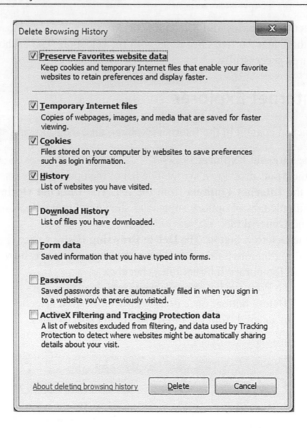

FIGURE 10.27   Delete browsing history.

10.6 FREQUENT PASSWORD CHANGES

The effective password management is very fundamental in maintaining high level of security for online browsing and shopping. The frequent change of the passwords is one of the important components of effective password management (Figure 10.28 for conceptual image).

We know that our passwords are always under threat from the cybercriminals and hackers. They use computer processing power to break our passwords. In such situations, to keep the hackers at bay, frequent change of the passwords helps improve the security of your online accounts related to shopping, banking, and others.

The standard recommendations regarding the password changes are 1–3 months. Normally, password change after 2 months is good for online shopping security. If you change your password after every 2 or 3 months, it is more convenient for you to manage the password easily.

According to the Better Business Bureau (BBB) recommendations, the account passwords must be changed after every month (30 days) for maintaining better security

FIGURE 10.28   Frequent password changes (conceptual image).

of the online accounts and secure shopping. Some experts recommend 2- month or 60-day time period after that the passwords should be changed. But frequent change of passwords is considered as a good thing in maintain good security for online shopping as well as for the Internet browsing purposes.

You can use manual as well as automatic password management options. In manual password management, you change the password and write down in your personal diary. The personal diary should be kept at very secure and locked place to avoid any leakage of the password.

In the present-day online web environment, there are many password management tools (we discussed password manager in Chapter 7 before) that can be used for the efficient management of your password. By using those password management tools, you can create strong passwords and manage all passwords through one single master password. But it has its own drawbacks too. In the scenario of using the password management tools, you need to memorize the master password. If you forget the master password, then you will go out of control of your other passwords that you save in the password management tools.

If you change your passwords even more frequently, for instance, within a few days, it can adversely affect your online security due to the following reasons:

- More chances of forgetting your passwords
- You many go out of the memorable combinations of the passwords
- Difficult to manage the wide range of passwords
- Chances of repetitive combinations, which are more guessable
- Your password pattern may be exposed

Only changing your passwords will not produce the desired results pertaining to your online shopping or Internet browsing, if those passwords are not as per password standards. Any weak password changed frequently will impact you adversely.

You should always choose the strongest password that has at least 14 characters that should also include the following:

- Capital and lowercase alphabetic letters
- Numeric characters
- Special symbols

So, always make a habit of changing your account passwords in between 30 and 60 days. This will offer you good security for online shopping as well as Internet browsing.

Other than the regular password changes as per company security policy or as recommended by the authorities dealing with the cybersecurity, you should also make sure to change the passwords in the following conditions:

- In case of any suspected activities on your account
- Sudden increase in the spam emails in your accounts
- If concerned company discloses that some security breaches have occurred
- If you find any malware, virus, or any other malicious activity on your computer, mobile, or any other device
- If you shared account password with someone else for a certain period, you should change the password after that period of time
- After you logged into any public insecure network such as public hotspots at airports, railway stations, or any other public place

In a nutshell, change your passwords frequently as recommended by the industry experts and standard authorities. And always, be smart and creative while creating stronger passwords.

10.7 UPDATING OS

Cybercriminals and hackers are always in search for the vulnerabilities in the operating systems (Figure 10.29) and other software applications. The first thing the hackers try to find vulnerabilities in is operating system, because a particular operating system is used by a huge number of devices across the globe. This huge user base makes the operating systems the first target of attack from the hackers.

Operating systems are normally developed with the help of a huge team of experts, developers, programmers, managers, and quality assurance engineers. All operating systems go through vigorous testing and quality checks, but despite all that, vulnerabilities emerge on a regular basis when the operating system is released in the real world for use.

The hackers continuously strive to break the operating system security by exploiting the vulnerabilities. Meanwhile, the security experts related to the OS development team continuously monitor the performance and security of the operating system and also get feedback from the customers on a regular basis.

If they find any kinds of bug or vulnerability, they immediately develop the patch to heal that vulnerability. Those new software patches are known as the OS updates. It is highly recommended to download those updates and install on the operating system so that known vulnerabilities can be patched and healed.

For making your online shopping and Internet browsing experience safe, secure, and free of worries, always keep your operating system up to date by downloading and installing the latest updates released by the concerned teams of operating systems.

Let us now talk about the procedure to update the most commonly used operating systems.

FIGURE 10.29   Various OSs.

10.7.1 Updating Windows 10

Windows 10 is the latest version of the Microsoft operating system (at the time of writing this book), which was released in July 2015. Many updates have already been released for this operating system, and numerous new releases are released time to time.

You can set automated updates for Windows 10, if you like. To download and install the manual update of the Windows 10 operating system, take the following steps:

- Open the **Settings** by pressing "**Windows + I**" shortcut key. Windows settings page appears.
- Choose the **Update & Security** option. More options appear.
- Choose **Windows Update** option. The Windows Update page appears as shown in Figure 10.30.

FIGURE 10.30   Windows update.

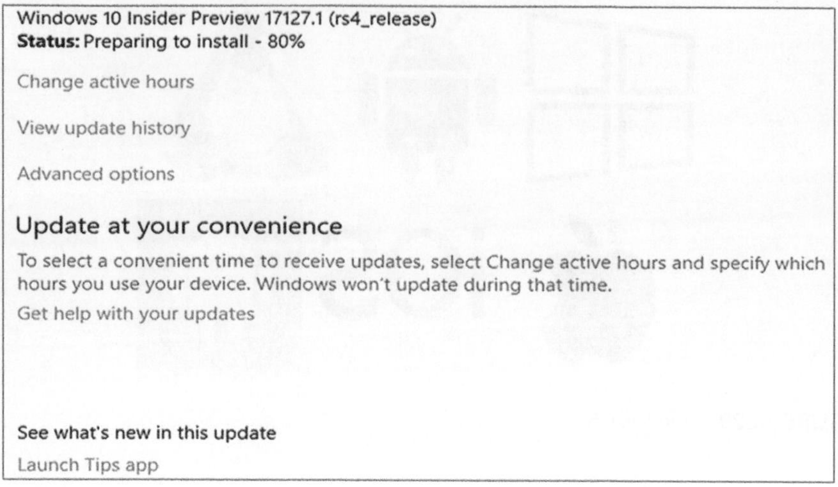

Windows 10 Insider Preview 17127.1 (rs4_release)
Status: Preparing to install - 80%

Change active hours

View update history

Advanced options

Update at your convenience

To select a convenient time to receive updates, select Change active hours and specify which hours you use your device. Windows won't update during that time.

Get help with your updates

See what's new in this update

Launch Tips app

FIGURE 10.31 Update download.

- Click the **Check for updates** button to check for new updates. The new updates are checked and found, if the updates are available online.
- The Important Updates Are Available message appears.
- Click the message to download the updates (Figure 10.31).
- The available updates start downloading and installing on your computer, as shown in the above snapshot.
- You will be prompted to restart your computer once the installations have been downloaded.
- Click the **Restart** button and wait for the updates to take effect. It may take many minutes to install the updates depending on the total size of the update.
- Have patience till all the updates are installed and computer restarts after many minutes.
- Windows 10 operating system is updated successfully.

Note: Like other versions of the Windows operating system, Windows 10 also takes many minutes to update the operating system.

10.7.2 Updating Windows 7

Windows 7 has been one of the most popular operating systems in recent years. Still this operating system is used by many people worldwide.

To update Windows 7 operating system, take the following steps:

- Click the ⊞ **Start** menu.
- Choose the **Control Panel** option. The list of control panel options appears (Figure 10.32).

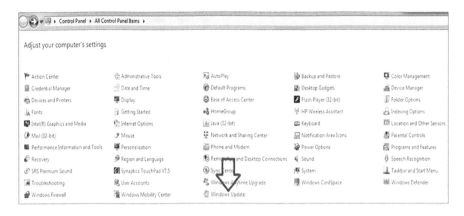

FIGURE 10.32   Control panel list.

- Click the Windows Update link as shown in Figure 10.32.
- The **Windows Update** page appears.
- Click the **Check for Updates** button as shown in Figure 10.33. The windows starts checking for the available updates.
- Windows starts checking for the available windows updates. A list of all available Windows updates will be displayed as shown in Figure 10.33.
- The available updates are divided into two parts – important updates and optional updates. Important updates very critical for the security of the computer, while the optional updates are less critical (Figure 10.34).
- Click the **Install Updates** button. The Windows updates start installing.
- Once the updates are installed, the system prompts for **Restart** to take the updates effect.
- Click the **Restart** button, if you want the newly updates take effect immediately.
- It will take many minutes to restart. Be patient until the system restarts.
- Your Windows updates are installed successfully.

FIGURE 10.33   Checking for updates.

FIGURE 10.34   Different types of Windows updates.

10.8 UPDATING APPS

We live in the world of software nowadays. Every computer as well as mobile device runs numerous applications to perform different functions and activities on your device. All those applications work on the foundation of firm ware and operating system. Any vulnerability in the software applications can also help the hackers to unleash the cyberattack on the devices.

Many applications are available for computers and mobile devices. Those applications are based on the operating systems, for example, windows applications, computer applications, mobile applications, and many others.

In this section, we will focus on the updating of the computer applications (Figure 10.35). The mobile application updates will be dealt in Chapter 11. Examples of computer applications include the following:

- Microsoft Skype
- Email Application
- Adobe Acrobat
- Java Applications
- Adobe Flash

Many applications are designed to search for the updates automatically and prompt the user about that update to download. But in many cases, the third-party applications do not update automatically on the computers. Updating those applications is cumbersome activity. You need to go to the products or their websites individually and search for the updates and download to install on your computer.

In many cases, some applications are not used for longer periods. Those applications lie without any updates; such applications can be the suitable target for the hackers to exploit the vulnerabilities and stage a cyberattack on the systems.

FIGURE 10.35 Updating apps – conceptual image.

10.8.1 Updating Google Chrome Application

To update Google Chrome, take the following steps:

- Open the **Google Chrome** application.
- Click the ⋮ symbol to customize and control Chrome. The list of available options appears (Figure 10.36).

FIGURE 10.36 Available options in Chrome.

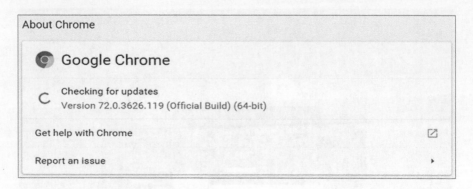

FIGURE 10.37   About Chrome.

- Click the **Help** option. More options appear.
- Choose the **About Google Chrome** option. The **About Chrome** page appears, as shown in Figure 10.37.
- Google Chrome automatically starts checking for updates as shown in Figure 10.37.
- Click the **Install** option, if new updates are found. Your browser is up to date now.

Similarly, applications such as Adobe Flash, Acrobat, or any other application can be updated through the **About** or the **Help** options on the settings of the applications. If you want to make your life easy, you can choose any good application updater software available in the market.

10.8.2 Important Computer Application Updaters

A few very important computer application updater software tools are listed below:

- Patch My PC Updater Tool
- Update Notifier Tool
- FileHippo Update Checker Tool
- AppFresh Update Checker Tool
- OutDateFighter Update Checker Tool

You can get some of those applications for free and some charge a little fee for using the services. These applications scan your entire computer and check if any application is outdated. If it finds any update for any applications, it alerts for the same. You can configure them to automatically search and download the updates of the applications, if available online.

10.9 USEFUL TIPS ON SAFE BROWSING AND ONLINE SHOPPING

There are certain useful tips and guidelines for safe browsing and online shopping, which are listed below (Figure 10.38):

- Always use your personal data carefully and professionally.
- Avoid to click unsolicited links and promotions.
- Never use public networks for shopping purposes.
- Always use secure connection with firewall enabled.
- Always keep your privacy settings open/active.
- Think twice before you download any software.
- Avoid freebies and tempting offers.
- Always use strong passwords.
- Change your passwords within 60 or 90 days.
- Always visit the secure websites that use HTTPS.
- Always shop from the trusted websites.
- Keep your OS and applications up to date.
- Clear your browser cache and browsing history regularly.
- Keep antivirus and anti-spyware up to date.
- Check you online shopping and bank statements regularly.
- Don't follow the links in the phishing emails.
- Try to use blurring software tools that blur your personal information while shopping.
- Mobile apps for trusted merchants are better for shopping as compared to the online shopping through browser.
- Try to use digital wallets rather than credit or debit cards.
- Try to pay through gift vouchers and other such prepaid cards for shopping.
- Check the credibility of the merchant.
- Send complaints immediately, if you find any suspicious activity on your account.

Helpful tips

FIGURE 10.38   Useful tips on safe browsing and online shopping (conceptual icon).

- Read delivery and return policy of the merchant carefully.
- Read privacy statements carefully.
- Maintain a record of your online purchases.
- Last but not the least, use your common sense always!

You should be aware of the fact that the online shoppers fall victim to cyberattacks and online web crimes due to careless use of credit cards, personal information, and using the faulty websites and fraudulent links.

If you follow these guidelines carefully, you would be able to save you from online frauds, and your financial information from being compromised online. Online research would be very much helpful for anything that you are not sure about. You should use search engines to know about any particular matter that you are not clear about.

SAMPLE QUESTIONS AND ANSWERS FOR WHAT WE HAVE LEARNED IN CHAPTER 10

Q1. What are the main points that are normally exploited by the cybercriminals?

A1: The main points that are normally exploited by the cybercriminals include the following:

- Introduction of poisonous links by using the black SEO
- Malicious links and emails for phishing purpose
- Text messages and popup notifications
- Identity theft techniques
- Social engineering methods
- Software vulnerabilities to send virus, Trojan horse, and worms
- Operating system vulnerabilities
- Vulnerabilities in browsers
- Fake websites and offers
- Exploit your personal information that you provide
- Rogue and public access point vulnerabilities
- Use of weak passwords
- Bad password management
- And yes, your own carelessness

Q2. What is HTTP?

A2: Hypertext Transfer Protocol precisely HTTP is an application-layer communication protocol that is used for establishing the Internet communication between client and server. A client is any software browser that is used to send the request for accessing certain resources located on the web server. The web server has the sever part of the HTTP that provides response to the requests originated from the HTTP client.

Q3. What is HTTPS?

A3: HTTPS is the secure version of HTTP. HTTPS uses a digital certificate signed by the certificate authority (CA). The websites purchase those certificates from the CAs for their websites. Normally, two major types of certificates are used in the HTTPS websites, which are listed below:

- Secure Socket Layer (SSL)
- Transport Layer Security (TLS)

Q4. What is SET?

A4: Secure Electronic Transactions, precisely SET is a comprehensive communication protocol for maintaining the full security of the online payments and financial transactions.

Q5. What are the main scoring algorithms used by Web Fraud Detection System (WFDS)?

A5: The main scoring algorithms used by the WFDS are as follows:

- Predictive Behavioral Scoring Model
- Rule-Based Scoring Model
- Hybrid Scoring Model

SOURCES

https://www.statista.com/topics/871/online-shopping/
https://www.statista.com/statistics/617136/digital-population-worldwide/
https://www.instantssl.com/compare-tsl-ssl-certificates
https://www.w3schools.com/tags/ref_httpmethods.asp
https://www.w3schools.com/whatis/whatis_http.asp
https://www.howtogeek.com/181767/htg-explains-what-is-https-and-why-should-i-care/
https://www.technorms.com/891/what-is-https-protocol-why-you-should-use-it-whenever-possible
https://www.digicert.com/csr-creation-ssl-installation-iis-10.htm#ssl_certificate_install
https://en.wikipedia.org/wiki/Secure_Electronic_Transaction
https://www.geeksforgeeks.org/secure-electronic-transaction-set-protocol/
https://searchfinancialsecurity.techtarget.com/definition/Secure-Electronic-Transaction
https://www.statista.com/statistics/272391/us-retail-e-commerce-sales-forecast/
https://searchsecurity.techtarget.com/feature/Introduction-to-Web-fraud-detection-systems
http://gotowebsecurity.com/web-fraud-detection/
https://www.disruptiveadvertising.com/ppc/ecommerce/2018-ecommerce-statistics/
https://searchsecurity.techtarget.com/feature/Choosing-the-best-web-fraud-detection-system-for-your-company
https://searchsecurity.techtarget.com/definition/card-not-present-fraud-card-not-present-transaction
https://blog.lastpass.com/2018/08/often-change-password.html/
https://carleton.ca/its/2017/change-your-password-regularly/

https://www.lifewire.com/free-software-updater-programs-2625200
https://lifehacker.com/five-best-software-update-tools-5384140
https://usa.kaspersky.com/resource-center/preemptive-safety/top-10-internet-safety-rules-and-what-not-to-do-online
https://www.pcmag.com/feature/364896/14-tips-for-safe-online-shopping
https://www.indoindians.com/tips-on-shopping-online-new-2/

Mobile Device Security

11

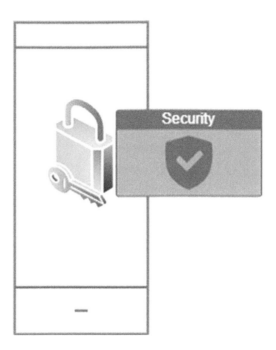

11.1 INTRODUCTION

According to the Statista information, more than 2.5 billion people will be using smart-phones in the world. The online shopping through mobile phones has already overtaken the online shopping done through the desktop computers about a year back. The online transactions through mobile accounted for about 55% in Europe. The average website visits through mobile accounted for about 63% in the United States in 2017.

These statistics clearly indicate the power of mobile phones. With the increased popularity of the mobile phones, the security issues related to mobile phones have also increased tremendously (conceptual images; Figures 11.1 and 11.2). According to the McAfee Mobile Threat Report Q1 2018, a gigantic increase of 36% in ad clicks was noticed in the first quarter of 2018 as compared to the same period in the previous year.

FIGURE 11.1   Conceptual image of mobile security.

FIGURE 11.2   Mobile security concept.

The other threats also increased substantially, such as Botnet activities (22%), spyware (23%), banking Trojans (12%), and others (2%–5%). The total market value of ad click fraud was estimated to be about US$40 billion in 2018. Thus, you can image the level of security issues on the arena of mobile market.

The major threats related to mobile security are listed below:

- Increasing menace of ad click frauds
- Increased Trojan attacks
- BotNet activities
- Crypto-mining malware attacks

- Spyware attacks
- Root malicious attacks

More than 25 million new mobile malware were detected during the year 2017. The number is increasing at an alarming level. This indicates a mobile security is going to drive the future of cybersecurity in the years to come.

11.2 IMPORTANCE OF MOBILE SECURITY

Mobile is one of the most extensively used electronic devices in the world nowadays. A huge ratio of the world population has one or more mobile phone. More than 2.5 billion people own a smartphone. A smartphone is a multipurpose device. The security of mobile device is very important because of the following things:

- It is used as your camera for recording your memorable movements with the help of photos and videos.
- It is your communication partner through voice calls, SMS, chats, video calls, emails, and other applications.
- It is used as a computer device for Internet browsing and online shopping.
- Smartphone is your guide to new area through maps and GPS (Global Positioning System).
- Mobile device is your entertainment partner.
- Mobile is used as the payment wallet for traditional shopping.
- Mobile device is used for physical access management and even for the digital access management tool.
- You store your valuable contacts and personal information.
- You use it as your temporary data storage.

If your deal with such a huge range of your day-to-day activities, then imagine how important it is to keep this device secure from any physical as well as cyber threats. You need to secure your mobile device to avoid any compromise on your privacy, data, and other valuable things you do with smartphone. So, you have to make sure that your smartphone is fully safe from any cybersecurity threats.

11.3 TYPES OF MOBILE PLATFORMS

The mobile operating platforms have evolved for over three decades now: from a very basic analogue mobile to the latest high-tech digital mobiles referred to as smartphones. Different manufacturers introduced different operating systems (OSs) for their own

FIGURE 11.3   Mobile platforms.

products from early 1990s or even before. Those OSs can be classified in the following categories (Figure 11.3):

- **(1973–1993):** Embedded OSs for function controls (1973–1993).
- **(1993–1999):** During this period, independent mobile OSs were introduced, which included Newton OS, IBM Simon, Palm OS, Symbian OS, Nokia S40 and others.
- **(2000–2010):** This period was the starting of the smartphones. The main OSs, which were launched during this period, include Windows CE, Blackberry, Maemo OS, iOS, Android, webOS, Bada OS, and Windows OS.
- **(2010 to Present):** During this period of time, there were a very few new launches of OS platforms. But during this period of time, the newer versions of Android, iOS, Windows, Blackberry, and others were launched. During this period, a huge competition between iOS, Android, Windows, and Blackberry started, which is still running. Nowadays, the main competition exists between Android and iOS in terms of market of OSs.

According to the latest global statistics about mobile platforms, Google Android is the market leader with a whopping ratio of 74.45% of all smartphones available in the marketplace, followed by the iOS phone with 22.85%. The market share of other major OSs in January 2019 is listed below:

- KaiOS with 1.1% share
- Windows with 0.3% share
- Samsung OS 0.28% share
- Others 0.41% share

In the present marketplace, Android and iOS are the top OSs worth describing here in this chapter.

Android

FIGURE 11.4   Android icon.

11.3.1 Android Operating System

Android (Figure 11.4) is the leading mobile OS in the world. It is developed by the Google Corporation in alliance with many other companies under Open Handset Alliance (OHA). This platform is based on the modified Linux kernel and released as an open source code.

Android OS is developed with the help of Java, C, C++, and other languages. The first version of Android OS was released in September 2008. The latest version of Android is named as Android 9 (Pie). It was released on August 6, 2018. Google Android is also associated with a few important proprietary services such as Google Play, Chrome, Google Mobile Services (GMS), Gmail, and Google Search.

Android OS has more than 2 billion monthly active users and the number is counting. There are more than 2.6 million Android applications on the Google Play store, which is the leading Android application platform.

The major manufacturers of Android-based mobile phones are listed below:

* Samsung Corporation (45.4%)
* Huawei Technologies (10.4%)
* Xiaomi Corporation (6.7%)
* Motorola Corporation (4.6%)
* Oppo Mobiles (4.6%)
* LG Corporation (3.6%)

11.3.2 iOS Operating System

iOS (Figure 11.5) is the second largest mobile OS after Android. The total market share of the mobile devices running on iOS is about 22.85% globally. This OS is developed by Apple Corporation. It is a proprietary system. This OS supports multiple devices of Apple Inc., such as iPhone, iPod Touch, and iPad.

The entire OS is written with different programming languages such as Objective-C, C++, C, and Swift. The first version of iOS was released on June 29, 2007. The latest stable version released by Apple Inc., is known as iOS 12.1.4, which was released in

FIGURE 11.5   iOS icon.

the first week of February 2019. The beta version of iOS 12.2 has also been released on February 19, 2019.

This OS is based on multiple layers. The main layers of this OS are listed below:

- Core operating system layer
- Core Services layer
- Media layer
- Cocoa Touch layer

Apple store has over 2 million mobile applications for iOS-based devices. This is the second largest application marketplace after Android. Apple is big brand name popular in the market of high-income people. A large number of iOS applications are paid applications as compared to other applications like Android applications or any other framework.

11.4 LOCKED BRANDED PHONES

The branded phones are normally locked and branded with a particular wireless service provider. The company that brands the mobile phone modifies the firmware to disable general features that can allow using the services of other phone operators.

The branded phones are normally offered at the low initial price and locked for a certain period with a particular operator. This way, the user is locked in with the operator. These phones normally have one SIM (Subscriber Identity Module) slot and do not allow any other company's services. The locked phones have also certain inbuilt applications of that particular service provider.

The major downside of the branded and locked phones is that the data of the user is routed through one carrier and the remote access is also enabled in certain cases. Thus, the security concerns increase while you use the branded and locked phones.

It is highly recommended to purchase the unbranded phones so that your data and personal information is not locked and compromised. You are also free to use any security applications to make your phone more secure.

11.5 ANDROID PHONE SECURITY GUIDELINES

Android OS is based on the Linux kernel, which is considered as one of the most powerful and secure platform. Owing to the power of Linux kernel, Android OS is considered as very secure platform (Figure 11.6). Another important aspect of Android OS is its open source nature, which allows a huge team of developers to keep the security of Android improving continuously.

A large number of developers continuously contribute to the improvement in the security and other features of the OS. New bugs are continuously identified and patched with the suitable fixes. A large community powered by the Google development teams is also very active in providing the quick patches to the vulnerabilities in the Android OSs.

One of the main problems with the Android OS update is that the companies that use the OS on their devices are not bound to the newly developed updates. So, the updating of the Android OS normally gets delayed.

11.5.1 Guidelines for Security

Despite the robust security capabilities, the Android phones security can be compromised by the sophisticated hackers. To make your Android phone from any security-related breaches, take care of the following guidelines:

- Always purchase the phone that runs the latest version of the Android OS.
- Data files and important information should be stored in the encrypted form. Android phones support encrypted data storage on the internal memories. You can also make arrangements to encrypt the data on the external memory like SD card.
- It is highly recommended to save your account credentials in Account Manager tools, which are very highly reliable and protected. Thus, your credentials become less prone to the security threats.
- Always download trusted Android applications on your mobile phone. Google Play store checks and verifies the secure applications before putting

FIGURE 11.6 Phone security.

on the Google Store. So always download Android applications from Google Play store.

- Always install an antivirus and anti-spyware software to safeguard your mobile device from popular cyber threats. Using the paid version of the trusted antivirus offers many other security features. So prefer to download the paid version.
- Before installing any application, read the permissions that the application needs to use your resources available on the mobile. If any application asks for more permissions that look not reasonable, don't use that application.
- Read the privacy policy of the applications that you want to run on your Android phone.
- Update all Android applications running on your mobile. Any vulnerabilities in Android applications can lead to cyberattack on your mobile phone and valuable data.
- Check and make sure that any application does not expose your information or personal data to the third party, especially to the content and service providers.
- Try to avoid using the public wireless networks or any other insecure network; this will help you remain away from any hackers and malware available on the networks.
- Check if your applications don't use the READ_LOGS permission. Normally, at the time of installation, the applications may ask for this permission. Never give this permission to the Android applications; this may lead to breach to your data, privacy, and security.
- Try to use virtual private network (VPN) connections for your Internet browsing and online shopping. This will save you from many security-related issues.
- Quick release of Android OS updates is a big problem with the vendors of the mobile phones. It is highly recommended to do some research about this issue and check how long does the company that you are interested to purchase a phone of takes to release the OS patches. Always buy Android phones of those companies that release patches very fast.
- Always lock your phone with a strong password. You can also lock your phone by using patterns, and others, but they are easier to break that strong passwords. The biometric capability offers the most robust security, if you have available this option on your phone.
- Android is the Google-powered OS system, which requires a Google account to use different services related to Google. So, always use the two-factor authentication for your mobile security. It will help you maintain your control over the accounts that are linked to your Google account.
- Always try to use different numbers for two-factor authentication. If you use the SIM that is inserted in the mobile that has also the Google account, then your SMS will go to the same number. If your mobile is lost, some immediately changes the passwords by using the two-way authentication; it will

be very difficult for you to get control over a lot of accounts on your mobile phone.

- Use the Android phone's device encryption features. You can enable the device encryption features by going to the **Settings**, then choosing the **Security** option, and finally selecting the **Encrypt Device** option on your Android phones.
- Always use the password management tools for better and consolidated security of your multiple accounts on your phone.
- Always turn off the wireless connections on your mobile when you are not using it. This will save the battery life and will increase the security of your phone.
- Never install the applications that you don't want to use for longer. If you installed any application that is not in use nowadays, remove it. This will help you increase the performance and security of your mobile phone.
- Never communicate important information through SMS text because they are not encrypted anywhere on the mobile operator's network. These messages can be accessed by the employers working with the mobile companies, and other authorities easily.
- Your voice calls can also be intercepted easily. So, always try to use the applications that transmit your communication over secure connection. For example, WhatsApp is using encrypted communication nowadays.
- Never handover your Android mobile to any unknown person.
- Install an Ad Blocker to avoid any kind of malicious activities regarding the online shopping scams.
- Always activate pop-up blocker on the browsers.
- It is recommended to disable JavaScript on your Android phone.
- Enable remote device locator so that you can easily locate your mobile phone in case you lose your mobile.
- Automatic backup should be activated to back up mobile data into the cloud. This will help you restore your data in case of any hacker attack.
- If you are willing to sale your mobile, you should have a factory reset before you handover your mobile to your client.

If you follow all the abovementioned guidelines and use your common sense while Internet browsing and online shopping through mobile, you would be able to secure your data and privacy from being compromised and exploited. Let's have a look at how to enable the biometric-based mobile screen lock protection.

11.5.2 How to Enable Biometric Security on Android Phone

Note: It is important to note that enabling biometric security on Android phones may vary a little bit depending on the manufacturers and version of the Android OS. Biometric is considered as the most reliable and robust mobile security nowadays.

To enable biometric security lock on your Android phone, take the following steps:

- Swipe your finger from top to bottom of the screen. The list of different options appears.
- Tap the ⚙ **Settings** icon with finger. The list of more options appears as shown in Figure 11.7.
- Tap the **Lock Screen and Security** option on the list. The list of security options appears.
- Scroll down to the screen lock type option.
- Tap the **Screen Lock Type** option. The list of screen lock types appears.
- Scroll down to the fingerprints option.
- Tap the **Fingerprints** option. The **Set Up Fingerprint Security** wizard appears as shown in Figure 11.8.
- Before you enable the fingerprint, you will be prompted to add any one of the three security lock options such as **Password**, **Pin,** or **Pattern**.
- Scroll down to the desired option. For instance, the **Password** option.
- Add password and confirm the same. Tap to go back to Lock Screen and Security page (Figure 11.9).
- Tap the **Fingerprint Scanner** option as shown in Figure 11.9. The fingerprint scanner page appears (Figure 11.10).

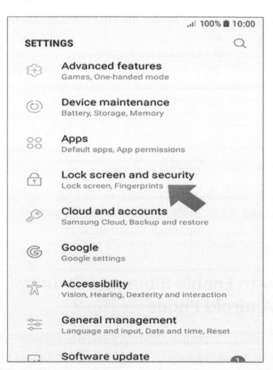

FIGURE 11.7   Settings page.

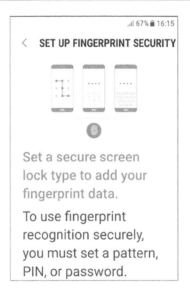

FIGURE 11.8   Set up fingerprint security.

FIGURE 11.9   Lock screen and security.

FIGURE 11.10   Fingerprint scanner option.

- Place your fingers on the home key as guided in the wizard till 100% scanning is completed.
- The fingerprint-based screen lock and password is added successfully on your Android phone.

11.6 IPHONE SECURITY GUIDELINES

Apple's iPhone (Figure 11.11) is considered as one of the secure OSs available in the marketplace. A dedicated team powered by the Apple Corporation supports this platform with quick fixes and patch releases.

As we know, hackers are always several steps (sometimes told, at least two steps ahead!) ahead of the security professionals in this very fast-paced environment of technology. So, it is always a good idea to take care of some of the basic guidelines for averting the data, privacy, and security breaches on iPhone mobiles.

11.6.1 Major Guidelines for iPhone Security

The major guidelines for iPhone security are listed below:

- Always take care of Siri security by not leaving your phone unattended.
- Implement iPhone Configuration Utility (iCU) in enterprise environments.
- Create stronger passwords for the accounts.

FIGURE 11.11   iPhone security.

- Use password manager tools for better password security.
- Don't use unauthorized iPhone applications.
- Disable the on-screen notifications.
- Enable the two-step authentication on your Apple account as well as iCloud.
- Disable auto-synch feature to iCloud.
- Disable the use of Siri on a locked screen.
- Always choose to use VPN connection.
- On browser, disable the auto-fill form feature.
- Don't allow your applications to access your personal information.
- Cookies on your browser should be turned off.
- Disable auto-connection to available Wi-Fi networks.
- Use the secure networks and avoid public networks.
- Turn off application protocols that are not in use.
- Always encrypt the local files on the phone.
- Backup your data files to the iCloud.
- Use encrypted communication at maximum.
- Always update your iPhone mobile applications.
- Keep your mobile OS up to date with the latest software releases.
- Use your common sense when browsing and shopping online.

If you strictly follow these guidelines, your privacy and data on your phone will remain safe and secure from the cybersecurity threats.

11.6.2 How to Enable Biometric Security on Apple iPhone

Almost all iPhone versions released after iPhone 5S have the fingerprint scanning capability. The fingerprint scanning capabilities in iPhone and iPad devices are known as touch ID. The touch ID works with the four-digit passcode, which you will have to enter for just once when you start your mobile.

The biometric scanning is automatically activated during the process of iOS Setup Assistant. If skipped at that time, you can configure it by taking the following mentioned step-by-step procedure to activate the biometric scanning security.

- Tap the **Settings** on the iPhone and choose **Touch ID & Passcode** option. The list of available options appears (Figure 11.12).
- Turn on the **Passcode** button. Passcode field appears.
- Enter the four-digit passcode, which should be unique and hard to guess. Passcode is saved automatically.
- Go back to **Touch ID & Fingerprint** screen as shown in the above figure.
- Tap the **Add a Fingerprint...** option. The **Place Your Figure** screen appears.
- Place your finger in different positions on the **Home** key. The device continues scanning and recording the prints of the figure.
- The progress of the fingerprint scanning can be seen on the screen as the red lines continue to increase as shown in Figure 11.13.

FIGURE 11.12   Touch ID & passcode.

FIGURE 11.13   Fingerprint scanning.

- When the scanning of your fingerprints with slight variation in its position is completed, the **Adjust Your Grip** screen appears (Figure 11.14).
- Hold the mobile in the position you would use for fingerprint scanning.
- Repeat the mobile grip positioning for multiple times. The **Success** screen appears, when the **Adjust Your Grip** scanning is completed.
- Your fingerprint security with the passcode has been successfully configured.

FIGURE 11.14   Adjust your grip screen.

- Now press the lock screen button to lock/sleep the screen.
- Press lock screen again to activate the lock screen.
- Put your finger on the Home key. The mobile scans your fingerprints and compares with the saved fingerprints.
- The screen unlocks automatically, if the fingerprint matches with the saved fingerprints.

Note: You can save multiple fingerprints on your iPhone devices.

11.7 WINDOWS PHONE SECURITY GUIDELINES

Windows phones (Figure 11.15) are powered by the Microsoft Windows OS for mobile devices. This is very intuitive and easy-to-use OS. Windows OS is one of the most popular OSs that are very well known to almost all people either at work or at home. Many people are already aware of the security features of Windows OS as well as the security guidelines.

The security guidelines for Windows mobile phone are mentioned below:

- Always purchase the Windows phone with the latest OS version.
- Always keep your OS up to date by installing any new update and releases.
- Always download the mobile applications from the trusted stores like Microsoft Store.

FIGURE 11.15 Windows phone security.

- Try to use the paid mobile apps that are free from apps and other pop-up annoyance.
- Always keep your Windows apps updated.
- Install the best antivirus and anti-malware tool in the marketplace.
- Activate multi-step authentication security.
- Always use screen lock pin to keep the phone secure.
- Enable the "Find My Phone" feature so that you can locate your mobile easily in case you lose your mobile.
- Use Internet Explorer browser with strong security settings.
- Don't allow your browser to store cookies on your phone.
- Never use the insecure public networks.
- Always visit the secure websites.
- Use VPN connection for secure browsing and shopping.
- Always try to back up your precious data regularly.
- Use the latest mobiles that have security microchips or Trusted Platform Modules (TPMs).
- Try to use facial recognition, fingerprints, or iris scanning for phone unlocking.
- Use enlightened mobile applications, if you are using your Windows phone in the corporate work environment.
- Use remote access feature only in very specific and compulsory conditions.
- Always shop from the trusted websites.
- Third-party application permissions should be given carefully.

If you follow these guidelines for your Windows mobile phone, you would be in comfortable position in terms of the security and safety of your mobile phone.

11.8 MOBILE APPLICATION MANAGEMENT

Millions of mobile apps are already in the marketplace and hundreds of thousands new apps are emerging in the IT world annually. A large number of mobile apps are used by every person on his or her mobile device. These applications are normally developed by the third-party mobile development companies.

Those companies have their own commercial interests; they use those applications for their business objectives in such a way that some security-related issues always remain in using those applications, if proper guidelines are not followed strictly.

Those applications use ads, data access permissions, and other such things to gain legitimate business objectives. The hackers normally exploit the vulnerabilities and weak points in the code and operations of the mobile applications to compromise your mobile security. It is the responsibility of the user whether personal or enterprise user to make sure that those applications are used as per security guidelines and any vulnerability is not allowed to put your data on stake.

In our modern business ecosystem, the concept of bring your own device (BYOD) is getting more and more popular. In this methodology of business system, the enterprises use the mobile devices of the employees at their work. The enterprises save a huge cost on purchasing the laptops, tablets, and mobiles for the employees by adopting BYOD concept. But this methodology also opens up the doors of cybersecurity.

The owner of the mobile device always configures and uses the applications as per his/her choice, and any vulnerabilities in those applications can lead to the compromise on the enterprise data security. Therefore, the enterprises use the Mobile Application Management (MAM) software (Figure 11.16) platforms which control and manage the

FIGURE 11.16   Mobile application management.

security of the applications and the enterprise data that those applications use. The MAM normally covers the following aspects of mobile cybersecurity:

- Assessing the mobile applications' security measures implemented by the developers of the mobile applications
- Auditing the vulnerabilities of the mobile applications
- Establishing the controls over the mobile applications
- Managing those applications for any updates
- Checking for any violation of the security policy
- Integration of apps in a container so that inter-app data is guarded
- Addition, modification, and deletion of the applications
- Blacklisting and white-listing of the applications and activities

All of the abovementioned activities can be performed effectively with the help of MAM software platforms.

As far as the management of the personal applications is concerned, you need to follow the guidelines for managing the mobile applications effectively. The effective management of mobile applications helps you improve the security of your mobile as well as your personal information and privacy.

The most important guidelines for mobile apps management to maintain a high level of security include the following:

- Always download mobile applications from the trusted stores such as Apple Store and Google Play.
- Before downloading any mobile application, make sure you read all details about the applications and the past user reviews.
- Take special care about the permissions that an app asks for at the time of installation of the application.
- Read each and every component on the application wizard; don't click next… Blindly.
- Choose the custom installations that suit your needs.
- Be very much picky while choosing the mobile apps.
- If undue permissions are sought, don't install that app.
- Always delete the applications that you don't use.
- Always update all applications regularly.
- Set the mobile applications on auto-update so that they can update on a regular basis.
- Always install one powerful antivirus and anti-malware application from the top-rated security service provider companies.
- Arrange the applications in good order so that you can easily track the desired application.
- Arranging applications in terms of their frequency of use is a good idea.
- Try to use a containerization method for application communication so that your valuable data is not compromised.
- Use encrypted connections for communication with the application servers.
- Manage an automatic key manager to manage the passwords of your application.

- Use strong passwords on the applications.
- If you find abnormal behavior of any application, remove it immediately.
- Share your experience to the other users on the review page so that other users can also benefit from your experience with a particular mobile application.

If you follow these security guidelines, you will be able to maintain a good level of mobile security on your mobile phone.

SAMPLE QUESTIONS AND ANSWERS FOR WHAT WE HAVE LEARNED IN CHAPTER 11

Q1. State the major threats related to mobile security.

A1: The major threats related to mobile security are listed below:

- Increasing menace of ad click frauds
- Increased Trojan attacks
- BotNet activities
- Crypto-mining malware attacks
- Spyware attacks
- Root malicious attacks

Q2. Why is securing mobile device so important?

A2: The security of mobile device is very important because of the following things:

- It is used as your camera for recording your memorable movements with the help of photos and videos.
- It is your communication partner through voice calls, SMS, chats, video calls, emails, and other applications.
- It is used as a computer device for Internet browsing and online shopping.
- Smartphone is your guide to new area through maps and GPS (Global Positioning System).
- Mobile device is your entertainment partner.
- Mobile is used as the payment wallet for traditional shopping.
- Mobile device is used for physical access management and even for the digital access management tool.
- You store your valuable contacts and your personal information.
- You use it as your temporary data storage.

Q3. What is Android?

A3: Android is the leading mobile operating system in the world. It is developed by the Google Corporation in alliance with many other companies under Open Handset Alliance (OHA). This platform is based on the modified Linux kernel and released as an open source code.

Q4. What is the main downside of the branded and locked phones?

A4: The major downside of the branded and locked phones is that the data of the user is routed through one carrier and the remote access is also enabled in certain cases. Thus, the security concerns increase while the user uses the branded and locked phones.

Q5. State a potential problem associated with the updating process of Android operation system.

A5: One of the main problems with the Android operating system update is that the companies that use the operating system on their devices are not bound to the newly developed updates. So, the updating of the Android operating system normally gets delayed.

SOURCES

https://www.statista.com/statistics/330695/number-of-smartphone-users-worldwide/
https://www.asymbo.com/55-of-online-transactions-in-europe-happen-on-mobile-devices-criteo-2018/
https://www.stonetemple.com/mobile-vs-desktop-usage-study/
https://www.mcafee.com/enterprise/en-us/assets/reports/rp-mobile-threat-report-2018.pdf
http://gs.statcounter.com/os-market-share/mobile/worldwide
https://en.wikipedia.org/wiki/Mobile_operating_system
https://www.appbrain.com/stats/top-manufacturers
https://www.cs.colorado.edu/~kena/classes/5448/s11/lectures/13_introtoios.pdf
https://www.statista.com/statistics/276623/number-of-apps-available-in-leading-app-stores/
https://www.zdnet.com/article/the-ten-best-ways-to-secure-your-android-phone/
https://www.zdnet.com/article/googles-october-android-patches-have-landed-theres-a-big-fix-for-dnsmasq-bug/
https://developer.box.com/docs/android-security-guidelines
https://heimdalsecurity.com/blog/smartphone-security-guide-keep-your-phone-data-safe/
https://www.stickypassword.com/help/fingerprint-authentication-on-android-1106
https://searchmobilecomputing.techtarget.com/tip/iPhone-security-FAQ-Risks-fixes-and-the-future-of-iPhone-security
https://www.kaspersky.com/blog/iphone-maximum-security-tips/6132/
https://developer.box.com/docs/ios-security-guidelines
https://discussions.apple.com/thread/7813128
https://support.apple.com/en-jo/HT201371#use
https://docs.microsoft.com/en-us/windows/security/threat-protection/windows-10-mobile-security-guide
https://www.thewindowsclub.com/7-tips-to-secure-your-windows-phone-7
https://www.upwork.com/hiring/mobile/mobile-application-security/
https://www.educba.com/mobile-apps-development-tools/

Cybersecurity Standards

12

12.1 INTRODUCTION

Industrial standards play a very critical role in all types of industries. The standards are the defined guidelines, best practices, and rules to achieve any certain objective in that particular industry. In this chapter, we will talk about a few important standards that deal with the cybersecurity in the field of information and communication technology commonly referred to as ICT (Figure 12.1).

There are many standard organizations, industry alliances, and government authorities that devise different types of standards for different activities related to ICT. The standard organizations develop standards through deep research with the help of the industry experts in the field of information technology. They develop certain formulas and criteria for different things, activities, and procedures such as:

- Security of the code of the web environment
- Criteria for the testing of the computer code

FIGURE 12.1 Cybersecurity standards.

- Assessment of the vulnerabilities in the web environments
- Possible impact of the vulnerabilities on the industries and the end-users
- Ways to avert any kinds of security threat
- Assessment of level of risk
- Assessing and implementing secure communication
- How to deal with the potential threats
- What preemptive measures can help avert any possible cyber threats

In a nutshell, the cybersecurity standards identify the most suitable ways and industry best practices that are implemented to establish an effective cybersecurity. The detailed documents of the guidelines are also created; those documents establish the relationship between other security standards and guidelines. A detailed scope of work, roles, implementation procedure, and audit process is created for smooth adoption of the standards in the organizations.

This is an international standard offered by ISO. It is also accepted all over the world. The organizations from any part of the world can adopt this standard for establishing information security control.

Let us discuss a few very important cybersecurity standards that are commonly adopted in the field of ICT.

12.2 ISO/IEC 27001 & 27002 STANDARDS

These two standards deal with the information technology control within the IT organizations. The standards are developed by the International Organization of Standards commonly referred to as ISO. These standards are also written as ISO 2700X, which denotes both the cybersecurity standards as mentioned above.

The objectives of this standard include the following:

- Establishing information security controls
- Reducing the security risk in the organization
- Streamlining the cybersecurity procedures
- Selection of the information security controls
- Management of information security controls
- Implementation and monitoring of the information security controls.

These standards allow the company to take the following steps:

- Choose the right controls over the information security processes for the organizations that are defined in the recommendations.
- Implement the already accepted controls that have already been used and proven in different industries for IT controls.
- Develop new information security controls that are in compliance with the set criteria in the ISO standards and also suit the requirements of the organization.

These standards are constantly revised in the changed environment of the security threat and security risk profiles. So, always have a look at the revised versions of the standards.

ISO also provides certificates to the organizations that fully adopt these standards and implement them in accordance with the set criteria. The organization also audits the implementation of the standards on a regular basis.

ISO certification requires charges even to access the detailed requirements. There are four modules based on fixed prices, which will allow the IT organizations to achieve the certification of the ISO information security control standards. ISO also has a wide range of their consultant companies that work all over the world and deal with the organizations that are interested in the implementation of information security control standards.

Mostly the organizations undergo a security audit by the representatives of the standard organizations annually to ascertain that the rules are being strictly followed as per set procedures in the written documents or standard operational procedures (SOPs).

There are many other standards for establishing complete cybersecurity governance. Those standards are in compliance with the information security control standard. So, any organization can choose the set of standards offered by the ISO international.

12.3 INFORMATION SECURITY FORUM (ISF) STANDARDS

Information Security Forum (ISF) is an IT governance organization that devises good practices for the organizations to deal with the risks associated to the information technology security. The main focus of this organization is to provide the industry with the risks of the existing as well as the emerging security threats.

The major areas that the ISF good practices cover include the following:

- Risk associated with the Agile software development methodology
- Privacy of information and intelligence about the emerging threats
- Security aspects of industrial control systems (ICSs)
- Assessing and establishing the co-relationship between the operational risk and the information risk

This is also an international set of good practice acceptable worldwide. These standards help the organizations in the following:

- Helping the leaders and teams exploit new areas for improving productivity and efficiency while maintaining high level of security against information risks
- Preparing the organizations to preempt the potential threats to reduce the risk through agility and preparedness
- Identifying the ways to implement the security standards in efficient and effective manner

This set of good practice improves the efficiency, agility, and effectiveness of the security personnel and organization leaders by improving their alertness and innovative thinking. This is a business-focused set of good practice.

12.4 PAYMENT CARD INDUSTRY DATA SECURITY STANDARD (PCI/DSS)

The Payment Card Industry Data Security Standard (PCI/DSS) is focused to the personal information of the online shopper. This standard is developed by the PCI Security Standard Council. The standard was developed to safeguard the bank and card information of the card users who use their cards for online shopping.

This standard directly impacts the millions of the people across the world. Security Standard Council helps the financial institutes and merchants to implement the standard guidelines devised by the council so that the card information of the people can be safeguarded easily.

The council includes the following financial organizations:

- American Express
- MasterCard Inc.
- Visa Inc.
- JCB International
- Discover Inc.

The PCI council focuses on the following organizations to help them safeguard the personal and financial information of the card users.

- Point-of-sales (POS) manufacturers
- Financial software developers
- Financial hardware developers
- Merchants of all sizes
- Financial institutes/banks

The main function of the council through its IT card security standards is to implement the card information security by the following:

- Implementing security-related technology, policy, and best practices to the existing and upcoming financial processes used at the merchant and financial institute end
- Helping hardware and software venders to implement the security features and capabilities in their products at the development level

At present, almost all financial institutes and merchants implement and follow the PCI/DSS guidelines and standards.

SAMPLE QUESTIONS AND ANSWERS FOR WHAT WE HAVE LEARNED IN CHAPTER 12

Q1. Why are industrial standards important?

A1: Industrial standards play a very critical role in all types of industries. The standards are the defined guidelines, best practices, and rules to achieve any certain objective in that particular industry.

Q2. Name two industrial standards that deal with the information technology control within an IT organization.

A2: ISO/IEC 27001 & 27002 Standards. These two standards deal with the information technology control within the IT organizations. The standards are developed by the International Organization of Standards commonly referred to as ISO.

SOURCES

https://leocybersecurity.com/wp-content/uploads/2017/11/14-List-of-Security-Standards-20171103.pdf
https://www.iso.org/standard/54533.html
https://www.itgovernance.co.uk/cybersecurity-standards
https://www.securityforum.org/tool/the-isf-standard-good-practice-information-security-2018/
https://www.pcisecuritystandards.org/pci_security/

Index